# Customization-Oriented Design of Product-Service System

Wenyan Song

# Customization-Oriented Design of Product-Service System

Springer

Wenyan Song
School of Economics and Management
Beihang University
Beijing, China

ISBN 978-981-13-0862-8     ISBN 978-981-13-0863-5 (eBook)
https://doi.org/10.1007/978-981-13-0863-5

Library of Congress Control Number: 2018943723

© Springer Nature Singapore Pte Ltd. 2019
This work is subject to copyright. All rights are reserved by the Publisher, whether the whole or part of the material is concerned, specifically the rights of translation, reprinting, reuse of illustrations, recitation, broadcasting, reproduction on microfilms or in any other physical way, and transmission or information storage and retrieval, electronic adaptation, computer software, or by similar or dissimilar methodology now known or hereafter developed.
The use of general descriptive names, registered names, trademarks, service marks, etc. in this publication does not imply, even in the absence of a specific statement, that such names are exempt from the relevant protective laws and regulations and therefore free for general use.
The publisher, the authors and the editors are safe to assume that the advice and information in this book are believed to be true and accurate at the date of publication. Neither the publisher nor the authors or the editors give a warranty, express or implied, with respect to the material contained herein or for any errors or omissions that may have been made. The publisher remains neutral with regard to jurisdictional claims in published maps and institutional affiliations.

Printed on acid-free paper

This Springer imprint is published by the registered company Springer Nature Singapore Pte Ltd.
The registered company address is: 152 Beach Road, #21-01/04 Gateway East, Singapore 189721, Singapore

# Preface

Many manufacturers today are striving to offer high value-added product-service system (PSS) due to the increasing competition and environmental pressure. PSS is a system consisting of products, services, networks of players, and supporting infrastructure, which are jointly capable of fulfilling specific client demands in an economical and sustainable manner. PSS design activities face a variety of challenges such as a high level of customization as well as its resulting challenges, i.e., hidden requirements in product use phase, potential conflicts of design attributes, and internal complexity of service processes. Specifically, due to a higher number of and more variable stakeholders involved in PSS, PSS requirements management with the methods for product requirements elicitation is challenged. Moreover, different value propositions to the stakeholders may also lead to potential conflicts between design attributes. Besides, when the external environment (e.g., customer requirements) changes greatly, the PSS providers have to rearrange service processes and resources, and even to redesign the whole PSS to adapt to the changed environment, which may cause the increase of service response time and cost. However, existing frameworks for PSS design are fragmented and insufficient to solve these issues in customization because most of them lack systematic and comprehensive support to specifically guide PSS customization from early requirements identification to design conflict resolving, and give quick response to customer with lower cost. Thus, it is necessary to develop a systematic and comprehensive framework with design process and methods to solve those issues.

Therefore, this book is devoted to the customization design of product-service system (PSS), making use of a systematic design process and a number of methods, especially Industrial Customer Activity Cycle Analysis, Service Quality Function Deployment, Service Function and Attribute Analysis, Modified Service Blueprint, Multi-Objective Optimization, and Multi-Criteria Recommendation Method.

In this book, we will offer a thorough and systematic introduction to the PSS customization process (e.g., requirements analysis, requirements specification, modularization, modular configuration, and recommendation) and various PSS customization methods such as Industrial Customer Activity Cycle Analysis, Modified Quality Function Deployment, Service Function and Attribute Analysis,

Modified Service Blueprint, Multi-Objective Optimization, Multi-Criteria Recommendation Method, etc. The book is structured as the following six chapters.

Chapter 1 introduces a PSS customization design framework that involves design activities and methods. The framework includes five successive stages, i.e., requirements analysis, requirements specification, modularization, modular configuration, and concept selection. These successive stages are introduced specifically in the following five chapters. Based on the PSS customization design framework in Chap. 1, Chap. 2 presents process and methods for PSS requirements analysis. In this chapter, a model of industrial customer activity cycle is utilized to efficiently elicit PSS requirements from the lifecycle perspective. Afterward, a rough group analytic hierarchy process method is utilized to find the critical requirements. Then, a rough DEMATEL (Decision Making Trial and Evaluation Laboratory) method is provided to evaluate the dependencies and correlations between the PSS requirements. A requirement forecast method based on Kano model and Grey-Markov chain is also presented to analyze the future requirements in this chapter. Chapter 3 introduces requirements specification of PSS, in which a modified QFD (Quality function deployment) is provided to convert the elicited PSS requirements into technical attributes. Then, the interactions and conflicts between technical attributes are identified with SFAA (Service Function and Attribute Analysis). TRIZ is used to resolve the conflicts between technical attributes. Chapter 4 introduces modularization of PSS. The modified service blueprint is used in Chap. 4 to identify all the PSS components. Then, correlation analysis is conducted to analyze the interdependencies between components. After that, fuzzy graph-based approach is utilized to cluster the PSS components into modules. Chapter 5 presents a modular configuration method for PSS. In this chapter, the PSS modules are configured into customizable solutions with a multi-objective optimization model which simultaneously considers the constraints of performance, cost, and response time. The configured PSSs are then preliminarily evaluated with a rough TOPSIS (Technique for Order Preference by Similarity to an Ideal Solution) approach. To help potential buyers effectively discover the most suitable PSS with lower search costs, Chap. 6 introduces personalized recommendation of PSS, in which a multi-criteria recommendation method based on rough collaborative filtering (CF) approach is used to achieve proactively suggesting proposals of customizable offerings to customers.

This book is useful for practitioners and researchers working in the fields of product-service system, product/service engineering, industrial and systems engineering, management science and engineering, engineering design, and engineering management. It can also be used as a textbook for postgraduate and senior undergraduate students. The book is especially valuable in manipulating the problems of PSS requirements analysis, design conflict, design reuse, and proactively response to customer. The methods in the book facilitate modular design of customized solutions and enhance PSS design efficiency. Presenting case studies, this book helps researchers and practitioners to understand the customization process and methods in the early development of PSS.

This work was supported by the National Natural Science Foundation of China (No. 71501006), the NSFC key program (No. 71632003), the Technical Research Foundation (JSZL2016601A004) and the Fundamental Research Funds for the Central Universities. Finally, I am grateful to my family for their constant love, encouragement, and support.

Beijing, China  Wenyan Song
April 2018

# Contents

| | | | |
|---|---|---|---|
| **1** | **Design Framework for Customizable Product-Service System** | | 1 |
| | 1.1 Product-Service System | | 1 |
| | 1.2 Basic Definitions of the Customization Framework | | 3 |
| | 1.3 The Proposed PSS Customization Framework | | 4 |
| | | 1.3.1 PSS Requirements Identification and Analysis | 5 |
| | | 1.3.2 PSS Requirements Specification | 7 |
| | | 1.3.3 PSS Modularization | 8 |
| | | 1.3.4 PSS Configuration and Concept Selection | 9 |
| | 1.4 Case Study: Elevator PSS Customization | | 10 |
| | | 1.4.1 Elevator PSS Requirements Analysis | 11 |
| | | 1.4.2 Elevator PSS Requirements Specification | 13 |
| | | 1.4.3 Elevator PSS Modularization | 15 |
| | | 1.4.4 Elevator PSS Configuration and Concept Selection | 17 |
| | 1.5 Comparisons and Discussion | | 19 |
| | References | | 21 |
| **2** | **Requirements Analysis for Customizable PSS** | | 23 |
| | 2.1 PSS Requirement | | 23 |
| | 2.2 PSS Requirements Analysis | | 24 |
| | 2.3 PSS Requirements Identification and Prioritization | | 25 |
| | | 2.3.1 PSS Requirement Elicitation | 26 |
| | | 2.3.2 PSS Requirement Prioritization | 29 |
| | | 2.3.3 Case Study: Air Compressor PSS Requirement Identification and Prioritization | 33 |
| | | 2.3.4 Comparisons and Discussion | 40 |
| | 2.4 PSS Requirement Interaction Analysis | | 43 |
| | | 2.4.1 The Method for PSS Requirement Interaction Analysis | 43 |

|  |  | 2.4.2 | Case Study: Elevator PSS Requirement Interaction Analysis | 48 |
|---|---|---|---|---|
|  |  | 2.4.3 | Comparisons and Discussion | 53 |
|  | 2.5 | Customer Requirement Forecast | | 60 |
|  |  | 2.5.1 | The Method for Customer Requirements Forecast | 60 |
|  |  | 2.5.2 | Case Study: Customer Requirements Forecast for Mobile Phone | 66 |
|  |  | 2.5.3 | Comparisons and Discussion | 70 |
|  | References | | | 73 |
| **3** | **Requirements Specification for Customizable PSS** | | | **75** |
|  | 3.1 | Specification of PSS Requirement | | 75 |
|  | 3.2 | PSS Requirement Conversion | | 76 |
|  |  | 3.2.1 | Preliminaries | 76 |
|  |  | 3.2.2 | The Method of PSS Requirement Conversion | 80 |
|  |  | 3.2.3 | Case Study: Conversion of Compressor Rotor Service Requirement | 86 |
|  |  | 3.2.4 | Comparisons and Discussion | 92 |
|  | 3.3 | PSS Design Conflict Identification and Resolution | | 95 |
|  |  | 3.3.1 | The Method for Identifying and Resolving PSS Design Conflicts | 96 |
|  |  | 3.3.2 | Case Study: Design Conflict Resolution for Elevator PSS | 103 |
|  |  | 3.3.3 | Discussion | 109 |
|  | References | | | 109 |
| **4** | **Modularization of PSS** | | | **111** |
|  | 4.1 | PSS Modularization | | 111 |
|  | 4.2 | The Method for Modularizing PSS | | 113 |
|  |  | 4.2.1 | Preliminaries | 113 |
|  |  | 4.2.2 | Service Components Identification | 114 |
|  |  | 4.2.3 | Correlation Analysis for Service Components | 116 |
|  |  | 4.2.4 | PSS Module Partition Based on Fuzzy Graph | 119 |
|  | 4.3 | Case Study: Modularizing Maintenance Service for Rotor of Compressor | | 120 |
|  |  | 4.3.1 | Identification of Rotor Maintenance Service Components | 121 |
|  |  | 4.3.2 | Correlation Analysis for Rotor Maintenance Service Components | 121 |
|  |  | 4.3.3 | Module Partition of Rotor Maintenance Service | 127 |
|  | 4.4 | Comparisons and Discussion | | 129 |
|  | References | | | 130 |

## Contents

**5 Modular Configuration for Customizable PSS** .................. 133
- 5.1 Problem Formulation of PSS Configuration Optimization ....... 133
- 5.2 Methodology for PSS Configuration Optimization ............ 135
  - 5.2.1 Modeling for PSS Configuration Optimization.......... 136
  - 5.2.2 Problem-Solving Process Based on NSGA-II........... 142
  - 5.2.3 Case Study: Configuration Optimization for Elevator PSS ......................................... 144
  - 5.2.4 Comparisons and Discussion ...................... 150
- 5.3 Design Concept Selection Under Subjective Environments ...... 153
  - 5.3.1 Preliminaries ................................. 153
  - 5.3.2 The Method for Design Concept Selection ............ 155
  - 5.3.3 Case Study: Design Concept Selection of Mini Fridge.... 161
  - 5.3.4 Comparisons and Discussion ...................... 166
- References ................................................ 174

**6 Personalized Recommendation of Customizable PSS to Customers**............................................. 177
- 6.1 The Proposed Method for Personalized PSS Recommendation ... 177
  - 6.1.1 Phase I: Weight Determination for PSS Recommendation Criteria ..................................... 178
  - 6.1.2 Phase II: Multi-criteria PSS Recommendation .......... 182
- 6.2 Case Study: Personalized Recommendation of Elevator PSS ..... 187
  - 6.2.1 Case Background............................... 187
  - 6.2.2 Implementation of the PSS Recommendation Approach .................................... 188
- 6.3 Comparisons and Discussion............................. 197
- 6.4 Theoretical and Practical Implications ..................... 201
- References ................................................ 202

# Chapter 1
# Design Framework for Customizable Product-Service System

In order to support PSS (Product-Service System) customization in early design phase, Song and Sakao (2017) develop a modular design framework that involves design activities and methods. The framework includes five successive stages, i.e. requirements analysis, requirements specification, modularization, modular configuration and concept selection. The proposed design framework is module-based and can be adjusted flexibly according to the user needs. In addition, it takes advantage of some existing methods. An elevator PSS design case study shows the feasibility and potentials of the design framework and its associated design process to its broad usage in industry.

## 1.1 Product-Service System

Under the pressure of increasing competition (Uppenberg and Strauss 2010), diversification of customer demands (Hu et al. 2011) and environmental pressures (Umeda et al. 2012), many manufacturing companies redefine their roles as solution providers by offering high value-adding services (Meier et al. 2010). Those manufacturing companies are on a journey of servitization towards a tightly-coupled integration of products and services (Beuren et al. 2013; Vandermerwe and Rada 1988). Servitization can be seen as a process to transfer from selling products to selling Product-Service System (PSS) and involves strategic innovation of a company's capabilities (Baines et al. 2007; Vandermerwe and Rada 1988). PSS are collections of physical technological elements and service elements that are integrated to resolve customer problems. It involves product and service shares in one system. PSS is "sold" as one package which is supposed to be integrated, customer-centered and lifecycle-oriented solution. Modern business models are used to operate such systems more efficiently about technical, economical and ecological aspects. Instead of purchase the customer pays for system functionality or for a defined result. The payment can be arranged in various ways such as pay-per-unit, pay-per-use or flat rates. For example, a company offers air compressors for pharmaceutical plants; but the customer pays based on the compressors usage. The main benefit for the customer is that the company provides clean compressed air for the pharmaceutical operation, and arranges it with the schedule to reduce fixed costs. In order to integrate the PSS into the organization, it is necessary to make a comprehensive determination of the customer's business processes, the company's support processes and usage of the PSS (Berkovich et al. 2011). PSS designers have to identify and analyze the requirements resulting from the business processes. In the example above, the solution provider needs to know all tasks performed in the pharmaceutical plants to offer the suitable compressor service at the right time and place.

By offering more functionalities and flexibility, PSS provides more customized solutions, and create more value for customers than conventional products and services (Halen et al. 2005). On this point, the possession of the PSS is the value resulting from the usage of integrated product and service components. The key to successful solutions is, in particular, how to satisfy demands and expectations of the customer and stakeholders in different aspects (Nuseibeh and Easterbrook 2000; Song et al. 2015a). The conventional model tends to provide standardized after-sales service such as spare part provision, on the contrary, PSS offers customized service portfolio to flexibly meet customer's requirements (Kindström and Kowalkowski 2009). There are different ways of categorization of PSS. Manzini (1999) categorizes PSS into two modes, i.e., use-oriented and result-oriented modes. Roy (2000) further extends the categories to include four modes, i.e., result services, shared utilization services, product-life extension services, and demand side management. Tukker (2004) proposes the concept of product-oriented services (e.g., maintenance and repair) adding services to current products, use-oriented services (e.g., product renting, sharing, and pooling) intensifying the use of products, and result-oriented services focusing on customer requirements fulfillment.

Effective customization depends on accurate requirements capturing and handling (Jiao and Tseng 2004). However, because of a higher number of and more variable stakeholders involved in PSS (Song et al. 2015a), PSS requirements management face challenges in improving the conventional methods for product requirements elicitation. Moreover, potential conflicts between design attributes may arise due to different value propositions of the stakeholders, which is not thoroughly addressed in PSS design researches (Berkovich et al. 2011; Vasantha et al. 2012). Besides, when customer requirements change in product use phase, it usually leads to rearrange service processes and resources, and even redesign the whole PSS to cope with the changes. This might increase service response time, it also means a waste of previous designs. Embedding modularity is effective to avoid this problem, because it brings benefits such as increased feasibility of change, increased variety, and ease of design and testing (Gershenson et al. 2003). Thus, customization involves different steps covering a wide range of activities from requirements elicitation to module-based configuration, and to achieve effective and efficient PSS customization, the systematic and comprehensive support is necessary. However, existing frameworks for PSS design are fragmented and insufficient to support customization and later PSS configuration, owing to lack of systematic and comprehensive support to specifically guide PSS customization from early requirements identification to design conflict resolving (Berkovich et al. 2011). The insufficient systematic methodical support for the customization process may cause implementation difficulty in practice of PSS customization.

Therefore, Song and Sakao (2017) propose a systematic and comprehensive framework with a design process for PSS customization. The design framework includes four successive design stages. The proposed framework would systematically provide designers with standardized design process reference from the beginning requirements identification to the later concept configuration. Specifically, early conflict resolving mechanism in the framework aims to reduce possible failures during subsequent detailed design and delivery. Modularization process and methods of the framework will facilitate frequent design reuse and easier trace-back of failures, and thus enhance design efficiency. The module-based configuration in the framework could help the service provider to achieve flexible PSS customization.

## 1.2 Basic Definitions of the Customization Framework

To provide a basis for design framework of PSS, the main terms are introduced and defined briefly in this section. These definitions provide a foundation for PSS design framework.

**Definition 1.1: PSS Design Conflict** In PSS design process, improvement or enhancement of one PSS design attribute may lead to deterioration of another. Then, it can be considered that conflict exists between the two design attributes. For example, design attribute of service response time often conflicts with design attribute of service cost, because reducing response time often needs to invest more costs.

**Definition 1.2: PSS Component** PSS component is the basic element of Product-Service System. Generally, it is a set of processes, operations, people or other objects. Service modules with different functions are composed of different PSS components. For example, the PSS components of a service planning module include service engineer, service dispatching, and service tool library.

**Definition 1.3: PSS Module** PSS module integrates PSS components with strong interdependencies among each other. PSS components of different modules have little interdependencies, which gives service modules a high degree of independence among each other facilitating exchangeability. A PSS module is a set of components for performing a service function. There are two kinds of PSS module, i.e. mandatory service module and optional service module. Mandatory service module provides mainly basic service functions (e.g., a module of installation and commissioning), while optional service module is designed to be function carrier to meet personalized requirements (e.g., a module of energy saving). Each service module contains different module instance (e.g., remote installation guidance is an instance of a module of installation and commissioning) which is the specific service content of with different service performance.

**Definition 1.4: PSS Configuration** PSS configuration can be thought of as selecting appropriate PSS module instances to combine for a PSS alternative under certain constraints (e.g., response time, cost, and profits) to meet customer requirements. For example, selecting appropriate module instances to get a portfolio to control the response time within 1 h.

**Definition 1.5: PSS Concept** PSS concept is a general description of total solution that consists of a series of service processes, activities and service resources. It is expected to improve the product function or overall performance during the product lifecycle. In this work, PSS concept refers to the combination of a set of existing PSS module instances to support customer activities during the product lifecycle. For example, a set of Online knowledge support, Expert advisory, Remote installation guidance, Regular telephone follow up, Original spare parts supply, Emergency repair, Monthly maintenance, Monitoring, Outsourced dispatching, Energy performance contracting, and Component failure alert is a configured elevator PSS concept.

## 1.3 The Proposed PSS Customization Framework

The proposed design framework is shown in Fig. 1.1. The PSS customization framework includes three levels: the top-level of PSS design process, the middle level of design methods and techniques and the bottom level of supporting data and knowledge. The top level of framework includes four parts, namely, PSS requirements identification and analysis, technical attributes and conflict resolving, PSS modularization, and PSS configuration and concept selection. The design process domains are progressively connected through the mapping of design information. PSS requirements identification and analysis aims to obtain key inputs for the customization. Conflicts between technical attributes are resolved to reduce possible defects in the customization process. The purpose of PSS modularization is to facilitate design reuse and prepare for module-based configuration. PSS configuration aims to develop a PSS that meets the requirements of customized solutions based on existing modules from the phase of modularization.

The middle level of design methods consists of specific design methods and techniques to support the PSS design process. The reasons why these methods and techniques are selected are explained in Table 1.1. The bottom level of information and knowledge support as inputs is necessary. Product lifecycle information in the figure consists of product health monitoring information and customer feedbacks. Table 1.2 summarizes critical elements of the framework and how they were built.

With the key elements in Table 1.2, the framework establishes throughput mechanism so that the output from one phase provides input to one or more of the following phases of PSS customization. As the framework shows, PSS customization

## 1.3 The Proposed PSS Customization Framework

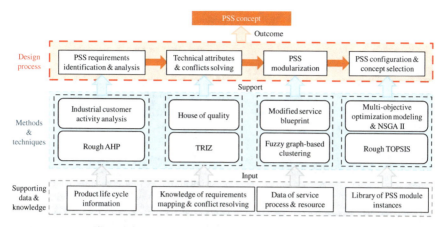

**Fig. 1.1** A design framework for sustainable Product-Service System (Song and Sakao 2017)

begins with requirements identification and ends with customized concept selection to obtain the most proper PSS solution. This process is shown with more details in Fig. 1.2. Firstly, the PSS requirements are elicited and analyzed to get systematic and structured requirements. Then, the identified structured PSS requirements are transformed into design attributes that designers can use. Potential design conflicts are also simultaneously identified and resolved to facilitate later modularization and configuration. After that, the PSS provider scans the service solutions and capabilities to identify PSS components, and clusters them into modules. Finally, optimization model for module-based configuration is built and solved respectively to effectively obtain reasonable customization concept.

### 1.3.1 PSS Requirements Identification and Analysis

Requirements are the starting point for conceptual design of PSS, and they are usually considered as metrics of PSS customized concepts. It not only needs to identify requirements in product use phase, but also to identify requirements that exist in other lifecycle phases, e.g., product acquisition, remanufacturing, recycling or disposal stage. In addition to these common requirements, environmental requirements (such as energy saving) should also be identified and analyzed.

PSS requirements identification is closely associated with different stakeholders, e.g., end users, product managers, and operators, etc. The method of I-CAC (Industrial customer activity analysis cycle) proposed in Song et al. (2013a) is used to acquire the PSS requirements around the customer activity cycle. Due to the diverse, imprecise and linguistic characteristic of PSS requirements, it is beneficial to group requirements into meaningful hierarchies to facilitate further analysis. Here, the identified requirements can be structured into groups. After that, designers use Rough

**Table 1.1** Reason for selecting the methods and techniques in the proposed framework (Song and Sakao 2017)

| Method and techniques | Reason for use in the framework |
|---|---|
| I-CAC (Industrial customer activity analysis) (Song et al. 2013a) | It systematically considers different stakeholders' involvement and the full stages of customer using product |
| Rough AHP (Analytic Hierarchy Process) (Song et al. 2013a) | The Rough AHP has the strengths in prioritizing the fuzzy, subjective, and uncertain PSS requirements |
| Rough HoQ (House of Quality) (Song et al. 2014) based on HoQ (Hauser and Clausing 1988) | As a customer-oriented approach, it can effectively convert the PSS requirements into design attributes with vagueness, which can be well understood and used by designers |
| 9-point rating scale assessment (Myint 2003) | It can indicate the degree of relationship between customer requirements and technical attributes |
| TRIZ (Theory of inventive problem solving) (Al'tshuller 1999) | Contradiction Matrix and 40 inventive principles in TRIZ are effective tools to guide designers to solve design conflicts |
| Modified service blueprint (Song et al. 2015b) | It can visually display the complex interactions between components in PSS for component identification |
| Fuzzy graph-based clustering (Song et al. 2015b) | As a clustering method, it can cluster components with high interdependencies into PSS module |
| Multi-objective optimization modeling (Song and Chan 2015) | It can be used to simultaneous optimization of multiple configuration objectives, e.g., PSS performance, cost, and response time |
| NSGA II (Non-dominated sorting genetic algorithm II) (Deb et al. 2002) | The NSGA-II avoids subjectivity in converting the multi-objective optimization model into the one with single objective |
| Rough TOPSIS (Technique for order of preference by similarity to ideal solution) (Song et al. 2013b) | It has strength in handling vagueness of PSS design concept evaluation with multi-criteria |

AHP (Rough Analytic Hierarchy Process) (Song et al. 2013a) based on the traditional AHP (Saaty 1988) to prioritize PSS requirements. Requirement priority analysis can help designers to distribute resources among the follow-up design activities. It will also serve as key inputs for PSS concept evaluation in the configuration stage. The specific methods will be discussed in Chap. 2.

## 1.3 The Proposed PSS Customization Framework

**Table 1.2** Key elements in the proposed framework and their sources (Song and Sakao 2017)

| Key elements of the framework | Sources |
|---|---|
| PSS requirements identification and analysis, using product life cycle information, and corresponding design process | Song et al. (2013a) |
| Technical attributes and conflict resolving, support of requirements mapping/conflict resolving, and corresponding design process | Sakao (2007), Song and Sakao (2016), and Li and Song (2016) |
| PSS modularization, using data of service process/resource and corresponding design process | Song et al. (2015b), and Sakao et al. (2017) |
| PSS configuration and concept selection, library of PSS modules, and corresponding design process | Song and Chan (2015), and Song et al. (2013b) |

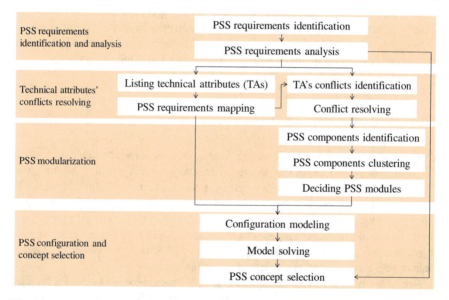

**Fig. 1.2** A design process of sustainable Product-Service System under the framework (Song and Sakao 2017)

### 1.3.2 PSS Requirements Specification

Based on the analysis of PSS requirements and experience of designers, the PSS technical attributes (TAs) can be derived. Then, in order to achieve the transformation of PSS requirements, the basic structure of House of Quality (HoQ) (Hauser and Clausing 1988) is used in this stage to convert the PSS requirements from different stakeholders into TAs, which can be fully understood and used by designers. These technical attributes include both basic PSS functions and environmental measures.

The designers judge the degree of correlations between PSS requirements and the service technical attributes using the 9-point rating scale assessment (Myint 2003). At the same time, the priorities of TAs are calculated according to the method proposed in Song et al. (2014), which provides critical inputs for the subsequent PSS configuration. The specific methods of requirement conversion will be discussed in detail in Chap. 3.

After accomplishing the PSS requirements mapping, correlation matrix in the roof of HoQ is used to identify possible conflicts between TAs. Negative correlations in roof of HoQ imply potential conflicts between technical attributes. Then, these negative correlations can be connected with conflict matrix of TRIZ and 40 inventive principles (Sakao 2007; Song and Sakao 2016). The conflicting TAs are standardized into the parameters in contradiction matrix of TRIZ. By searching contradiction matrix of TRIZ, the preliminary conflict resolving principles can be obtained. With the guidance of the initial conflict resolution principles, designers can get the final concrete conflict resolution. In this way, potential conflict between TAs can be solved. Identifying and resolving conflicts in the early design phase will address PSS potential failure, reduce conflicting goals, and increase customer satisfaction. The specific methods of design conflict resolving will be discussed in detail in Chap. 3.

### 1.3.3 PSS Modularization

In order to quickly respond to personalized requirements, some common components can be used in the process of PSS design. In this way, service process simplification, service resource sharing, and service cost reduction are expected to be achieved. PSS module contains components with strong interdependencies. While PSS components in different modules have little interdependencies, which ensures that the modules are highly interchangeable. Heterogeneous elements (such as service personnel, service object and service process) make the structure of PSS more complicated. Specific steps of PSS modularization are described as follows.

Firstly, all the related PSS components are identified. Modified service blueprint (Song et al. 2015b) is used to identify all the relevant PSS components including service processes, service objects and service resources. Modified service blueprint contains five different functional areas, namely product using domain, product management domain, visualized service domain (foreground), invisible service domain (background) and resources domain.

Secondly, interdependencies between different components are analyzed with pair-wise comparison method from the perspective of process, function and resource.

Finally, components are clustered into PSS modules with clustering methods, e.g. fuzzy graph-based approach (Song et al. 2015b) which can visually show the interdependency between different components. These PSS modules can be reused in future design. The specific methods will be discussed in detail in Chap. 4.

## *1.3.4 PSS Configuration and Concept Selection*

Configuration is an efficient method for rapid PSS customization to enhance customer satisfaction. Modular PSS configuration refers to the selection of suitable service module instances that are combined into complete PSS solutions to meet the specific customer requirements.

The steps of PSS configuration are described as follows: Firstly, identify the relationship between technical attributes and module instances. In this way, technical attributes can be converted into configuration requirements of the module instances. Secondly, obtain appropriate module instances in accordance with the configuration requirements and constraints to obtain an optimized service portfolio. Specifically, a module instance is selected for each module in the mandatory modules. After that, select the optional module from the optional module collection and then select a module instance for each optional module. Thirdly, PSS concept composed by the module instances (mandatory and optional) can be obtained.

In fact, PSS configuration can be regarded as the combinatorial optimization of service modules to maximize fulfillment of customer requirements. According to relationships between technical attributes and module instances, appropriate service module instances are selected from the existing set of module instances. This is a typical problem with constrained multi-objective combinatorial optimization, because PSS configuration optimization model often simultaneously takes service performance, cost, and response time as the optimization objectives. After that, the multi-objective optimization model can be solved by NSGA II (Non-dominated sorting genetic algorithm II) (Deb et al. 2002) and other methods, to obtain the optimized configuration set. The specific implementation steps and processes of configuration optimization (Song and Chan 2015) will be introduced in Chap. 5. The optimized configuration collection contains all the feasible solutions of the customized PSS concepts, which can meet the constraints and pre-set goals. Then, the most proper concept can be selected with a method of rough TOPSIS (Song et al. 2013b) in subjective environments (the specific implementation steps are provided in Chap. 5).

In the proposed framework, the correlations between technical attributes (converted from PSS requirements) and module instances are identified to link them with the specific configuration requirements. In the meantime, the configuration set of feasible PSS solutions is assessed with customer preference and requirements. All of these ensure that the PSS customization framework can achieve closed-loop process, i.e., from the beginning of requirements identification to the end of requirements fulfillment by flexible configuration. Moreover, conflict resolving before PSS configuration can reduce conflicting goals of the configuration decision-making, which will largely alleviate burden of solving multi-objective optimization model for PSS configuration.

## 1.4 Case Study: Elevator PSS Customization

To demonstrate the proposed PSS design framework, it was applied to an elevator manufacturing Company M. A single case was chosen in order to gain an in-depth view of the framework implementation. The case Company M was selected, as it decided to change from an elevator manufacturer to an elevator solution provider. In this section, implementation of the proposed design framework of PSS in Company M is first briefly introduced. Further, effects of PSS design framework are analyzed and discussed.

Company M is a leader in elevator manufacturing who provides different types of elevators including passenger/freight elevator, hospital elevator, escalator, and elevator monitoring system, etc. The company did not consider satisfying the personalized requirements when providing some standard after-sales service. Moreover, customers complained much about the failure of subsequent service delivery, and some critical service requirements during elevator lifecycle were often overlooked, as they had not been expressed by customers. In this respect, Company M decided to offer customized PSS to ensure efficiency and effectiveness of elevator operation. The PSS customization project team in Company M consisted of company director, marketing engineers, designers, service engineers, and customer service managers, and they used the framework in the project. The first author and some other researchers (postgraduates) took the role as participatory consultants (or even part-time project engineers) to help Company M to discuss its problems as well as to create and implement solutions.

The data was obtained through several visits and two graduate student internships at Company M. Interview can provide a basis for discussion of particular aspects of a framework implementation and it is also a flexible and appropriate method for finding strategic information. Therefore, semi-structured interviews with (sixteen) practitioners were mainly conducted to adjust the initial framework to the evaluator PSS customization project and verify the effectiveness of the framework. The involved 16 practitioners consisted of one company director, two operations managers, seven designers, three service managers, and three service engineers at Company M. The duration of interviews was 1–1.5 h. Beside the interviews, the objective data (e.g., about elevator service process, service cost) were collected from analysis of available reports (e.g., operations analysis report of customer service center) and observations (e.g., maintenance and repair process), because these methods need a minimal level of interaction between the researchers and practitioners and, therefore, is bound to a minimal level of bias in the results.

## 1.4 Case Study: Elevator PSS Customization

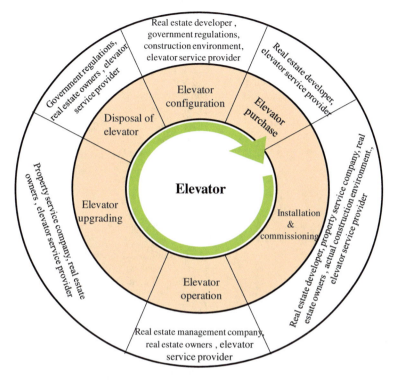

**Fig. 1.3** Customer activity cycle of elevator in Company M (Song and Sakao 2017)

### 1.4.1 Elevator PSS Requirements Analysis

Figure 1.3 shows the customer activity cycle for elevator. The central portion of the circle describes an elevator. The middle ring of Fig. 1.3 includes different customer activities during the elevator use phase, e.g., elevator configuration, purchase analysis, installation and commissioning, and elevator operation, etc. The outer ring in Fig. 1.3 contains stakeholders (e.g., real estate developer, real estate owners, and elevator manufacturer) who play different roles in different phase of customer activity cycle. In different phase of customer activity cycle, interviews were conducted to elicit requirements of stakeholder. The original requirements from interviews were decomposed, merged and simplified into a requirement hierarchical structure (see Table 1.3).

After identifying elevator PSS requirements, five experts from various fields were invited to judge the importance of each requirement. The five experts were representative of the real estate owners, building developer representative, elevator service manager, property service manager and representative of elevator service engineers. The final importance of PSS requirements (also see Table 1.3) was calculated with the method of rough group AHP proposed in Song et al. (2013a). As can be seen from

**Table 1.3** Customer requirements of passenger elevator service (Song and Sakao 2017)

| Customer activity cycle | Customer requirement | Sub-requirement | Requirement importance |
|---|---|---|---|
| Elevator configuration and purchase, | Quickly acceptance test and being in use of elevator ($R_1$) | Professional and customized advisory on purchasing and using elevator ($R_{11}$) | 0.018 |
| Installation and commissioning | | Timely and professional installation including construction and commissioning ($R_{12}$) | 0.052 |
| Elevator operation | Safe and reliable operation of elevator ($R_2$) | Fewer accidents (e.g. elevator dropping) resulting in casualties ($R_{21}$) | 0.797 |
| | | Fewer failures (e.g. circuit breakdown) resulting in shutdown of elevator ($R_{22}$) | 0.217 |
| | | Long service life of elevator ($R_{23}$) | 0.132 |
| | Low operating costs of elevator ($R_3$) | Lower maintenance costs (e.g., labor cost, consumable cost and spare part cost) ($R_{31}$) | 0.162 |
| Elevator upgrading | Flexible service with quick response ($R_4$) | Quick response to service request of customer ($R_{41}$) | 0.361 |
| | | Various types of service contracts to satisfy personalized needs ($R_{42}$) | 0.098 |
| | Lifecycle energy saving of elevator($R_5$) | Low power consumption and efficient energy use in elevator lifecycle ($R_{51}$) | 0.099 |

Table 1.3, requirement $R_{21}$ (fewer accidents) was ranked the first in requirement list. $R_{41}$ (quick service response) came in the second place, because the service response time would affects customer satisfaction and experience. For the high-rise building, especially commercial high-rise building, the shut-down of elevator not only brings inconvenience of daily travel, but also may lead to security incidents. Therefore, $R_{22}$ (fewer failures of shut-down) was also given a high priority.

1.4 Case Study: Elevator PSS Customization

**Table 1.4** The technical attributes of elevator service (Song and Sakao 2017)

| Technical attribute | Name | Description |
|---|---|---|
| $TA_1$ | Professional level of elevator purchase guidance | Capability to provide guidance for customer to select the most suitable elevator in terms of the building environment |
| $TA_2$ | Efficiency of installation and commissioning | Efficiency of installation and commissioning services for quick start and safe use of elevator |
| $TA_3$ | Coverage of condition monitoring | Scope of condition monitoring to guarantee grasping real-time running state of the elevator |
| $TA_4$ | Accuracy of failure diagnosis | Failure diagnosis accuracy based on expert knowledge and elevator condition information |
| $TA_5$ | Level of maintenance | Maintenance service level to keep the elevator in good condition |
| $TA_6$ | Effectiveness of elevator operation training | Customer's knowledge/skill of safe use and basic maintenance acquired from training |
| $TA_7$ | Level of repair service | Repair service capability to quickly restore elevator's functionality |
| $TA_8$ | Cost of spare parts supply | Cost of interchangeable part kept in an inventory and supplied for the repair or replacement of failed units |
| $TA_9$ | Coverage of service network | Scope of service network that ensures the availability of the elevator service for customers |
| $TA_{10}$ | Time of service dispatching | Time of dispatching service technicians to meet certain service response requirement |
| $TA_{11}$ | Availability of emergency repair | Repair service availability in emergency circumstances, e.g., rescuing people trapped in the elevator |
| $TA_{12}$ | Technical level of elevator retrofit and upgrading | Retrofits and upgrading technology level for safe and efficient operation in the later stage of elevator lifecycle |

## *1.4.2 Elevator PSS Requirements Specification*

After acquiring the PSS requirements and their requirements, service technical attributes were obtained from the current service resources and functions in the company. Those elevator service technical attributes are illustrated in Table 1.4. $TA_{12}$ could help to save power by upgrading the elevator with an energy feedback system.

**Table 1.5** Correlations between PSS requirements and technical attributes (Song and Sakao 2017)

| | TA$_1$ | TA$_2$ | ... | TA$_9$ | TA$_{10}$ | TA$_{11}$ | TA$_{12}$ | Weights of elevator service requirements |
|---|---|---|---|---|---|---|---|---|
| R$_{11}$ | 9,9,7,7,9 | | ... | 1,1,3,1,3 | | | | 0.018 |
| R$_{12}$ | 3,3,1,3,3 | 9,7,9,9,9 | ... | 5,3,3,3,5 | 5,5,5,3,5 | 3,5,3,3,5 | | 0.052 |
| R$_{21}$ | 1,1,3,1,3 | 5,5,5,3,5 | ... | | | 7,5,5,5,5 | 5,5,7,7,5 | 0.797 |
| R$_{22}$ | 3,1,3,3,3 | 5,5,3,5,3 | ... | | | | 5,3,3,3,3 | 0.217 |
| ... | | | | | | | | ... |
| R$_{42}$ | | | ... | 9,7,7,7,7 | 7,5,5,7,7 | 7,9,7,9,9 | | 0.098 |
| R$_{51}$ | 5,7,7,5,7 | 3,3,3,3,3 | ... | | | | 7,9,7,7,9 | 0.099 |
| Weights of elevator service technical attributes | 0.0815 | 0.0834 | | 0.0826 | 0.0829 | 0.0834 | 0.0839 | – |

Then, the elevator service design engineers analyzed correlations between PSS requirements and the service technical attributes under the structure of HoQ. The weights of the elevator service technical attributes are listed in Table 1.5. TAs' Weights were calculated with rough HoQ in Song et al. (2014). Table 1.5 also illustrates relationships between PSS requirements and technical attributes. The service design team consisting of five designers evaluated the correlations between technical attributes and requirements. The degree of correlations was evaluated by the five designers with the method of 9-point rating scale assessment (Myint 2003). Then the design group analyzed the correlations between different service technical attributes to find those attributes with negative correlations in the HoQ. The five designers participated in conflict identification process. Improvement or enhancement of one elevator service technical attribute may cause the deterioration of another. In this case, there is a conflict between the two elevator service technical attributes. Here, an identified conflict between TA$_9$ (Wide coverage of service network) and TA$_{10}$ (Short time of service dispatching), is used to show the conflict resolving process.

Firstly, the design team analyzed the relationships between different elevator service technical attributes to identify attributes with negative correlations, and they found TA$_9$ (Coverage of service network) and TA$_{10}$ (Time of service dispatching) were negatively correlated. Therefore, the design team considered that there may be potential conflicts between TA$_9$ and TA$_{10}$. Actually, under conditions of limited service resources, wide coverage of service network would make dispatching time increase, and ultimately lead to the increase of customer waiting time.

Secondly, two TRIZ experts were invited to help to represent the TA$_9$ and TA$_{10}$ with the standardized parameters in TRIZ. TA$_9$ was represented with the 33rd TRIZ parameter "Ease of operation" (Simplicity: The process is NOT easy if it needs a lot of people, complex steps in the operation, requires special tools, etc. "Hard" processes have low yield and "easy" process have high yield; they are easy to do right) (Al'tshuller et al. 1999). While TA$_{10}$ was represented with the 25th TRIZ parameter "Loss of time" (Time is the duration of an activity. Improving the loss of time means reducing the time taken for the activity) (Al'tshuller 1999).

Thirdly, the contradiction matrix in TRIZ was examined to find out the favorable inventive principles. The TRIZ parameter "33. Ease of operation" was detected by the design team as "improving parameter" in the columns, while "25. Loss of time" was detected as "worsening parameter" in the rows. Then, to find the recommend inventive principles, designers searched through the intersection of the improving and worsening TRIZ parameters in contradiction matrix. Four inventive principles were recommended to resolve conflict between TA9 and TA10. They were principle 4 (Asymmetry), 28 (Mechanics substitution), 10 (Preliminary action) and 34 (Discarding and recovering) respectively.

After discussion with TRIZ experts, the design team decided to choose inventive principle 10 (Preliminary action) to resolve the conflict. According to the subprinciple of the inventive principle 10 ["Pre-arrange objects such that they can come into action from the most convenient place and without losing time for their delivery" (Al'tshuller 1999)], it was necessary to provide service skill training for works in advance to keep the service facilities in good state. Specifically, in order to reduce customer waiting time, a precise dispatching method based on GIS (Geographic Information System) was proposed to optimize service route and resources in advance.

### 1.4.3 Elevator PSS Modularization

Firstly, the modified service blueprint (Song et al. 2015b) was used to represent the entire scenario of elevator PSS in Fig. 1.4. In Fig. 1.4, there are different customers-involved activities in the visualized service domain, for example, elevator operation training, installation and maintenance relying on supports of components in the resources domain (e.g., service engineer and service tool library). The non-visualized service domain (due to the limited space) consists of installation tasks assignment, maintenance planning, and upgrading analysis, etc. The activity of "safe operation of elevator" in product using domain is mainly to achieve reliable and efficient use of elevator. Product management domain consists of three activities, i.e., real-time data acquisition, remote inspection and malfunction alarm. All the activities in both product domain and service domain require supports from resource domain. Therefore, the service components of the elevator PSS in each domain can be identified with the modified service blueprint (represented by the boxes in Fig. 1.4). A total of 50 elevator service components were identified in the modified service blueprint.

Secondly, interdependencies between the 50 identified components (see Table 1.6) were analyzed by means of pair-wise comparison method to obtain the interdependencies between elevator service components.

Finally, the fuzzy graph-based modularizing method proposed in Song et al. (2015b) was used to group the service components into 13 PSS modules. All the elevators PSS modules are listed in Table 1.6. The PSS components in Table 1.6 were identified from Fig. 1.4, and the elevator PSS modules were obtained using the method in Song et al. (2015b). Only part of the elevator PSS modules is provided in Table 1.6 due to the limited space.

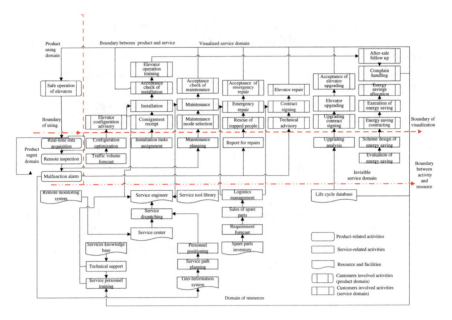

**Fig. 1.4** The modified service blueprint for elevator PSS (Song and Sakao 2017)

**Table 1.6** Elevator PSS module and components (Song and Sakao 2017)

| No. | Elevator PSS module | Elevator PSS components |
|---|---|---|
| | | Elevator PSS components |
| 1 | Service knowledge support | Services knowledge base, Technical support, Service personnel training |
| 2 | Purchase consulting | Elevator configuration advisory, Elevator configuration optimization, Traffic volume forecast |
| 3 | Installation and commissioning | Elevator operation training, Acceptance check of installation, Installation, Consignment receipt, Installation tasks assignment |
| 4 | Customer care | After-sale follow up, Complaints handling |
| 5 | Elevator service planning | Service engineer, Service dispatching, Service center, Service tool library |
| 6 | Repair | Elevator repair, Repair contract signing, Technical advisory |
| … | … | … |
| 12 | Life-cycle data analysis | Lifecycle database |
| 13 | Energy-saving of elevator | Evaluation of energy saving, Scheme design of energy saving, Energy saving contracting, Execution of energy saving, Energy savings allocation |

## *1.4.4 Elevator PSS Configuration and Concept Selection*

The elevator service modules and module instances are provided in Table 1.7. The designers and managers in Company M provided the service module instances (▲: mandatory module, △: optional module) and the data about their cost and response time in Table 1.7. The module instances in Table 1.7 can be used in the first configuration step to establish configuration requirements. Besides, the modules and module instances in Table 1.7 are the key input for the multi-objective configuration optimization modeling of elevator PSS in the second configuration step. The different specifications of module instances (i.e., cost, response time, and module property) in Table 1.7 constitute constraints of the configuration optimization model. Moreover, these module instances with different specifications can be combined into the final solutions for the third step of configuration.

Firstly, the relationship between each technical attribute obtained in Table 1.4 and module instance in Table 1.7 was identified. Scores of 9, 3, 1, and 0 were used to indicate very strong, strong, weak, and no relationship between technical attributes and PSS module instances, respectively (Song and Chan 2015). Thus, correlations between technical attributes and module instances were determined.

Secondly, the multi-objective configuration optimization model was built based on correlations and constraints. The goal of elevator PSS configuration optimization model was built to search for a proper module instance portfolio to achieve relative optimum of overall PSS performance, i.e., the optimized service solution should have the best service performance, shortest response time and lowest service cost. The elevator PSS configuration was required to meet constraints including: Company M's expected profit margin is 25%; The highest price of elevator service that customer can afford is RMB¥300,000; And the tolerable total response time of customer is 50 h.

Thirdly, the model was solved with the NSGA II to obtain the optimized PSS configuration set. The selected optimized elevator PSS concept with rough TOPSIS (Song et al. 2013b) from the solution set is A1. Elevator PSS concept A1 is a set of Online knowledge support with internet, Personalized expert advisory for elevator purchase, Remote installation guidance with internet, Regular telephone follow-up, Maintenance with non-original spare parts, Collaborative emergency repair with partners, Traditional spare parts supply, Maintenance/semimonthly, Operation monitoring, Outsourced dispatching, Energy management contracting (EMC) based on the energy-saving performance, and Proactive lifecycle alert of component failure based on real-time monitoring. Concept A1 includes 12 modules, its total service cost is RMB¥173,200, and total response time is 31.1 h.

**Table 1.7** Elevator service modules and module instances (Song and Sakao 2017)

| Service module name | Module instance | Cost (ten thousand yuan) | Response time (h) | Module property |
|---|---|---|---|---|
| Service knowledge support | Online knowledge support with internet | 1.25 | 0.3 | ▲ |
| | Remote knowledge support with telephone | 1.54 | 0.3 | ▲ |
| | On-site technology training by experts | 2.55 | 1.5 | ▲ |
| Purchase consulting | Personalized expert advisory for elevator purchase | 0.50 | 3.5 | ▲ |
| | Standardized online self-advisory for elevator purchase | 0.30 | 0.2 | ▲ |
| Installation and commissioning | Remote installation guidance with internet | 1.25 | 8 | ▲ |
| | On-site installation guidance from experts | 0.62 | 16 | ▲ |
| | Turnkey service for installation and commissioning | 2.50 | 8 | ▲ |
| Customer care | Regular telephone follow-up | 1.55 | 0.5 | ▲ |
| | Random telephone follow-up | 0.96 | 6.2 | ▲ |
| | Follow-up based on customer complaints | 1.24 | 5.5 | ▲ |
| ... | ... | ... | ... | ... |
| Lifecycle data analysis (optional) | Proactive lifecycle alert of component failure based on real-time monitoring | 0.64 | 0.5 | △ |
| | Maintenance information inquiry and reporting after failure occurs | 0.88 | 0.5 | △ |
| Energy-saving of elevator (optional) | Energy management contracting (EMC) based on the energy-saving performance | 3.58 | 8 | △ |
| | Disposable payment for energy-saving retrofit based on project | 5.16 | 8 | △ |

## 1.5 Comparisons and Discussion

**Table 1.8** Comparisons with former frameworks (Song and Sakao 2017)

| Key features of framework | The proposed framework | Aurich et al. (2006) | Kindström and Kowalkowski (2009) | Pezzotta et al. (2013) | Lee et al. (2010) |
|---|---|---|---|---|---|
| I-CAC-based requirements identification | √ | No | P | P | √ |
| Conflict resolving | √ | No | No | No | No |
| Modularization | √ | √ | No | No | No |
| Configuration for customization | √ | √ | No | P | No |
| End-to-end process | √ | P | No | P | P |
| Case/example | Elevator | Heavy road construction machine | Multiple case study (10 companies) | Truck repair | Clothes TakeIN |

### 1.5 Comparisons and Discussion

Table 1.8 shows comparisons of the proposed framework with the former PSS design frameworks. "√" in Table 1.8 indicates that the framework has the critical feature, "No" indicates that the framework does not have the critical feature, and "P" indicates that the framework partially has the critical feature. The previous framework does not have comprehensive coverage as the proposed one. The proposed framework provides end-to-end process to complete PSS customization from requirement identification to requirement fulfillment with configured PSS solutions based on modules, which has not been considered in previous framework. With a widened scope, the proposed framework's major differences as compared with existing life cycle design methods, which are reported by review articles such as (Ramani et al. 2010; Umeda et al. 2012), or general design methods exist in its orientation to customization and PSS. Specifically, differently with the other frameworks in Table 1.8, the proposed framework identifies requirements from the perspective of the customer's activity using product as well as facilitates conflict resolving and modularization. Especially, the framework by Pezzotta et al. (2013) and that by Lee et al. (2010) lack mechanisms of conflict resolving and modularization. Although the framework by Aurich et al. (2006) provides perspective of modularization and configuration for PSS design, it does not use the information of customer activity in requirement identification process. The technical attributes' conflicts resolving is also beyond the framework of Aurich et al. (2006). The framework of Kindström and Kowalkowski (2009) is based on multiple case study, but it lacks specific design process and methodical supports from requirements identification to PSS configuration.

The case study of elevator PSS design is an illustrative example of a design process that helps to enhance understanding of PSS customization process and can serve as a basis for further research in this area. In more details, the case study has shown the following advantages of the proposed framework.

(1) The framework provides a systematic PSS design process, as well as quantitative methods to reduce the randomness in PSS conceptual design process. Furthermore, the framework includes throughput mechanism so that the output of one phase provides input to one or more of the following phases. E.g., PSS requirement identification and analysis provide critical inputs for PSS configuration. Hence, designers can get a systematical and standardized design process reference from the framework, from the initial requirements identification to the later concept configuration. Collectively, the framework simplifies modular design of customized solutions and provides systematic design supports from the requirement identification to the PSS concept configuration.

(2) The framework involves conflict resolving in the early PSS design. Manipulating the conflicts of potential design attributes helps to reduce possible defects during subsequent process of detailed design and delivery. This is particularly relevant in considering the environmental requirements or requirements from different lifecycle phases, because it makes more likely for conflicts to occur. Besides, conflict resolving in early design phase reduces possible failures and ensures to fulfill requirements. Contrary to other articles dealing with conflicts in physical products (e.g., Chang and Chen 2004), the proposed framework is innovative by addressing service aspects.

(3) Modular design thinking is introduced into the PSS customization framework. The modularization feature also helps to modify a specific existing PSS module by handling requirement changes without undermining the entire PSS structure. For example, to solve conflicts between TA9 (Coverage of service network) and TA10 (Time of service dispatching), a precise dispatching solution based on GIS (Geographic Information System) was proposed. In the modularization process, the component of "automatic positioning based on GIS" replaces the previous component of "manual entry of geo-information reported by user" without substantially redesigning the module of service dispatching.

(4) The synergy between the different methods and technologies under the framework is also a motivation to develop the framework, and has been illustrated in the case study. For instance, the HoQ has advantages in identifying the negative relationships (conflicts) between TAs (e.g., conflict between TA9 and TA10), while TRIZ has strength in conflict resolving due to its knowledge-based nature. The recommended inventive principle 10 (Preliminary action) in TRIZ effectively resolves the conflict between TA9 and TA10. This shows clear benefits of a comprehensive framework as compared with a mere set of individual methods.

(5) Based on the module-based PSS configuration in the framework, the service provider can achieve flexible and optimized customization. Conflict resolving before PSS configuration can reduce conflicting goals when setting configuration optimization objectives, which will greatly alleviate burden of solving

multi-objective PSS configuration model. This also reflects the synergy between the different design phases of the framework.

# References

Al'tshuller, G. S. (1999). *The innovation algorithm: TRIZ, systematic innovation and technical creativity*. Technical Innovation Center, Inc

Aurich, J. C., Fuchs, C., & Wagenknecht, C. (2006). Life cycle oriented design of technical Product-Service Systems. *Journal of Cleaner Production, 14*(17), 1480–1494.

Baines, T. S., Lightfoot, H. W., Evans, S., Neely, A., Greenough, R., Peppard, J., Roy, R., Shehab, E., Braganza, A., Tiwari, A., & Alcock, J. R. (2007). State-of-the-art in product-service systems. *Proceedings of the Institution of Mechanical Engineers, Part B: Journal of Engineering Manufacture, 221*(10), 1543–1552

Berkovich, M., Leimeister, J. M., & Krcmar, H. (2011). Requirements engineering for product service systems. *Business & Information Systems Engineering, 3*(6), 369–380.

Beuren, F. H., Ferreira, M. G. G., & Miguel, P. A. C. (2013). Product-service systems: a literature review on integrated products and services. *Journal of Cleaner Production, 47*, 222–231.

Chang, H. T., & Chen, J. L. (2004). The conflict-problem-solving CAD software integrating TRIZ into eco-innovation. *Advances in Engineering Software, 35*(8–9), 553–566.

Deb, K., Pratap, A., Agarwal, S., & Meyarivan, T. A. M. T. (2002). A fast and elitist multiobjective genetic algorithm: NSGA-II. *IEEE Transactions on Evolutionary Computation, 6*(2), 182–197.

Gershenson, J. K., Prasad, G. J., & Zhang, Y. (2003). Product modularity: Definitions and benefits. *Journal of Engineering Design, 14*(3), 295–313.

Hauser, J. R., & Clausing, D. (1988). *The house of quality*.

Hu, S. J., Ko, J., Weyand, L., ElMaraghy, H. A., Lien, T. K., Koren, Y., Bley, H., Chryssolouris, G., Nasr, N., & Shpitalni, M. (2011). Assembly system design and operations for product variety. *CIRP Annals-Manufacturing Technology, 60*(2), 715–733.

Jiao, J., & Tseng, M. M. (2004). Customizability analysis in design for mass customization. *Computer Aided Design, 36*(8), 745–757.

Kindström, D., & Kowalkowski, C. (2009). Development of industrial service offerings: A process framework. *Journal of service Management, 20*(2), 156–172.

Lee, S. W., Maeng, J. W., Hong, Y. K., Park, H. J., & Kim, Y. S. (2010). Product-service system design processes and cases. *The Asian Conference on Design and Digital Engineering (ACDDE 2010)*, 126–129.

Li, X., & Song, W. (2016). A rough VIKOR-based QFD for prioritizing design attributes of product-related service. *Mathematical Problems in Engineering*.

Manzini, E. (1999, February). Strategic design for sustainability: towards a new mix of products and services. In *Proceedings of the First International Symposium on Environmentally Conscious Design and Inverse Manufacturing, 1999. EcoDesign'99* (pp. 434–437). IEEE

Meier, H., Roy, R., & Seliger, G. (2010). Industrial product-service systems—IPS2. *CIRP Annals-Manufacturing Technology, 59*(2), 607–627.

Myint, S. (2003). A framework of an intelligent quality function deployment (IQFD) for discrete assembly environment. *Computer and Industrial Engineering, 45*(2), 269–283.

Nuseibeh, B., & Easterbrook, S. (2000, May). Requirements engineering: a roadmap. In *Proceedings of the Conference on the Future of Software Engineering* (pp. 35–46). ACM

Pezzotta, G., Pirola, F., Akasaka, F., Cavalieri, S., Shimomura, Y., & Gaiardelli, P. (2013). A service engineering framework to design and configure product-service systems. *IFAC Proceedings Volumes, 46*(7), 263–268.

Ramani, K., Ramanujan, D., Bernstein, W. Z., Zhao, F., Sutherland, J., Handwerker, C., Choi, J. K., Kim, H. C., & Thurston, D. (2010). Integrated sustainable life cycle design: a review. *Journal of Mechanical Design, 132*(9), 091004

Roy, R. (2000). Sustainable product-service systems. *Futures, 32*(3–4), 289–299.

Saaty, T. L. (1988). *What is the analytic hierarchy process?* (pp. 109–121). Berlin, Heidelberg: Springer.

Sakao, T. (2007). A QFD-centred design methodology for environmentally conscious product design. *International Journal of Production Research, 45*(18–19), 4143–4162.

Sakao, T., Song, W., & Matschewsky, J. (2017). Creating service modules for customising product/service systems by extending DSM. *CIRP Annals, 66*(1), 21–24.

Song, W., & Chan, F. T. (2015). Multi-objective configuration optimization for product-extension service. *Journal of Manufacturing Systems, 37,* 113–125.

Song, W., Ming, X., & Han, Y. (2014). Prioritising technical attributes in QFD under vague environment: a rough-grey relational analysis approach. *International Journal of Production Research, 52*(18), 5528–5545.

Song, W., Ming, X., Han, Y., & Wu, Z. (2013a). A rough set approach for evaluating vague customer requirement of industrial product-service system. *International Journal of Production Research, 51*(22), 6681–6701.

Song, W., Ming, X., Han, Y., Xu, Z., & Wu, Z. (2015a). An integrative framework for innovation management of product-service system. *International Journal of Production Research, 53*(8), 2252–2268.

Song, W., Ming, X., & Wu, Z. (2013b). An integrated rough number-based approach to design concept evaluation under subjective environments. *Journal of Engineering Design, 24*(5), 320–341.

Song, W., & Sakao, T. (2016). Service conflict identification and resolution for design of product-service offerings. *Computer and Industrial Engineering, 98,* 91–101.

Song, W., & Sakao, T. (2017). A customization-oriented framework for design of sustainable product/service system. *Journal of Cleaner Production, 140,* 1672–1685.

Song, W., Wu, Z., Li, X., & Xu, Z. (2015b). Modularizing product extension services: An approach based on modified service blueprint and fuzzy graph. *Computer and Industrial Engineering, 85,* 186–195.

Tukker, A. (2004). Eight types of product-service system: eight ways to sustainability? Experiences from SusProNet. *Business Strategy and the Environment, 13*(4), 246–260.

Umeda, Y., Takata, S., Kimura, F., Tomiyama, T., Sutherland, J. W., Kara, S., Herrmann, C., & Duflou, J. R. (2012). Toward integrated product and process life cycle planning—An environmental perspective. *CIRP Annals-Manufacturing Technology, 61*(2), 681–702

Uppenberg, K., & Strauss, H. (2010). *Innovation and productivity growth in the EU services sector*. Luxembourg: European Investment Bank.

Van Halen, C., Vezzoli, C., & Wimmer, R. (2005). Methodology for product service system innovation: how to develop clean, clever and competitive strategies in companies. Uitgeverij Van Gorcum

Vandermerwe, S., & Rada, J. (1988). Servitization of business: Adding value by adding services. *European Management Journal, 6*(4), 314–324.

Vasantha, G. V. A., Roy, R., Lelah, A., & Brissaud, D. (2012). A review of product-service systems design methodologies. *Journal of Engineering Design, 23*(9), 635–659.

# Chapter 2
# Requirements Analysis for Customizable PSS

Since the success of the PSS largely depends on the understanding and satisfying of different requirements, requirements analysis has become a critical factor in PSS development. However, PSS are mixed product-service offerings with features of heterogeneity, interaction, stakeholder participation and customization, which makes the PSS requirement difficult to be captured, analyzed and forecasted. In this chapter, a model of industrial customer activity cycle (Song et al. 2013a) is utilized to efficiently elicit PSS requirements from the lifecycle perspective. Afterward, a rough group analytic hierarchy process method (Song et al. 2013a) is utilized to find the critical requirements. Then, a rough DEMATEL (Decision Making Trial and Evaluation Laboratory) method is provided to evaluate the dependencies and correlations between the PSS requirements (Song and Cao 2017). A requirement forecast model based on Kano model and Grey-Markov chain (Song et al. 2013b). is also presented to analyze the future requirements in this chapter.

## 2.1 PSS Requirement

Jung (2006) defines requirement as a request that a product fulfills certain properties or functions, and it contains a describing attribute and a defining value (quantification). A requirement is a defined behavior, characteristic or property, to be assumed for an object, a person or an activity which must assure a certain result in a value creation process (Kruse 1996). Objects, actors/stakeholders, activities and values, which all are relevant in the PSS context, are considered by this definition. PSS requirement is one of the fundamental driving forces for service-oriented manufacturing transformation. Different product usage scenarios in different environments generate different PSS requirements (Song 2017). In this respect, PSS development is largely driven by requirements. To successfully achieve service transformation, conventional manufacturer must have a deep understanding of users' requirements and their behavior patterns. The accurate requirement identification, rational analysis and effective mapping is critical to obtain a satisfactory PSS design solution. Moreover, requirement management is also one of the basic processes of product, service and system development. However, PSS are mixed product-service offerings which have features of heterogeneity, interaction, stakeholder participation and modularization, etc. These features enable the PSS requirement to have characteristics as follows.

First, PSS requirements are heterogeneous. Not only product requirements, but also service requirements are included. Compared with product requirements, it is more difficult to accurately express and portray the intangible service requirements. Second, elements of customer perception and experience, which are difficult to be identified and expressed directly, should be contained by PSS requirements. These implicit elements must be converted into specific explicit items by designers. Third, product requirements and service requirements can interact with each other, because relations of enhancements, synergies, and substitutions may exist between these heterogeneous PSS requirements. In addition, potential conflicts may also exist between the different PSS requirements. The reason is that PSS is a Socio-technical System (Bruijn and Herder 2009) of value co-creation. PSS involves many stakeholders, and they often have different value propositions, which may cause requirement conflicts. Finally, PSS requirements can change with the product life cycle and users' behavior of operating the product.

## 2.2 PSS Requirements Analysis

Customer requirement analysis is of great important in the development phase of a new product or service. One of key elements to successful product-service design and delivery is requirements identification and processing. It is the beginning of PSS development project. The task of requirements elicitation is to identify requirements' sources and elicit the requirements according to the identified stakeholders and other sources. Actually, PSS is a value co-creation system focusing on user activities with multi-stakeholders' participation in co-creating process (Xu et al. 2014). Thus, it is necessary to consider the impact of the stakeholders' interactions in PSS requirement generation process. In this way, we can broaden the breadth of requirement identification. However, the conventional requirement identification methods for product or service are no longer fully applicable. In addition, the implicit requirements of PSS are usually reflected in user interactions with the product (e.g. perception and experience of using product). So, it is essential to further extract PSS implicit requirements behind the user's behavior, which will enhance the depth of requirement identification and understanding. Moreover, the normative expression of requirement, accuracy and reusability of the requirement still need to be explored. Previous researches consider less about the relationships between different PSS requirements, which will result in inaccurate analysis of requirements (e.g. priorities of PSS requirements).

In engineering practice of PSS, requirements of customers are not only limited to features of product, but also include the functions and results of service activities. However, as the two different types of objects in PSS, product and service have typical characteristics of heterogeneity. The heterogeneous requirement analysis will influence the integration design of product and service. As a combination of product requirement and service requirement, some problems of matching the physical product requirement and intangible service requirement have not been solved. Interactions (e.g. requirement conflict and substitution) between product requirement and service requirement are still not well considered. Besides, service requirements involve much human perceptions and judgments, which lead to the ambiguity and subjectivity in process of PSS requirement analysis. Although some approaches for gaining customer's preferences are reported in the literatures, the problem of analysis customer's PSS preferences is still not well addressed.

The lifecycle of PSS is different with that of traditional products. The company developing PSS also offers services in combination with the product, which means that the later operation of the product is also critical. The operator model has changed from "develop and forget" to "develop, operate and advance". To achieve the successful operation and advancement, it is essential to better understand future customer requirements (Xu et al. 2017). In fact, customer requirements are dynamic and may vary extremely in different time. The trend of customer individuality is also one of the important features characterizing these PSS. Thus, it is necessary to analyze dynamic requirements and forecast their future trends, because this helps find out which requirement might become critically important in the near future and which might become less important from the point of view of customers (Wu et al. 2005). In addition, forecasting future customer requirements early on could help companies provide better products or services, delight customers, and eventually increase customer satisfaction (Shen et al. 2001). Requirements trend can be dug out from the vast amounts of PSS operation information, which helps service providers to improve their offerings and achieve PSS innovation. For example, by forecasting future trends of customer requirements, service-oriented manufacturer can push customized solutions to meet users' unique demands, which helps to change from passive response model to active service model. The active service will not only shorten the service response time, but also improve customer satisfaction and increase customer value. Some researchers have studied on requirement forecasting of product or service.

## 2.3 PSS Requirements Identification and Prioritization

A rough group AHP method is proposed by Song et al. (2013a) to evaluate the PSS requirement elicited from industrial customer activity cycle analysis. This method integrates the advantage of AHP in requirement evaluation structure and the strength of rough set theory in manipulating vagueness and subjectivity. With the aid of the proposed method, it is expected that the critical customer requirements can be easily found for further design of PSS. In sum, this section is to provide a systematic method for requirements elicitation and prioritization under vague environment. In the proposed approach, the whole requirement assessment process is divided into two main parts as shown in Fig. 2.1. Below, each functional part is analyzed in detail.

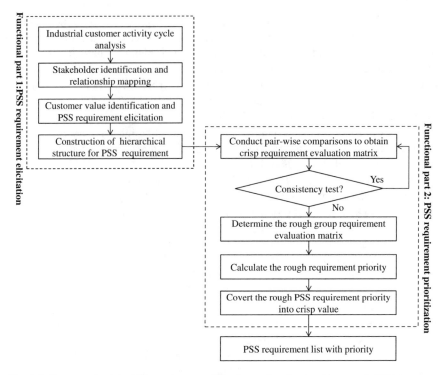

**Fig. 2.1** Framework of the PSS requirement elicitation and evaluation (Song et al. 2013a)

## 2.3.1 PSS Requirement Elicitation

The beginning of PSS development project is requirement elicitation. The first functional part is to obtain an understanding of the problem that PSS is to solve. In this functional part, industrial customer activity cycle is reviewed, stakeholders are identified, and customer value and requirement is elicited. This process is typically performed by a requirement engineer team with enough expertise and experience in implementing elicitation techniques.

**Step 1. Construct model of Industrial Customer Activity Cycle (I-CAC)**

In contrast to the conventional product thinking, value is not embedded in the industrial product but is generated by supporting the industrial customer's activities related to the use of the product. To facilitate the use of industrial product, designers should consider both pre-use activities (e.g. installation, training) and post-use activities (e.g. disposal). Therefore, to obtain industrial customer's requirement systematically and effectively, this section introduces a tool named Industrial Customer Activity Cycle (I-CAC) analysis. An I-CAC contains three kinds of activities, pre-what goes on before the industrial customer obtains the expected result, during-what happens while they derive the core benefit, and post-what happens after long use of the product. Each

## 2.3 PSS Requirements Identification and Prioritization

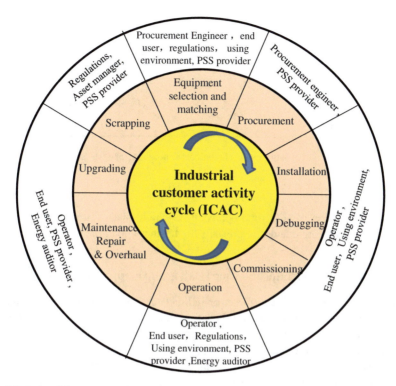

**Fig. 2.2** Industrial customer activity cycle (I-CAC) and stakeholders (Song et al. 2013a)

category consists of several key activities. As is shown in the middle ring of Fig. 2.2, in the phase of Pre-use, customers firstly conduct product selection and matching to choose the most suitable products to meet their production need. This activity would be significant to the overall function and operation efficiency. Activities (such as bargaining, delivery, inspection and payment, etc.) are included in the Procurement. After procurement, it is necessary to ensure the quick and reliable equipment starting and running with installation, debugging, and commissioning of the product. In the phase of during use, operation of industrial product mainly focuses on the efficient use and collecting relevant information of the product. To improve equipment operation efficiency and reduce equipment life cycle costs, MRO (Maintenance, Repair and Overhaul) is adopted, which includes activities such as disassembly, diagnosis, spare part supply, etc. In the final phase of Post-use, Upgrading and Scrapping are related activities equipment dismantling, assessment, refurbishment and recycling, etc.

Designers can actually determine the benefit, costs or even, the environmental effects, only when a product interacts with customer in an activity. The I-CAC model could be tailored for the actual context of different types of industrial products. A

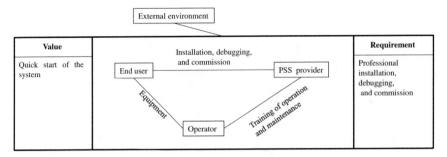

**Fig. 2.3** An illustration of requirement elicitation in the phase of installation, debugging, and commission (Song et al. 2013a)

key concept here is the life time perspective, which takes a broader, holistic and longer-term perspective and often reveals the business potential of the whole value chain.

**Step 2. Stakeholder identification and relationship mapping in the I-CAC model**

Firstly, different stakeholders (direct or indirect) are identified throughout the life cycle so that the designer can gain their common value later. A stakeholder could either be from the external or internal organizational environment. There are various stakeholders around the Industrial Customer Activity Cycle (I-CAC), each with different types of stakes in the decisions made during the development of a PSS. The stakeholders include end users/customers, spare part suppliers, laws and regulations, procurement engineer, operator, and PSS providers, etc. (see outer ring in Fig. 2.2). Those stakeholders play different roles in different phase of customer activity cycle. For instance, end users in the activity of product selection and matching mainly presents their requirements of the product, while in the operation activity, they use the result or function of the product.

Secondly, the relationships between the stakeholders need to be identified around the customer activity, because the value and requirements are embed in those relationships. Interactions between stakeholders include: exchanging information and knowledge, operating products, executing instructions and providing supporting tasks or spare parts. An illustration of stakeholders' interactions in activity of installation, debugging, and commission is shown in the middle of Fig. 2.3. The PSS provider installs, debugs and trials the industrial product to meet the end user's requirements. Meanwhile, the end user obtains the function of the product from the operator's work (operation of the equipment). To ensure that operator provides reliable results with the product, PSS provider also offers training and maintenance. Other stakeholders' interactions can be obtained in the same way.

## Step 3. Customer value identification and requirement elicitation

The customer value is the benefit obtained by customers when their requirements are fulfilled. It is also the common vision of stakeholders for the PSS. The expression of customer value should clearly describe the added value provided by the new PSS in different activities, for example, once the procurement contracts is signed, the customer value is "quick start of the system". When customer's common value has been identified, relevant stakeholders' requirement related with the value could be determined. To support this process, several methods exist for gathering and collecting the information from the different stakeholders. Those methods include, for example, interviews, focus groups, brainstorming, use cases, checklists and questionnaires. For example, PSS is often complex and automated system, professional installation, debugging, and commission is valuable for customers, which would increase the customer's satisfaction. Industrial customer needs the PSS provider to guide the installation and adjust the key parameters of the equipment at the starting period. Therefore, the value of "Quick start of the system" can be translated into the requirement of "Professional installation, debugging, and commission" (see Fig. 2.3).

## Step 4. Construction of hierarchical structure for PSS requirement

Due to the diverse, imprecise and linguistic characteristics of customer requirements, it is necessary to classify them into meaningful hierarchies or categories for easy understanding and analysis. Affinity Diagram (Cohen 1995) can be used to organize customer requirements, because it is a method of arranging random data into natural and logical groups. The PSS requirement management team firstly interprets the elicited customer requirements into simple and representative expressions. Then, these phrases would be combined into many affinity groups, and the phrase that could capture the primary theme and key points of the group would be selected as the header while its group members could be stratified into a tree structure. With this effort spent, customer requirements can be organized as a tree-like structure with an increasing number of items moving from left to right. Figure 2.4 shows a sample IPS2 requirement hierarchy.

## *2.3.2 PSS Requirement Prioritization*

Requirements need to be ranked by designers so that they can make decisions on which requirements to fulfill when different requirements cannot be fulfilled at the same time. The conventional prioritization methods always ignore the vagueness and subjectivity of decision information in uncertain environment. Therefore, in this section, in order to deal with vague and subjective information in PSS requirement prioritization, a rough group AHP based on the rough set theory in is proposed. The rough set theory can enable stakeholders to well express their true perception and evaluation without any priori information.

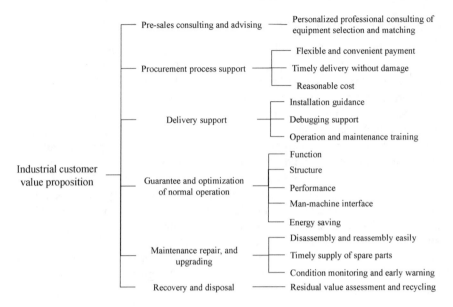

**Fig. 2.4** Hierarchical structure for PSS requirement (Song et al. 2013a)

**Step 1. Construction of pair comparison matrix and consistency test**

Invite expert team to make pair-wise comparisons of PSS requirement to obtain crisp evaluation matrix. The $k$th expert pair-wise comparison matrix $M_k$ is as follows:

$$M_k = \begin{bmatrix} 1 & r_{12}^k & \cdots & r_{1n}^k \\ r_{21}^k & 1 & \cdots & r_{2n}^k \\ \vdots & \vdots & \ddots & \vdots \\ r_{n1}^k & r_{n2}^k & \cdots & 1 \end{bmatrix} \quad k = 1, 2, \ldots m \qquad (2.1)$$

where $r_{ij}^k$ is the $k$th expert's judgment for the $i$th PSS requirement's importance compared with the $j$th requirement, $m$ is the number of experts, and $n$ is the number of PSS requirement. It is necessary for testing consistency of pair-wise comparison matrix. Consistency test can be conducted as follows.

$$CI = \frac{\lambda \max - n}{n - 1} \qquad (2.2)$$

$$CR^* = \left(\frac{CI}{RI(n)}\right), \qquad (2.3)$$

## 2.3 PSS Requirements Identification and Prioritization

**Table 2.1** Random index $RI(n)$ (Song et al. 2013a)

| Dimension | 1 | 2 | 3    | 4   | 5    | 6    | 7    | 8    | 9    |
|-----------|---|---|------|-----|------|------|------|------|------|
| RI        | 0 | 0 | 0.58 | 0.9 | 1.12 | 1.24 | 1.32 | 1.41 | 1.45 |

$CI$ is consistency index, and $\lambda_{max}$ is the largest eigenvalue of matrix $M_k$, $n$ is the dimension of the matrix $M_k$, $CR^*$ is consistency ratio, and $RI(n)$ is random index that depends on the dimension of the matrix (Saaty 1977) (see Table 2.1).

When $CR^* < 0.1$, pair-wise comparison matrix pass the consistency test, experts' evaluations on the PSS requirement are in consistency and acceptable. While $CR^* > 0.1$, experts need to adjust their judgments until pass the consistency test.

After consistency test, PSS requirement management team could then build group requirement evaluation matrix $\tilde{R}$ as follows:

$$\tilde{R} = \begin{bmatrix} 1 & \tilde{r}_{12} & \cdots & \tilde{r}_{1n} \\ \tilde{rl}_{21} & 1 & \cdots & \tilde{r}_{2n} \\ \vdots & \vdots & \ddots & \vdots \\ \tilde{r}_{n1} & \tilde{r}_{n2} & \cdots & 1 \end{bmatrix} \quad (2.4)$$

where $\tilde{r}_{ij} = \{r_{ij}^1, r_{ij}^2, \cdots, r_{ij}^k, \cdots, r_{ij}^m\}$

**Step 2. Determination of the rough group requirement evaluation matrix**

Assume that there is a set of $m$ classes of human judgments, $J = \{r_{ij}^1, r_{ij}^2, \ldots, r_{ij}^k, \ldots, r_{ij}^m\}$ ordered in the manner of $r_{ij}^1 < r_{ij}^2 < \cdots < r_{ij}^k < \cdots < r_{ij}^m$. $U$ is the universe including all the objects and $Y$ is an arbitrary object of $U$, and then the lower approximation of $r_{ij}^k$ and the upper approximation of $r_{ij}^k$ can be defined as:

Lower approximation: $\underline{Apr}(r_{ij}^k) = \cup \{Y \in U/J(Y) \leq r_{ij}^k\}$ \quad (2.5)

Upper approximation: $\overline{Apr}(r_{ij}^k) = \cup \{Y \in U/J(Y) \geq r_{ij}^k\}$ \quad (2.6)

Convert the crisp judgment sequence $\tilde{r}_{ij}$ in matrix $\tilde{R}$ into rough number form to obtain rough group evaluation matrix R. The geometric mean is adopted to synthesize individual judgments, because it preserves the reciprocal property of pair-wise comparison matrixes without violation of the Pareto principle (Forman and Peniwati 1998).

Thus, the judgment, $r_{ij}^k$, can be represented with a rough number defined by its lower limit $\underline{\lim}(r_{ij}^k)$ and upper limit $\overline{\lim}(r_{ij}^k)$ as follows:

$$\underline{\lim}(r_{ij}^k) = \left(\prod_{m=1}^{N_{ijL}} x_{ij}\right)^{1/N_{ijL}} \quad (2.7)$$

$$\overline{\lim}(r_{ij}^k) = (\prod_{m=1}^{N_{ijU}} y_{ij})^{1/N_{ijU}} \tag{2.8}$$

$x_{ij}$ and $y_{ij}$ are the elements of lower and upper approximation for $r_{ij}^k$. $N_{ijL}$ and $N_{ijU}$ are the number of objects included in the lower approximation and upper approximation of $r_{ij}^k$ respectively.

Then, the rough number form $RN(r_{ij}^k)$ of $\tilde{r}_{ij}$ can be obtained using Eqs. (2.5)–(2.8),

$$RN(r_{ij}^k) = [\underline{\lim}(r_{ij}^k), \overline{\lim}(r_{ij}^k)] = [r_{ij}^{kL}, r_{ij}^{kU}], \tag{2.9}$$

where $r_{ij}^{kL}$ and $r_{ij}^{kU}$ are the lower limit and upper limit of rough number $RN(r_{ij}^k)$ in the $k$th pair-wise comparison matrix. The interval of boundary region (i.e. $r_{ij}^{kU} - r_{ij}^{kL}$) indicates the degree of vagueness. A rough number with a smaller interval of boundary region is interpreted as more precise one.

Thus, the rough sequence $RN(\tilde{r}_{ij})$ can be obtained as follows,

$$RN(\tilde{r}_{ij}) = \{[r_{ij}^{1L}, r_{ij}^{1U}], [r_{ij}^{2L}, r_{ij}^{2U}], \ldots, [r_{ij}^{mL}, r_{ij}^{mU}]\} \tag{2.10}$$

The average rough interval $\overline{RN(\tilde{r}_{ij})}$ can be obtained as follows:

$$\overline{RN(\tilde{r}_{ij})} = [r_{ij}^L, r_{ij}^U] \tag{2.11}$$

$$r_{ij}^L = (\prod_{k=1}^{m} r_{ij}^{kL})^{1/m} \tag{2.12}$$

$$r_{ij}^U = (\prod_{k=1}^{m} r_{ij}^{kU})^{1/m} \tag{2.13}$$

$r_{ij}^L$ and $r_{ij}^U$ are lower limit and upper limit of rough number $[r_{ij}^L, r_{ij}^U]$ respectively. $m$ is the number of experts.

Then the rough group decision matrix R can be obtained as follows:

$$R = \begin{bmatrix} [1,1] & [r_{12}^L, r_{12}^U] & \cdots & [r_{1n}^L, r_{1n}^U] \\ [r_{21}^L, r_{21}^U] & [1,1] & \cdots & [r_{2n}^L, r_{2n}^U] \\ \vdots & \vdots & \ddots & \vdots \\ [r_{n1}^L, r_{n1}^U] & [r_{n2}^L, r_{n2}^U] & \cdots & [1,1] \end{bmatrix} \tag{2.14}$$

**Step 3. Calculate rough weights of PSS requirement**

Calculate rough weights of each PSS requirement $\widetilde{RW_i}$ in different hierarchy with the following equation.

## 2.3 PSS Requirements Identification and Prioritization

$$\widetilde{RW_i} = [RW_i^L, RW_i^U] \tag{2.15}$$

$$RW_i^L = \sqrt[n]{\prod_{j=1}^{n} r_{ij}^L}, \quad RW_i^U = \sqrt[n]{\prod_{j=1}^{n} r_{ij}^U} \tag{2.16}$$

$I = 1, 2, \ldots, n$.

In the same way, rough weights of PSS requirement can be get in any other hierarchies.

Finally, each requirement's overall priority is calculated using multiplication synthesis method from level top to bottom level.

**Step 4. Prioritization of PSS requirements**

To covert the rough PSS requirement weight into crisp value, here the authors introduce the optimistic indicator λ ($0 \leq \lambda \leq 1$) to transform the rough weight $\widetilde{RW_i}$ into crisp value $RW_i$. If decision makers are more optimistic about their judgments, then λ can select a bigger value (λ>0.5). If decision makers are more pessimistic about their evaluations, λ should select a smaller value (λ<0.5). If decision makers keep a moderate attitude, in other words, neither more optimistic nor more pessimistic, λ selects a certain value 0.5. The transformation calculation is as follows:

$$RW_i = (1 - \lambda)RW_i^L + \lambda RW_i^U \tag{2.17}$$

According to the weights from the above steps, all the requirements of PSS can be prioritized, and the important value-based requirements can also be focused.

### 2.3.3 Case Study: Air Compressor PSS Requirement Identification and Prioritization

In this section, PSS requirement identification and prioritization for a rotary oil-free air compressor is used to demonstrate the application of the proposed approach in the real world. In this case, the rotary oil-free air compressor is primarily designed and sold to pharmaceutical plants that need clean compressed air for washing bottles and starting pneumatic valves. Company H is a Fortune 500 manufacturer who is specialized in providing different air compressors and related services for industry: pharmaceutical industry, metallurgical industry, shipbuilding, and mining, etc. The company H now pays more attention to the selling industrial services related to their air compressors throughout the customer activity lifecycle, such as air compressor selection consulting, installation and debugging, MRO, and energy saving solutions, etc. The objective of the PSS requirement evaluation in this case study is to identify key requirements for further PSS design, and thereby improving the customer satisfaction and loyalty.

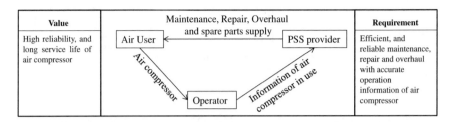

**Fig. 2.5** The value and requirement around the customer activity of MRO (Song et al. 2013a)

### Stage 1: Air compressor PSS requirement elicitation

Firstly, main activities of the customer are analyzed using survey based on Industrial Customer Activity Cycle (I-CAC). The activities are pre-sales consulting, procurement, installation, debugging and commissioning of air compressor, operation and use, maintenance, repair and overhaul, etc. Since the pharmaceutical plant has its own special channel to recycle the scrapped compressor, the disposal of air compressor is not considered here.

Secondly, the related stakeholders around customer activities are identified. Interactions between stakeholders and the nature of their relationships such as exchanging information, products, or instructions are also identified. For example, the stakeholders and their relationships in the MRO activity are captured in Fig. 2.5. There are three main stakeholders, i.e. air user, PSS provider, and operator. The air user proposes the air demand, the operator meet this demand with the air compressor operation and the PSS provider is mainly responsible for reliable air supply with professional MRO and spare parts supply in this phase. Similarly, the stakeholders and their relationships in other customer activities can be acquired.

Thirdly, the customer value, which is the common focus of stakeholders for the PSS, is identified with the interviews and focus groups. Value here is actually the definition of the PSS in terms of the requirement the industrial service is going to meet. For instance, to achieve the value of "High reliability, and long service life of air compressor", the requirement "Efficient, and reliable maintenance, repair and overhaul with accurate operation information of air compressor" has to be fulfilled. That is, the requirement is the cost of achieving the value. Similarly, the value in the delivery of air compressor is mainly "Using immediately without time consuming for the starting period". This value is related with the requirement "Filed guidance and training at the starting period". Thus, in this way, the rest of requirements can be acquired.

## 2.3 PSS Requirements Identification and Prioritization

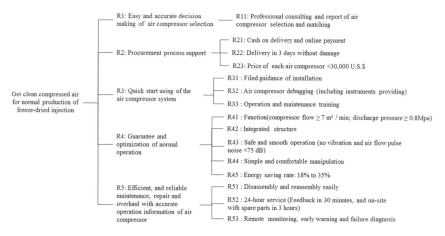

**Fig. 2.6** Hierarchical structure for PSS requirement of rotary oil-free air compressor (Song et al. 2013a)

Fourthly, Affinity Diagram is used to structure customer requirements. The elicited customer requirements are firstly interpreted into simple and representative expressions. For example, ambiguous requirement in Fig. 2.5 (Efficient, and reliable maintenance, repair and overhaul with accurate operation information of air compressor) is represented by three concrete sub-requirements, i.e. "Disassembly and reassembly easily", "24-h service (Feedback in 30 min, and on-site with spare parts in 3 h)" and "Remote monitoring, early warning and failure diagnosis". Similarly, other requirements could be also interpreted. Then, all the phrases would be bundled into many affinity groups, and the header with its group members could be obtained in Fig. 2.6.

### Stage 2: Air compressor PSS requirement prioritization

### Step 1: Construct pair comparison matrix and test consistency

An expert team is built to evaluate PSS requirement which consists of 5 experienced team members. They are procurement engineer, operator, end user, MRO engineer and PSS designer. The work experience of experts ranged from four to ten years in their own domains. Pair-wise comparisons between PSS requirements are conducted in each hierarchy until each comparison matrix can get through the consistency test.

Take the $R_4$ (Guarantee and optimization of normal operation) for example ($R_{41}$: Compressor flow $\geq 7$ m$^3$/min, discharge pressure $\geq 0.8$ Mpa; $R_{42}$: Integrated structure; $R_{43}$: no vibration and air flow pulse, noise $< 75$ dB; $R_{44:}$: Simple and comfortable manipulation; and $R_{45:}$ Energy saving rate: 18% to 35%) to illustrate computation process. The five experts' comparison matrixes of requirement importance for $R_4$ are as follows:

$$M_1 = \begin{array}{c} \\ R_{41} \\ R_{42} \\ R_{43} \\ R_{44} \\ R_{45} \end{array} \begin{array}{c} R_{41}\ R_{42}\ R_{43}\ R_{44}\ R_{45} \\ \begin{bmatrix} 1 & 5 & 3 & 3 & 5 \\ 1/5 & 1 & 1/2 & 1/2 & 1 \\ 1/3 & 2 & 1 & 1 & 3 \\ 1/3 & 2 & 1 & 1 & 3 \\ 1/5 & 1 & 1/3 & 1/3 & 1 \end{bmatrix} \end{array} \quad M_2 = \begin{array}{c} \\ R_{41} \\ R_{42} \\ R_{43} \\ R_{44} \\ R_{45} \end{array} \begin{array}{c} R_{41}\ R_{42}\ R_{43}\ R_{44}\ R_{45} \\ \begin{bmatrix} 1 & 7 & 3 & 5 & 3 \\ 1/7 & 1 & 1/3 & 1/2 & 1/3 \\ 1/3 & 3 & 1 & 3 & 1 \\ 1/5 & 2 & 1/3 & 1 & 1/3 \\ 1/3 & 3 & 1 & 3 & 1 \end{bmatrix} \end{array}$$

$$M_3 = \begin{array}{c} \\ R_{41} \\ R_{42} \\ R_{43} \\ R_{44} \\ R_{45} \end{array} \begin{array}{c} R_{41}\ R_{42}\ R_{43}\ R_{44}\ R_{45} \\ \begin{bmatrix} 1 & 5 & 1/2 & 2 & 3 \\ 1/5 & 1 & 1/8 & 1/2 & 1/2 \\ 2 & 8 & 1 & 5 & 5 \\ 1/2 & 2 & 1/5 & 1 & 3 \\ 1/3 & 2 & 1/5 & 1/3 & 1 \end{bmatrix} \end{array} \quad M_4 = \begin{array}{c} \\ R_{41} \\ R_{42} \\ R_{43} \\ R_{44} \\ R_{45} \end{array} \begin{array}{c} R_{41}\ R_{42}\ R_{43}\ R_{44}\ R_{45} \\ \begin{bmatrix} 1 & 3 & 1/3 & 2 & 1 \\ 1/3 & 1 & 1/8 & 1 & 1/3 \\ 3 & 8 & 1 & 7 & 3 \\ 1/2 & 1 & 1/7 & 1 & 1/2 \\ 1 & 3 & 1/3 & 2 & 1 \end{bmatrix} \end{array}$$

$$M_5 = \begin{array}{c} \\ R_{41} \\ R_{42} \\ R_{43} \\ R_{44} \\ R_{45} \end{array} \begin{array}{c} R_{41}\ R_{42}\ R_{43}\ R_{44}\ R_{45} \\ \begin{bmatrix} 1 & 5 & 3 & 3 & 1/2 \\ 1/5 & 1 & 1/2 & 1/2 & 1/8 \\ 1/3 & 2 & 1 & 1 & 1/5 \\ 1/3 & 2 & 1 & 1 & 1/5 \\ 2 & 8 & 5 & 5 & 1 \end{bmatrix} \end{array}$$

According to Formula (2.2) and (2.3), consistency ratio $CR_1 = 0.010 < 0.1$, $CR_2 = 0.017 < 0.1$, $CR_3 = 0.029 < 0.1$, $CR_4 = 0.004 < 0.1$, and $CR_5 = 0.002 < 0.1$, so the consistency of each pair-wise comparison matrix of the requirement $R_4$ (Guarantee and optimization of normal operation) is acceptable.

Then, the group evaluation matrix of requirement $\tilde{R}_4$ can be obtained by combining the above five pair-wise matrixes together.

$$\tilde{R}_4 = \begin{bmatrix} 1,1,1,1,1 & 5,7,5,3,5 & 3,3,1/2,1/3,3 & 3,5,2,2,3 & 5,3,3,1,1/2 \\ 1/5,1/7,1/5,1/3,1/5 & 1,1,1,1,1 & 1/2,1/3,1/8,1/8,1/2 & 1/2,1/2,1/2,1,1/2 & 1,1/3,1/2,1/3,1/8 \\ 1/3,1/3,2,3,1/3 & 2,3,8,8,2 & 1,1,1,1,1 & 1,3,5,7,1 & 3,1,5,3,1/5 \\ 1/3,1/5,1/2,1/2,1/3 & 2,2,2,1,2 & 1,1/3,1/5,1/7,1 & 1,1,1,1,1 & 3,1/3,3,1/2,1/5 \\ 1/5,1/3,1/3,1,2 & 1,3,2,3,8 & 1/3,1,1/5,1/3,5 & 1/3,3,1/3,2,5 & 1,1,1,1,1 \end{bmatrix}$$

The same procedure can be conducted to other PSS requirements and sub-requirements to get their comparison matrixes.

**Step 2: Determination of the rough group requirement evaluation matrix**

Get the rough group comparison matrix R with the original group comparison matrix from the step 1. To get the rough form of group comparison matrix, it is necessary to transform the elements $\tilde{r}_{ij}$ in group PSS requirement evaluation matrix $\tilde{R}_4$ into the rough number form according to Formulas (2.5)–(2.9).

## 2.3 PSS Requirements Identification and Prioritization

Take the element in $\tilde{r}_{42} = \{5, 7, 5, 3, 5\}$ in $\tilde{R}_4$ to illustrate the rough number conversion process,

$$\underline{Lim}(3) = 3 \quad \overline{Lim}(3) = \sqrt[5]{3 \times 5 \times 5 \times 5 \times 7} = 4.829$$
$$\underline{Lim}(5) = \sqrt[4]{5 \times 5 \times 5 \times 3} = 4.401 \quad \overline{Lim}(5) = \sqrt[4]{5 \times 5 \times 5 \times 7} = 5.439$$
$$\underline{Lim}(7) = \sqrt[5]{3 \times 5 \times 5 \times 5 \times 7} = 4.829$$

Thus, $r_{42}^k$ can be represented in the rough number form $RN(r_{12}^k)$,

$$RN(r_{12}^1) = RN(r_{12}^3) = RN(r_{12}^5) = RN(5) = [4.401, 5.439],$$
$$RN(r_{12}^2) = RN(7) = [4.829, 7],$$
$$RN(r_{12}^4) = RN(3) = [3, 4.829].$$

According to the Eqs. (2.10)–(2.13), the average rough interval of $\overline{RN(\tilde{r}_{42})} = [4.152, 5.586]$. Similarly, the rough number form and average rough interval for other elements in the group decision matrix $\tilde{R}_4$ can be acquired.

Therefore, the rough group comparison matrix $R_4$ can be obtained,

$$R_4 = \begin{bmatrix} [1.000, 1.000] & [4.152, 5.586] & [0.804, 2.338] & [2.324, 3.473] & [1.069, 3.140] \\ [0.179, 0.241] & [1.000, 1.000] & [0.180, 0.377] & [0.514, 0.642] & [0.238, 0.573] \\ [0.428, 1.244] & [2.650, 5.550] & [1.000, 1.000] & [1.484, 4.167] & [0.715, 3.027] \\ [0.288, 3.473] & [1.558, 1.945] & [0.240, 0.674] & [1.000, 1.000] & [0.400, 1.668] \\ [0.318, 0.935] & [1.746, 4.193] & [0.330, 1.400] & [0.599, 2.499] & [1.000, 1.000] \end{bmatrix}$$

In the same way, the other PSS requirements' group comparison matrixes in rough number form can also be obtained.

### Step 3: Calculate rough weights of PSS requirement

Calculate rough weights of PSS requirement and sub- requirement (see Table 2.2) in the light of Formula (2.15) and (2.16).

Similarly, the rough weights for the first hierarchy of PSS requirements can be obtained as follows.

$$RW_{R_0} = \{w_{R_1}, w_{R_2}, w_{R_3}, w_{R_4}, w_{R_5}\} = \{[0.788, 1.454], [0.360, 0.743], [0.237, 0.287], [2.495, 3.575], [1.745, 3.081]\}$$

The final overall weight is calculated using multiplication synthesis method from top level to bottom level. The results are also listed in Table 2.2. Normalized weights for other PSS requirements are also calculated similarly in Table 2.2.

### Step 4: PSS requirement prioritization

Then, PSS requirement management team introduces the optimistic indicator $\lambda$ = 0, 0.5, and 1 respectively, transform the normalized rough weight of requirement into crisp value with formula (2.17) (see Table 2.3).

**Table 2.2** Rough weight of PSS requirement (Song et al. 2013a)

| PSS requirement | Sub-requirement | Rough weight | Normalized rough weight |
|---|---|---|---|
| $R_1$ (Easy and accurate decision making of air compressor selection), [0.788, 1.454] | $R_{11}$ [1.000, 1.000] | [0.788, 1.454] | [0.082, 0.151] |
| $R_2$ (Procurement process support), [0.360, 0.743] | $R_{21}$ [0.329, 0.427] | [0.118, 0.318] | [0.012, 0.033] |
| | $R_{22}$ [1.296, 1.968] | [0.466, 1.463] | [0.048, 0.152] |
| | $R_{23}$ [1.355, 2.057] | [0.488, 1.529] | [0.051, 0.159] |
| $R_3$ (Quick start using of the air compressor system), [0.237, 0.287] | $R_{31}$ [0.680, 1.278] | [0.161, 0.367] | [0.017, 0.038] |
| | $R_{32}$ [0.418, 0.925] | [0.099, 0.266] | [0.010, 0.028] |
| | $R_{33}$ [1.230, 2.420] | [0.292, 0.695] | [0.030, 0.072] |
| $R_4$ (Guarantee and optimization of normal operation), [2.495, 3.575] | $R_{41}$ [1.527, 2.696] | [3.809, 9.639] | [0.395, 1.000] |
| | $R_{42}$ [0.331, 0.507] | [0.825, 1.812] | [0.086, 0.188] |
| | $R_{43}$ [1.037, 2.443] | [2.588, 8.736] | [0.269, 0.906] |
| | $R_{44}$ [0.533, 1.500] | [1.330, 5.363] | [0.138, 0.556] |
| | $R_{45}$ [0.643, 1.688] | [1.605, 6.035] | [0.167, 0.626] |
| $R_5$ (Efficient, and reliable MRO with accurate operation information of air compressor), [1.745, 3.081] | $R_{51}$ [0.373, 0.775] | [0.650, 2.387] | [0.067, 0.248] |
| | $R_{52}$ [1.024, 1.788] | [1.786, 5.510] | [0.185, 0.572] |
| | $R_{53}$ [0.986, 1.920] | [1.720, 5.915] | [0.178, 0.614] |

**Table 2.3** Crisp requirement weight and rank of PSS requirement under different vagueness (Song et al. 2013a)

| PSS requirement | $\lambda = 0$ | | $\lambda = 0.5$ | | $\lambda = 1$ | |
|---|---|---|---|---|---|---|
| | Crisp weight | Rank | Crisp weight | Rank | Crisp weight | Rank |
| $R_{11}$ | 0.082 | 8 | 0.116 | 9 | 0.151 | 11 |
| $R_{21}$ | 0.012 | 14 | 0.023 | 14 | 0.033 | 14 |
| $R_{22}$ | 0.048 | 11 | 0.100 | 11 | 0.152 | 10 |
| $R_{23}$ | 0.051 | 10 | 0.105 | 10 | 0.159 | 9 |
| $R_{31}$ | 0.017 | 13 | 0.027 | 13 | 0.038 | 13 |
| $R_{32}$ | 0.010 | 15 | 0.019 | 15 | 0.028 | 15 |
| $R_{33}$ | 0.030 | 12 | 0.051 | 12 | 0.072 | 12 |
| $R_{41}$ | 0.395 | 1 | 0.698 | 1 | 1.000 | 1 |
| $R_{42}$ | 0.086 | 7 | 0.137 | 8 | 0.188 | 8 |
| $R_{43}$ | 0.269 | 2 | 0.587 | 2 | 0.906 | 2 |
| $R_{44}$ | 0.138 | 6 | 0.347 | 6 | 0.556 | 6 |
| $R_{45}$ | 0.167 | 5 | 0.396 | 3 | 0.626 | 3 |
| $R_{51}$ | 0.067 | 9 | 0.158 | 7 | 0.248 | 7 |
| $R_{52}$ | 0.185 | 3 | 0.378 | 5 | 0.572 | 5 |
| $R_{53}$ | 0.178 | 4 | 0.396 | 4 | 0.614 | 4 |

## 2.3 PSS Requirements Identification and Prioritization

The weight of PSS requirement can be seen in Table 2.3. When experts are more cautious ($\lambda = 0$), the priority of PSS requirement is as follows:

$R_{41} > R_{43} > R_{52} > R_{53} > R_{45} > R_{44} > R_{42} > R_{11} > R_{51} > R_{23} > R_{22} > R_{33} > R_{31} > R_{21} > R_{32}$.

When experts have a moderate propensity ($\lambda = 0.5$), the priority of PSS requirement is as follows:

$R_{41} > R_{43} > R_{45} > R_{53} > R_{52} > R_{44} > R_{51} > R_{42} > R_{11} > R_{23} > R_{22} > R_{33} > R_{31} > R_{21} > R_{32}$.

When experts have much optimistic propensity ($\lambda = 1$), the priority of PSS requirement is as follows:

$R_{41} > R_{43} > R_{45} > R_{53} > R_{52} > R_{44} > R_{51} > R_{42} > R_{23} > R_{22} > R_{11} > R_{33} > R_{31} > R_{21} > R_{32}$.

We invite the designers and lead customers to evaluate the prioritizing results from the rough group AHP method, and the interview results show the prioritization are more accurate than that of the past. Both the lead customers and designers confirm that the results reflect their real judgments and evaluations.

If the manager takes different risk-bearing attitude, i.e. adopt different indicator $\lambda$, the crisp weight of PSS requirement would be different. For example, for the requirement $R_{11}$, the weigh is respectively $0.082(\lambda = 0)$, $0.116(\lambda = .5)$ and $0.151(\lambda = 1)$. This difference would lead to their different design priority and resource allocation.

The results indicate that $R_{41}$ (*Function: compressor flow* $\geq 7$ m³/min; *discharge pressure* $\geq 0.8$ *Mpa*), $R_{43}$ (*Safe and smooth operation*), $R_{45}$ (*Energy saving rate: 18–35%*), $R_{53}$ (*Remote monitoring, early warning and failure diagnosis*), and $R_{52}$ (*24-h service: Feedback in* 30 *min, and on-site with spare parts in* 3 *h*) are top 5 requirements which should be given much priority. The weight rankings of some PSS requirements such as $R_{51}$ (*Disassembly and reassembly easily*) and $R_{11}$ (*Professional consulting and report of air compressor selection and matching*) are dependent on the propensity of experts.

$R_{41}$ and $R_{43}$ are considered to be the top 2 important requirements because they are the core value of compressed air user. In this respect, importance of $R_{41}$ and $R_{43}$ would influence the selection of PSS business model in the later design phase, i.e. product-orientated, availability-orientated or result-orientated. Besides, according to the field survey, power consumption of compressed air system's accounts for about 20% of the total power consumption in the customer company. Energy consuming costs of an air compressor account for about 70% of it lifecycle cost. Therefore, $R_{45}$ is also given higher priority, and it is necessary to consider using variable frequency adjusting technology, heat recovery, and pipeline optimization to save energy in the following design phase. The experts highlight the $R_{53}$, because it is necessary to know exactly where the problem is located when or even before a problem occurs. With fulfillment of $R_{53}$, the maintenance of air compressor would be easier and cost effective for the PSS provider.

## 2.3.4 Comparisons and Discussion

In order to reveal the advantages of the I-CAC method in supporting elicitation of PSS requirements in the Company H, we compare this method with that Company H used previously. The company mainly uses collection template of requirement which contains some fixed items such as product function, reliability, and warranty, etc. Table 2.4 presents the comparison between the I-CAC method and the method used by Company H before.

Requirement manager and engineers believed that the method provided a logical, understandable, and step-by-step method to analyze PSS requirements. They also said they often use the I-CAC method to check whether some requirements have been covered or not. In addition, requirement manager and customer representatives regarded that the final priority was reasonable and acceptable because it well reflected true perception of customer's expectation. The requirement manager also recommended developing a computer system to support the requirement elicitation and evaluation.

The customer requirement evaluation with fuzzy group AHP using symmetrical triangular fuzzy number (Kwong and Bai 2002) has also been applied in the case study for further comparison. The comparison results of rough and fuzzy approach are shown in Fig. 2.7.

The customer requirements' weights from rough group AHP and fuzzy group AHP are almost different with each other (see Fig. 2.7). For example, $R_{41}$ is considered as the most important customer requirement in rough approach ($w_{41} = 0.395$, when $\lambda = 0$; $w_{41} = .698$, when $\lambda = 0.5$; $w_{41} = 1.000$, when $\lambda = 1$). However, in the fuzzy approach, the most important customer requirement is $R_{53}$ ($w_{53} = .420$, when $\lambda = $ ; $w_{53} = .710$, when $\lambda = .5$; $w_{53} = 1.000$, when $\lambda = 1$). The other PSS requirements also have different ranks, such as $R_{43}$, $R_{45}$, and $R_{52}$, etc. The difference in the weights in two methods is caused by the different subjectivity and vagueness manipulation mechanisms.

**Table 2.4** Comparison between the I-CAC method and the method Company H used before (Song et al. 2013a)

|  | System perspective | Lifecycle consideration | Stakeholders interaction | Value focus |
|---|---|---|---|---|
| I-CAC model | Consider product and service requirement systematically | Focus on full customer activity cycle (i.e. pre-use, during use, and post use) | Consider different stakeholders interaction around customer activity | Core benefit of customer, e.g. clean compressed air |
| Company H's method used previously | Fragmented and fixed requirement template | Focus on the static requirements before selling product to customer | Mainly focus on end user, and often ignores other stakeholders | The product function, e.g. flow and pressure |

## 2.3 PSS Requirements Identification and Prioritization

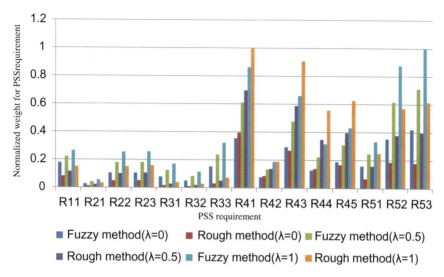

**Fig. 2.7** Comparison between rough and fuzzy customer requirement evaluation approach (Song et al. 2013a)

In fact, the fuzzy interval that denotes the degree of subjectivity and vagueness is fixed. For example, in the fuzzy comparison process of $R_4$, the five selected experts rate "$R_{41}$" relative to "$R_{42}$" are 5, 7, 5, 3, and 5, which are represented in form of fixed fuzzy interval [4, 6], [6, 8], [4, 6], [2, 4], and [4, 6], respectively (see Fig. 2.8). The geometric mean of the five experts' judgments is [3.776, 5.860] in the fuzzy approach. However, the actual situation of the judgments can not be fully reflected with this average fuzzy interval, because the boundary interval that denotes estimation range in customer requirement evaluation process varies across experts who have different knowledge, experience, and expertise. On the contrary, in rough group AHP approach, the ratings of 5, 7, 5, 3, and 5 are converted into the flexible interval form [4.401, 5.439], [4.829, 7], [4.401, 5.439], [3, 4.829] and [4.401, 5.439] respectively (see also in Fig. 2.8). This rough conversion brings a general description of the opinion of experts and presents a more holistic judgment. The group average interval from the rough method is [4.152, 5.586] which not only reflects the size of weight but also the actual estimation range. Therefore, the rough AHP provides a more accurate approach to describe the status of customer requirement of PSS. The same results can be also found in other customer requirements' evaluation process. In addition, it is not necessary for the rough group AHP method to subjectively pre-set the fuzzy membership function for interval number conversion, which is common in fuzzy methods.

The degree of vagueness measured by the interval of the boundary region influences the final weights of PSS requirements. For instance, in the rough method, the degree of vagueness for requirement $R_{11}$ is 0.069 (rough weight of $R_{11}$ is [0.082, 0.151]), and its weight is 0.116 ($\lambda = .5$). However, in the fuzzy method, the degree of

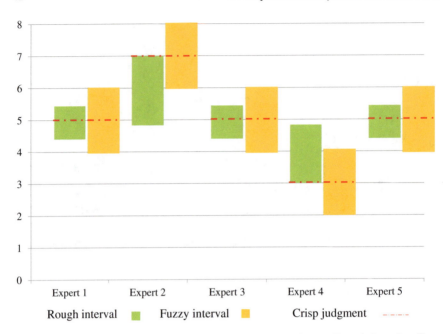

**Fig. 2.8** Different vagueness manipulations for judgments on requirement $R_{41}$ relative to $R_{42}$ (Song et al. 2013a)

vagueness for requirement $R_{11}$ is 0.087, and its weight is 0.222 ($\lambda = .5$). The reason for this divergence is that the fuzzy method overestimates the vagueness degree (the boundary region) for requirement $R_{11}$ (0.087 > 0.069). The same can be found in the other requirements' weights.

Furthermore, the small change of expert group' preference and inconsistency can be identified by the rough group AHP method, because it can flexibly adjust its boundary based on consensus of experts' preferences. For example, value of judgments 5, 5, 5, 5 and 7 can be converted into fuzzy interval [4, 6], [4, 6], [4, 6], [4, 6], and [6, 8], and rough interval [5, 5.348], [5, 5.348], [5, 5.348], [5, 5.348], and [5.348, 7]. When experts re-adjust their judgments as 5, 7, 5, 3, and 5, the fuzzy intervals are transformed into [4, 6], [6, 8], [4, 6], [2, 4], and [4, 6], and rough intervals are converted into [4.401, 5.439], [4.829, 7], [4.401, 5.439], [3, 4.829] and [4.401, 5.439]. Obviously, the newly transformed fuzzy interval still has a fixed boundary 2, which is not realistic in the practice because it cannot distinguish the change and inconsistency of experts' judgments. In the fuzzy approaches, all the cognitive differences are assumed to be equidistant. This would ultimately affect the quality of decision making in PSS requirement evaluation.

In short, the features revealed by the rough set approach are as follows: First, a systematic process for PSS requirement elicitation is provided based on the Industrial Customer Activity Cycle (I-CAC), and it considers the interaction of different stakeholders. It also helps to generate the PSS requirement from the perspective of lifecycle and customer value. Second, PSS requirement evaluation using rough group AHP has a flexible boundary that well reflects the subjective and vague judgments of experts. Third, the proposed PSS requirement evaluation method can avoid relying much on priori information (e.g. pre-set membership functions in fuzzy methods). Fourth, the rough group method can discern the change of decision makers' preferences and manipulates the inconsistency of experts' judgments in the process of the requirement evaluation.

## 2.4 PSS Requirement Interaction Analysis

Due to different stakeholder's preference and PSS heterogeneity, some PSS requirements may interact with others and even with the environment. Thus, it is necessary to understand the dependencies and correlations between the underlying PSS requirements. Song and Cao (2017) develop a rough group DEMATEL method to assess the interactions between PSS requirements. The method combines the advantage of group DEMATEL in interaction evaluation structure under group decision-making environment and the strength of rough set theory in dealing with vagueness and subjectivity without much priori information. With the help of the proposed method, PSS designers can easily find the critical requirements and their interactions for future PSS recommendation in Chap. 6. In sum, the proposed method provide a systematic approach for requirement interactions evaluation and analysis under vague environment. Figure 2.9 shows the whole PSS requirement interaction assessment process.

### 2.4.1 The Method for PSS Requirement Interaction Analysis

**Step 1. Acquisition of PSS requirements**

Requirement acquisition is the beginning of PSS design project. In this step, PSS requirements are obtained using the industrial customer activity cycle (I-CAC) (Song et al. 2013a) in Sect. 2.3. The final acquired PSS requirements are denoted as $SR_1$, $SR_2$, ..., $SR_n$. Some requirements are more prominent than the others, for example, the requirement "*Quick service response*" may lead to the increase of the service cost. Therefore, it will have impact on the requirement "*Lower service cost*". Thus, in the process of PSS requirement analysis, the two requirements should not be treated equally. Designers should emphasize more the highest predominant requirement among the others as well as the interactions between the requirements.

**Step 2. Construction of group direct-relation matrix**

$m$ experts are invited to make pair-wise comparisons in terms of crisp scores for the PSS requirement interactions (Very high influence = 4, High influence = 3, Low

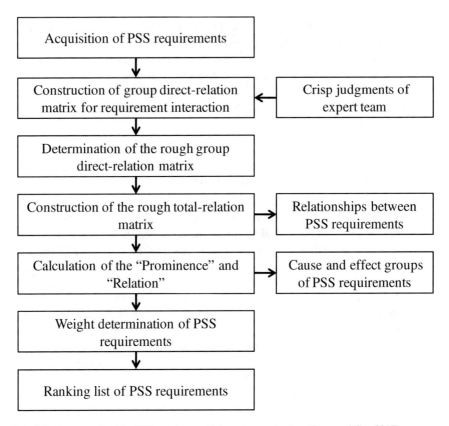

**Fig. 2.9** Framework of the PSS requirement interaction evaluation (Song and Cao 2017)

influence = 2, Very low influence = 1, No influence = 0) (Lin 2013). The experts include the manager, engineer, designer, and customer representatives, etc. The $k$th experts's direct-relation matrix $M_k$ is presented as follows:

$$M_k = \begin{bmatrix} 0 & r_{12}^k & \cdots & r_{1n}^k \\ r_{21}^k & 0 & \cdots & r_{2n}^k \\ \vdots & \vdots & \ddots & \vdots \\ r_{n1}^k & r_{n2}^k & \cdots & 0 \end{bmatrix} \quad k = 1, 2, \ldots m \quad (2.18)$$

where $r_{ij}^k$ is the $k$th expert's crisp judgment for the $i$th PSS requirement's influence on the $j$th requirement, $m$ is the number of experts, and $n$ is the number of PSS requirement.

## 2.4 PSS Requirement Interaction Analysis

Thus, the group direct-relation matrix $\tilde{R}$ can be obtained as follows:

$$\tilde{R} = \begin{bmatrix} \tilde{0} & \tilde{r}_{12} & \cdots & \tilde{r}_{1n} \\ \tilde{r}_{21} & \tilde{0} & \cdots & \tilde{r}_{2n} \\ \vdots & \vdots & \ddots & \vdots \\ \tilde{r}_{n1} & \tilde{r}_{n2} & \cdots & \tilde{0} \end{bmatrix} \quad (2.19)$$

where $\tilde{r}_{ij} = \{r_{ij}^1, r_{ij}^2, \cdots, r_{ij}^k, \cdots, r_{ij}^m\}$.

**Step 3. Determination of the rough group direct-relation matrix**

Assume that there is a set of $m$ classes of expert judgments on PSS requirement interactions, $J = \{r_{ij}^1, r_{ij}^2, \cdots, r_{ij}^k, \cdots, r_{ij}^m\}$ ordered in the manner of $r_{ij}^1 < r_{ij}^2 < \cdots < r_{ij}^k < \cdots < r_{ij}^m$. $U$ is the universe including all the objects and $P$ is an arbitrary object of $U$, and then the lower approximation of $r_{ij}^k$ and the upper approximation of $r_{ij}^k$ can be defined as:

$$\text{Lower approximation:} \quad \underline{Apr}(r_{ij}^k) = \cup\{P \in U/J(P) \leq r_{ij}^k\} \quad (2.20)$$

$$\text{Upper approximation:} \quad \overline{Apr}(r_{ij}^k) = \cup\{P \in U/J(P) \geq r_{ij}^k\} \quad (2.21)$$

Then, the judgment $r_{ij}^k$ can be represented by a rough number defined by its lower limit $\underline{Lim}(r_{ij}^k)$ and upper limit $\overline{Lim}(r_{ij}^k)$ as follows:

$$\underline{Lim}(r_{ij}^k) = \frac{\sum_{m=1}^{N_{ijL}} x_{ij}}{N_{ijL}} \quad (2.22)$$

$$\overline{Lim}(r_{ij}^k) = \frac{\sum_{m=1}^{N_{ijU}} y_{ij}}{N_{ijU}} \quad (2.23)$$

$x_{ij}$ and $y_{ij}$ are the elements of lower and upper approximation for $r_{ij}^k$. $N_{ijL}$ and $N_{ijU}$ are the number of objects included in the lower approximation and upper approximation of $r_{ij}^k$ respectively.

Then, all the crisp judgments on PSS requirement interactions $r_{ij}^k$ in direct-relation matrix $M_k$ can be converted into rough number (Zhai et al. 2009) form $RN(z_{ij}^{(k)})$ can be obtained using Eqs. (2.20)–(2.23),

$$RN(r_{ij}^k) = [\underline{Lim}(r_{ij}^k), \overline{Lim}(r_{ij}^k)] = [r_{ij}^{kL}, r_{ij}^{kU}], \quad (2.24)$$

where $r_{ij}^{kL}$ and $r_{ij}^{kU}$ are the lower limit and upper limit of rough number $RN(r_{ij}^k)$ in the $k$th direct-relation matrix. The interval of boundary region (i.e., $r_{ij}^{kU} - r_{ij}^{kL}$) indicates the degree of vagueness. A rough number with a smaller interval of boundary region is interpreted as more precise one.

Thus, a rough sequence $RN(\tilde{r}_{ij})$ can be obtained as follows,

$$RN(\tilde{r}_{ij}) = \{[r_{ij}^{1L}, r_{ij}^{1U}], [r_{ij}^{2L}, r_{ij}^{2U}], \cdots, [r_{ij}^{mL}, r_{ij}^{mU}]\} \quad (2.25)$$

The average rough interval $\overline{RN(\tilde{r}_{ij})}$ can be obtained by using rough computation principles (2.26)–(2.28):

$$\overline{RN(\tilde{r}_{ij})} = [r_{ij}^{L}, r_{ij}^{U}] \quad (2.26)$$

$$r_{ij}^{L} = (\sum_{k=1}^{m} r_{ij}^{kL})/m \quad (2.27)$$

$$r_{ij}^{U} = (\sum_{k=1}^{m} r_{ij}^{kU})/m \quad (2.28)$$

$r_{ij}^{L}$ and $r_{ij}^{U}$ are lower limit and upper limit of rough number $[r_{ij}^{L}, r_{ij}^{U}]$ respectively. $m$ is the number of decision makers.

Then the rough group direct-relation matrix R can then be obtained as follows:

$$R = [\overline{RN(\tilde{r}_{ij})}]_{n \times n} = \begin{bmatrix} [0,0] & [r_{12}^{L}, r_{12}^{U}] & \cdots & [r_{1n}^{L}, r_{1n}^{U}] \\ [r_{21}^{L}, r_{21}^{U}] & [0,0] & \cdots & [r_{2n}^{L}, r_{2n}^{U}] \\ \vdots & \vdots & \ddots & \vdots \\ [r_{n1}^{L}, r_{n1}^{U}] & [r_{n2}^{L}, r_{n2}^{U}] & \cdots & [0,0] \end{bmatrix} \quad (2.29)$$

**Step 4. Construction of the rough total-relation matrix**

The linear scale transformation is used as a normalization formula to transform the PSS requirement scales into comparable scales. The normalized rough group direct-relation matrix $R'$ is obtained as follows:

$$R' = [\overline{RN(\tilde{r}_{ij})}']_{n \times n} = \begin{bmatrix} \overline{RN(\tilde{r}_{11})}' & \overline{RN(\tilde{r}_{12})}' & \cdots & \overline{RN(\tilde{r}_{1n})}' \\ \overline{RN(\tilde{r}_{21})}' & \overline{RN(\tilde{r}_{22})}' & \cdots & \overline{RN(\tilde{r}_{2n})}' \\ \vdots & \vdots & \ddots & \vdots \\ \overline{RN(\tilde{r}_{n1})}' & \overline{RN(\tilde{r}_{n2})}' & \cdots & \overline{RN(\tilde{r}_{nn})}' \end{bmatrix} \quad (2.30)$$

where

$$\overline{RN(\tilde{r}_{ij})}' = \frac{\overline{RN(\tilde{r}_{ij})}}{\gamma} = \left[\frac{r_{ij}^{L}}{\gamma}, \frac{r_{ij}^{U}}{\gamma}\right], \quad (2.31)$$

## 2.4 PSS Requirement Interaction Analysis

$$\gamma = \max_{1 \le i \le n} \left( \sum_{j=1}^{n} r_{ij}^{U} \right). \tag{2.32}$$

The rough total-relation matrix $T$ can be acquired as follows:

$$T = [t_{ij}]_{n \times n}, \tag{2.33}$$

$$t_{ij} = [t_{ij}^{L}, t_{ij}^{U}], \tag{2.34}$$

$$T^{s} = [t_{ij}^{s}]_{n \times n} = R'^{s}(I - R'^{s})^{-1}, s = L, U. \tag{2.35}$$

where $t_{ij}^{L}$ and $t_{ij}^{U}$ are the lower limit and upper limit of rough interval $t_{ij}$ in the total-relation matrix $T$, and $I$ is the unit matrix.

### Step 5. Calculation of the "Prominence" and "Relation"

After obtaining the rough total-relation matrix $T$, the sum of rows and the sum of columns are separately denoted as $X_i$ and $Y_j$ within the rough total-relation matrix $T$ through the following formulas:

$$X_i = [x_i^{L}, x_i^{U}] = \left[ \sum_{j=1}^{n} t_{ij}^{L}, \sum_{j=1}^{n} t_{ij}^{U} \right] \tag{2.36}$$

$$Y_j = [y_j^{L}, y_j^{U}] = \left[ \sum_{i=1}^{n} t_{ij}^{L}, \sum_{i=1}^{n} t_{ij}^{U} \right] \tag{2.37}$$

where $x_{ij}^{L}$ and $x_{ij}^{U}$ are the lower limit and upper limit of rough interval $X_i$, $y_{ij}^{L}$ and $y_{ij}^{U}$ are the lower limit and upper limit of rough interval $Y_i$.

To effectively determine the "Prominence" and "Relation", it is necessary to convert the $X_i$ and $Y_j$ into crisp values. The de-"roughness" of $X_i$ is conducted as follows:

(1) Normalization

$$\tilde{x}_i^{L} = (x_i^{L} - \min_i x_i^{L}) / \Delta_{\min}^{\max} \tag{2.38}$$

$$\tilde{x}_i^{U} = (x_i^{U} - \min_i x_i^{L}) / \Delta_{\min}^{\max} \tag{2.39}$$

$$\Delta_{\min}^{\max} = \max_i x_i^{U} - \min_i x_i^{L} \tag{2.40}$$

where $\tilde{x}_i^{L}$ and $\tilde{x}_i^{U}$ are the normalized form of the $x_i^{L}$ and $x_i^{U}$, respectively.

(2) Determination of a total normalized crisp value

$$\alpha_i = \frac{\tilde{x}_i^{L} \times (1 - \tilde{x}_i^{L}) + \tilde{x}_i^{U} \times \tilde{x}_i^{U}}{1 - \tilde{x}_i^{L} + \tilde{x}_i^{U}} \tag{2.41}$$

(3) Computation of final crisp values $x_i$ for $X_i$

$$x_i = \min_i x_i^L + \alpha_i \Delta_{\min}^{\max} \tag{2.42}$$

Similarly, we can obtain the final crisp values $y_j$ for $Y_j$.

The vector $m_i$ named "Prominence" is made by adding $x_i$ to $y_j$. Similarly, the vector $n_i$ named "Relation" is made by subtracting $x_i$ to $y_j$.

$$m_i = x_i + y_j, \quad i = j \tag{2.43}$$

$$n_i = x_i - y_j, \quad i = j \tag{2.44}$$

The vector $m_i$ reveals how much importance the criterion has. The larger the value of $m_i$ the greater the overall prominence (visibility/importance/influence) of PSS requirement $i$ in terms of overall relationships with other PSS requirements. The vector $n_i$ divide the criteria into the cause and effect groups. When the value $n_i$ is positive, the criterion belongs to the cause group. Then the PSS requirement $i$ is a net cause for other PSS requirements. If the value $n_i$ is negative, the criterion belongs to the effect group. Then the PSS requirement $i$ is reliant on fulfillment of other PSS requirements. Therefore, the causal diagram can be acquired by mapping the dataset of the $(m_i, n_i)$, providing valuable insight for making decisions.

**Step 6. Weight determination of PSS requirement**

The importance of the $i$th PSS requirement $\omega_i$ is calculated with the following equation:

$$\omega_i = \sqrt{m_i^2 + n_i^2} \tag{2.45}$$

The importance of any PSS requirement can be normalized as follows:

$$W_i = \frac{\omega_i}{\sum_{1 \leq i \leq n} \omega_i} \tag{2.46}$$

$W_i$ is the normalized weight of the $i$th PSS requirement. The weight of each PSS requirement indicates its predominance among the others requirements.

## 2.4.2 Case Study: Elevator PSS Requirement Interaction Analysis

This section takes elevator PSS requirement interaction evaluation as an example to verify the proposed approach. Company M is a leading manufacturer providing different types of elevators, such as passenger/freight elevator, hospital elevator,

## 2.4 PSS Requirement Interaction Analysis

**Table 2.5** The elevator PSS requirements (Song and Cao 2017)

|  | Elevator PSS requirements |
|---|---|
| $SR_1$ | Professional procurement advice |
| $SR_2$ | Professional installation and commissioning |
| $SR_3$ | Wide scope of condition monitoring |
| $SR_4$ | Accurate failure diagnosis |
| $SR_5$ | Reliable and timely maintenance |
| $SR_6$ | Elevator operation training |
| $SR_7$ | High availability of repair |
| $SR_8$ | Lower cost of spare parts |
| $SR_9$ | Wide coverage of service center |
| $SR_{10}$ | Quick service response |
| $SR_{11}$ | Safe and efficient operation |
| $SR_{12}$ | Low energy consumption |

escalator, and elevator monitoring system, etc. To achieve sustainable growth in competitive market, Company M decides to provide PSS to customers. The elevator PSS is hybrid offering including elevator product, installation service, maintenance, repair, remote monitoring, elevator upgrading and spare parts supply, etc. The aim of the elevator PSS requirement interaction evaluation is to identify key interaction between them, and then to provide valuable suggestions for managers to determine which requirement needs more attention and make reasonable resource allocation in the early stage of PSS development.

**Step 1. Acquisition of elevator PSS requirements**

In this step, elevator PSS requirements are elicited by using the industrial customer activity cycle (I-CAC) (Song et al. 2013a ). Both the elevator lifecycle and operation environment are also analyzed in this stage. Table 2.5 provides the acquired twelve elevator PSS requirements.

**Step 2. Construction of group direct-relation matrix**

Five experts are invited to judge the influence degrees between different requirements in terms of crisp scores 4, 3, 2, and 1 (Very high influence = 4, High influence = 3, Low influence = 2, Very low influence = 1, No influence = 0). The expert team includes the 1 service manager, 1 service engineer, 1 elevator designer, and 2 customer representatives. According to the formula (2.18), the 1st decision maker's direct-relation matrix $M_1$ can be obtained in Table 2.6. Similarly, the 2nd–5th decision maker's direct-relation matrix can also be obtained. Then, we can acquire the group direct-relation matrix $\tilde{R}$ in the light of the Formula (2.19) (see Table 2.7).

**Table 2.6** The 1st decision maker's direct-relation matrix $M_1$ (Song and Cao 2017)

| | $SR_1$ | $SR_2$ | $SR_3$ | $SR_4$ | $SR_5$ | $SR_6$ | $SR_7$ | $SR_8$ | $SR_9$ | $SR_{10}$ | $SR_{11}$ | $SR_{12}$ |
|---|---|---|---|---|---|---|---|---|---|---|---|---|
| $SR_1$ | 0 | 2 | 2 | 1 | 2 | 3 | 1 | 3 | 2 | 1 | 2 | 3 |
| $SR_2$ | 0 | 0 | 1 | 2 | 2 | 2 | 0 | 1 | 0 | 0 | 3 | 3 |
| $SR_3$ | 1 | 1 | 0 | 4 | 3 | 0 | 3 | 2 | 3 | 4 | 4 | 2 |
| $SR_4$ | 0 | 0 | 1 | 0 | 3 | 1 | 3 | 1 | 0 | 2 | 2 | 2 |
| $SR_5$ | 1 | 1 | 3 | 4 | 0 | 1 | 4 | 4 | 2 | 1 | 4 | 4 |
| $SR_6$ | 1 | 3 | 1 | 2 | 3 | 0 | 2 | 1 | 1 | 2 | 4 | 4 |
| $SR_7$ | 0 | 0 | 1 | 2 | 3 | 1 | 0 | 1 | 0 | 3 | 3 | 2 |
| $SR_8$ | 1 | 0 | 0 | 0 | 3 | 0 | 3 | 0 | 0 | 0 | 2 | 0 |
| $SR_9$ | 0 | 2 | 2 | 1 | 3 | 1 | 4 | 3 | 0 | 3 | 0 | 0 |
| $SR_{10}$ | 0 | 0 | 2 | 1 | 3 | 1 | 3 | 3 | 2 | 0 | 0 | 0 |
| $SR_{11}$ | 0 | 0 | 0 | 0 | 0 | 0 | 2 | 3 | 0 | 0 | 0 | 2 |
| $SR_{12}$ | 0 | 0 | 2 | 0 | 0 | 0 | 0 | 0 | 0 | 0 | 0 | 0 |

## 2.4 PSS Requirement Interaction Analysis

**Table 2.7** The group direct-relation matrix of the elevator PSS requirements (Song and Cao 2017)

| | $SR_1$ | $SR_2$ | $SR_3$ | $SR_4$ | $SR_5$ | ... | $SR_{10}$ | $SR_{11}$ | $SR_{12}$ |
|---|---|---|---|---|---|---|---|---|---|
| $SR_1$ | 0, 0, 0, 0, 0 | 2, 1, 1, 2, 1 | 2, 1, 2, 2, 1 | 1, 1, 0, 1, 0 | 2, 2, 1, 2, 2 | ... | 1, 1, 0, 0, 0 | 2, 3, 2, 2, 2 | 3, 4, 4, 3, 4 |
| $SR_2$ | 0, 0, 0, 0, 0 | 0, 0, 0, 0, 0 | 1, 1, 0, 0, 1 | 2, 1, 2, 2, 2 | 2, 3, 3, 2, 3 | ... | 0, 1, 0, 0, 0 | 3, 3, 3, 3, 2 | 3, 3, 4, 4, 4 |
| $SR_3$ | 1, 0, 0, 0, 1 | 1, 2, 0, 1, 0 | 0, 0, 0, 0, 0 | 4, 4, 4, 3, 4 | 3, 2, 3, 3, 3 | ... | 4, 3, 4, 4, 4 | 4, 3, 3, 3, 2 | 2, 2, 3, 3, 2 |
| $SR_4$ | 0, 0, 0, 0, 0 | 0, 0, 0, 0, 0 | 1, 0, 0, 1, 0 | 0, 0, 0, 0, 0 | 3, 2, 3, 2, 2 | ... | 2, 3, 2, 4, 3 | 2, 2, 2, 3, 3 | 2, 1, 1, 3, 2 |
| $SR_5$ | 1, 1, 0, 1, 0 | 1, 0, 1, 0, 0 | 3, 2, 3, 3, 3 | 4, 2, 3, 3, 4 | 0, 0, 0, 0, 0 | ... | 1, 1, 1, 1, 0 | 4, 3, 3, 3, 3 | 4, 4, 3, 3, 4 |
| $SR_6$ | 1, 2, 1, 0, 0 | 3, 3, 3, 2, 2 | 1, 0, 2, 1, 1 | 2, 2, 3, 3, 3 | 3, 2, 3, 4, 4 | ... | 2, 0, 1, 2, 0 | 4, 4, 3, 4, 3 | 4, 2, 2, 4, 3 |
| $SR_7$ | 0, 0, 0, 0, 1 | 0, 1, 0, 0, 1 | 1, 1, 2, 1, 0 | 2, 2, 1, 3, 1 | 3, 3, 3, 3, 2 | ... | 3, 3, 4, 2, 4 | 3, 2, 3, 3, 2 | 2, 1, 1, 2, 1 |
| $SR_8$ | 1, 1, 0, 1, 1 | 0, 0, 0, 0, 0 | 0, 1, 1, 0, 1 | 0, 0, 0, 0, 0 | 3, 2, 2, 3, 2 | ... | 0, 1, 0, 0, 0 | 2, 2, 1, 2, 2 | 0, 1, 0, 0, 0 |
| $SR_9$ | 0, 0, 0, 0, 0 | 2, 1, 1, 1, 0 | 2, 2, 1, 3, 3 | 1, 1, 2, 1, 0 | 3, 2, 2, 2, 2 | ... | 3, 4, 2, 3, 4 | 0, 0, 0, 0, 0 | 0, 0, 0, 0, 0 |
| $SR_{10}$ | 0, 0, 0, 0, 0 | 0, 0, 0, 0, 0 | 2, 1, 3, 1, 2 | 1, 0, 1, 1, 0 | 3, 3, 2, 2, 3 | ... | 0, 0, 0, 0, 0 | 0, 1, 1, 0, 0 | 0, 0, 0, 0, 0 |
| $SR_{11}$ | 0, 0, 0, 0, 0 | 0, 0, 0, 0, 0 | 0, 1, 0, 0, 1 | 0, 0, 0, 0, 0 | 0, 0, 0, 0, 0 | ... | 0, 1, 1, 0, 0 | 0, 0, 0, 0, 0 | 2, 3, 3, 3, 2 |
| $SR_{12}$ | 0, 0, 0, 0, 0 | 0, 0, 0, 0, 0 | 2, 2, 1, 2, 2 | 0, 0, 0, 0, 0 | 0, 0, 0, 0, 0 | ... | 0, 0, 0, 0, 0 | 0, 0, 0, 0, 0 | 0, 0, 0, 0, 0 |

## Step 3. Determination of the rough group direct-relation matrix

According to the Formula (2.20)–(2.25), all the crisp judgments in group direct-relation matrix of the elevator PSS requirements are converted into rough number form. For example, for the judgment sequence $\widetilde{r}_{12} = \{2, 1, 1, 2, 1\}$,

$$\underline{Lim}(1) = \frac{1}{3}(1+1+1) = 1, \quad \overline{Lim}(1) = \frac{1}{5}(2+1+1+2+1) = 1.4$$

$$\underline{Lim}(2) = \frac{1}{5}(2+1+1+2+1) = 1.4 \quad \overline{Lim}(2) = \frac{1}{2}(2+2) = 2.$$

According to the Formula (2.20)–(2.24), the rough interval form of $\{0, 1, 1, 0, 2, 2, 0, 2\}$ can be obtained, i.e., $\{[1.4, 2], [1, 1.4], [1, 1.4], [1.4, 2], [1, 1.4]\}$. The average rough interval $\overline{RN(\widetilde{r}_{12})}$ can then be obtained by using rough computation principles (2.26)–(2.28):

$$\overline{RN(\widetilde{r}_{12})} = [r_{12}^L, r_{12}^U]$$

$$r_{12}^L = (1.4 + 1 + 1 + 1.4+1)/5 = 1.16 \quad r_{12}^U = (2+1.4+1.4+2+1.4)/5 = 1.64$$

$$\overline{RN(\widetilde{r}_{12})} = [1.16, 1.64]$$

Similarly, we can get rough number form for other judgment in group direct-relation matrix $\widetilde{R}$ (see Table 2.8).

## Step 4. Construction of the rough total-relation matrix

The rough group direct-relation matrix of the elevator PSS requirements is then normalized according to the Formulas (2.30)–(2.32). The normalized rough group direct-relation matrix is shown in Table 2.9.

Then the rough total-relation matrix $T$ (see Table 2.10) can be acquired by using the Formulas (2.33)–(2.35).

## Step 5. Calculation of the "Prominence" and "Relation"

After obtain the rough total-relation matrix $T$, the sum of rows $X_i$ and the sum of columns $Y_j$ (see Table 2.11) are calculate with the Formulas (2.36)–(2.37).

According to the Formulas (2.38)–(2.42), the sum of rows $X_i$ and the sum of columns $Y_j$ in Table 2.11 are converted into crisp values ($x_i$ and $y_j$) to effectively determine the "Prominence" $m_i$ and "Relation" $n_i$. The crisp values are presented in Table 2.12. The "Prominence" $m_i$ in DEMATEL represents the strength of influences both dispatched and received. On the other hand, if "Relation" $n_i > 0$, then the PSS requirement $i$ dispatches the influence to other PSS requirements more than it receives. If "Relation" $n_i < 0$, the PSS requirement $i$ receives the influence from other PSS requirements more than it dispatched.

2.4 PSS Requirement Interaction Analysis

**Table 2.8** The rough group direct-relation matrix of the elevator PSS requirements (Song and Cao 2017)

|        | $SR_1$           | $SR_2$           | $SR_3$           | ... | $SR_{11}$        | $SR_{12}$        |
|--------|------------------|------------------|------------------|-----|------------------|------------------|
| $SR_1$ | [0.000, 0.000]   | [1.160, 1.640]   | [1.360, 1.840]   | ... | [2.040, 2.360]   | [3.360, 3.840]   |
| $SR_2$ | [0.000, 0.000]   | [0.000, 0.000]   | [0.360, 0.840]   | ... | [2.640, 2.960]   | [3.360, 3.840]   |
| $SR_3$ | [0.160, 0.640]   | [0.360, 1.253]   | [0.000, 0.000]   | ... | [2.650, 3.350]   | [2.160, 2.640]   |
| $SR_4$ | [0.000, 0.000]   | [0.000, 0.000]   | [0.160, 0.640]   | ... | [2.160, 2.640]   | [1.360, 2.253]   |
| $SR_5$ | [0.360, 0.840]   | [0.160, 0.640]   | [2.640, 2.960]   | ... | [3.040, 3.360]   | [3.360, 3.840]   |
| $SR_6$ | [0.360, 1.253]   | [2.360, 2.840]   | [0.650, 1.350]   | ... | [3.360, 3.840]   | [2.467, 3.533]   |
| $SR_7$ | [0.040, 0.360]   | [0.160, 0.640]   | [0.650, 1.350]   | ... | [2.360, 2.840]   | [1.160, 1.640]   |
| $SR_8$ | [0.640, 0.960]   | [0.000, 0.000]   | [0.360, 0.840]   | ... | [1.640, 1.960]   | [0.040, 0.360]   |
| $SR_9$ | [0.000, 0.000]   | [0.650, 1.350]   | [1.747, 2.640]   | ... | [0.000, 0.000]   | [0.000, 0.000]   |
| $SR_{10}$ | [0.000, 0.000] | [0.000, 0.000]   | [1.360, 2.253]   | ... | [0.160, 0.640]   | [0.000, 0.000]   |
| $SR_{11}$ | [0.000, 0.000] | [0.000, 0.000]   | [0.160, 0.640]   | ... | [0.000, 0.000]   | [2.360, 2.840]   |
| $SR_{12}$ | [0.000, 0.000] | [0.000, 1.640]   | [1.960, 0.000]   | ... | [0.000, 0.000]   | [0.000, 0.000]   |

**Step 6. Weight determination of elevator PSS requirement**

The importance of the elevator PSS requirements can then be calculated with the Eqs. (2.45) and (2.46). Both the importance and the normalized weights of the PSS requirements are provided in Table 2.13.

### 2.4.3 Comparisons and Discussion

The proposed rough group DEMATEL is used to find the PSS requirements of significance, and their weights are presented in Fig. 2.10. As shown in Fig. 2.10, the most important three elevator PSS requirements with weights greater than 0.1 are $SR_5$ (Reliable and timely maintenance), $SR_3$ (Wide scope of condition monitoring), and $SR_7$ (High availability of repair). The ranking of weight value of criteria is as follows: $SR_5$ (Reliable and timely maintenance), $SR_3$ (Wide scope of condition monitoring), $SR_7$ (High availability of repair), $SR_{11}$ (Safe and efficient operation), $SR_{10}$

**Table 2.9** The normalized rough group direct-relation matrix (Song and Cao 2017)

|  | $SR_1$ | $SR_2$ | $SR_3$ | ... | $SR_{11}$ | $SR_{12}$ |
|---|---|---|---|---|---|---|
| $SR_1$ | [0.000, 0.000] | [0.042, 0.059] | [0.049, 0.067] | ... | [0.074, 0.085] | [0.122, 0.139] |
| $SR_2$ | [0.000, 0.000] | [0.000, 0.000] | [0.013, 0.030] | ... | [0.096, 0.107] | [0.122, 0.139] |
| $SR_3$ | [0.006, 0.023] | [0.013, 0.045] | [0.000, 0.000] | ... | [0.096, 0.121] | [0.078, 0.096] |
| $SR_4$ | [0.000, 0.000] | [0.000, 0.000] | [0.006, 0.023] | ... | [0.078, 0.096] | [0.049, 0.082] |
| $SR_5$ | [0.013, 0.030] | [0.006, 0.023] | [0.096, 0.107] | ... | [0.110, 0.122] | [0.122, 0.139] |
| $SR_6$ | [0.013, 0.045] | [0.085, 0.103] | [0.024, 0.049] | ... | [0.122, 0.139] | [0.089, 0.128] |
| $SR_7$ | [0.001, 0.013] | [0.006, 0.023] | [0.024, 0.049] | ... | [0.085, 0.103] | [0.042, 0.059] |
| ... | ... | ... | ... | ... | ... | ... |
| $SR_{12}$ | [0.000, 0.000] | [0.000, 0.000] | [0.059, 0.071] | ... | [0.000, 0.000] | [0.000, 0.000] |

**Table 2.10** The rough total-relation matrix of the elevator PSS requirements (Song and Cao 2017)

|  | $SR_1$ | $SR_2$ | $SR_3$ | ... | $SR_{11}$ | $SR_{12}$ |
|---|---|---|---|---|---|---|
| $SR_1$ | [0.007, 0.025] | [0.053, 0.094] | [0.082, 0.158] | ... | [0.128, 0.203] | [0.173, 0.256] |
| $SR_2$ | [0.003, 0.016] | [0.006, 0.021] | [0.039, 0.095] | ... | [0.130, 0.185] | [0.160, 0.224] |
| $SR_3$ | [0.012, 0.049] | [0.021, 0.083] | [0.053, 0.130] | ... | [0.164, 0.267] | [0.140, 0.238] |
| $SR_4$ | [0.003, 0.017] | [0.004, 0.023] | [0.034, 0.101] | ... | [0.113, 0.184] | [0.084, 0.168] |
| $SR_5$ | [0.019, 0.056] | [0.013, 0.059] | [0.131, 0.210] | ... | [0.172, 0.258] | [0.175, 0.269] |
| $SR_6$ | [0.017, 0.067] | [0.090, 0.135] | [0.058, 0.158] | ... | [0.173, 0.271] | [0.149, 0.270] |
| $SR_7$ | [0.006, 0.033] | [0.011, 0.051] | [0.055, 0.137] | ... | [0.127, 0.207] | [0.085, 0.166] |
| ... | ... | ... | ... | ... | ... | ... |
| $SR_{12}$ | [0.001, 0.003] | [0.001, 0.006] | [0.063, 0.080] | ... | [0.010, 0.019] | [0.008, 0.017] |

## 2.4 PSS Requirement Interaction Analysis

**Table 2.11** The sum of rows and the sum of columns for rough total-relation matrix (Song and Cao 2017)

|  | $X_i$ | $Y_j$ |
|---|---|---|
| $SR_1$ | [0.986, 1.781] | [0.110, 0.373] |
| $SR_2$ | [0.684, 1.234] | [0.243, 0.618] |
| $SR_3$ | [1.429, 2.355] | [0.741, 1.571] |
| $SR_4$ | [0.710, 1.391] | [0.823, 1.549] |
| $SR_5$ | [1.234, 2.134] | [1.263, 2.087] |
| $SR_6$ | [0.984, 2.057] | [0.299, 0.659] |
| $SR_7$ | [0.818, 1.630] | [1.190, 2.164] |
| $SR_8$ | [0.533, 1.031] | [1.154, 1.945] |
| $SR_9$ | [1.013, 1.876] | [0.558, 1.135] |
| $SR_{10}$ | [0.853, 1.618] | [0.857, 1.730] |
| $SR_{11}$ | [0.285, 0.589] | [1.244, 2.051] |
| $SR_{12}$ | [0.144, 0.238] | [1.191, 2.052] |

**Table 2.12** The "Prominence" and "Relation" values for the elevator PSS requirements (Song and Cao 2017)

|  | $x_i$ | $y_j$ | $m_i$ | $n_i$ |
|---|---|---|---|---|
| $SR_1$ | 1.418 | 0.139 | 1.558 | 1.279 |
| $SR_2$ | 0.901 | 0.321 | 1.223 | 0.580 |
| $SR_3$ | 2.082 | 1.162 | 3.243 | 0.920 |
| $SR_4$ | 1.004 | 1.199 | 2.203 | −0.195 |
| $SR_5$ | 1.809 | 1.828 | 3.638 | −0.019 |
| $SR_6$ | 1.608 | 0.381 | 1.990 | 1.227 |
| $SR_7$ | 1.217 | 1.851 | 3.068 | −0.634 |
| $SR_8$ | 0.696 | 1.664 | 2.360 | −0.968 |
| $SR_9$ | 1.499 | 0.783 | 2.281 | 0.716 |
| $SR_{10}$ | 1.232 | 1.340 | 2.572 | −0.108 |
| $SR_{11}$ | 0.339 | 1.792 | 2.131 | −1.452 |
| $SR_{12}$ | 0.148 | 1.765 | 1.913 | −1.616 |

(Quick service response), $SR_8$ (Lower cost of spare parts), $SR_{12}$ (Low energy consumption), $SR_9$ (Wide coverage of service center), $SR_6$ (Elevator operation training), $SR_4$ (Accurate failure diagnosis), $SR_1$ (Professional procurement advice), and $SR_2$ (Professional installation and commissioning).

The arrows in Fig. 2.11a shows the interrelationships among each of the individual elevator PSS requirement based on the proposed rough method. Since the number of relationships can include all the possibilities, those relationships that are over thresholds are only mapped. Due to the large number of PSS requirements, higher threshold values (0.2 and 0.25) were selected from the crisp form of the elements in the rough total-relation matrix T (Table 2.10). The thick arrow is drawn from requirement $i$ to requirement $j$ when $t_{ij}^* > 0.25$, the thin arrow when $0.25 \geq t_{ij}^* > 0.2$,

**Table 2.13** The importance and the normalized weights of the PSS requirements (Song and Cao 2017)

| | $\omega_i$ | $W_i$ |
|---|---|---|
| $SR_1$ | 2.016 | 0.066 |
| $SR_2$ | 1.353 | 0.044 |
| $SR_3$ | 3.371 | 0.110 |
| $SR_4$ | 2.211 | 0.072 |
| $SR_5$ | 3.638 | 0.119 |
| $SR_6$ | 2.338 | 0.076 |
| $SR_7$ | 3.133 | 0.102 |
| $SR_8$ | 2.551 | 0.083 |
| $SR_9$ | 2.391 | 0.078 |
| $SR_{10}$ | 2.574 | 0.084 |
| $SR_{11}$ | 2.579 | 0.084 |
| $SR_{12}$ | 2.504 | 0.082 |

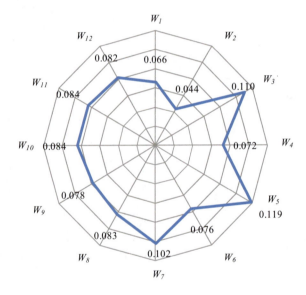

**Fig. 2.10** The radar graph of PSS requirement weights (Song and Cao 2017)

and no arrow when $t_{ij}^* \leq 0.2$, respectively. Here, $t_{ij}^*$ is the crisp form of the rough intervals in the rough total-relation matrix T. Similarly, the relationship digraph based on the crisp DEMATEL can also be obtained in Fig. 2.11b.

Figure 2.11a shows that the requirement $SR_3$ (Wide scope of condition monitoring) obtains seven interactive arrows as the most interactive requirement. The PSS requirement with several interactive arrows in the relationship digraph means that it has a frequent interactive relation with other PSS requirements. Different with Fig. 2.11a based on the rough group DEMATEL, Fig. 2.11b based on the crisp group DEMATEL indicates that the requirement $SR_5$ (Reliable and timely maintenance) obtains nine interactive arrows as the most interactive requirement. In Fig. 2.11a,

## 2.4 PSS Requirement Interaction Analysis

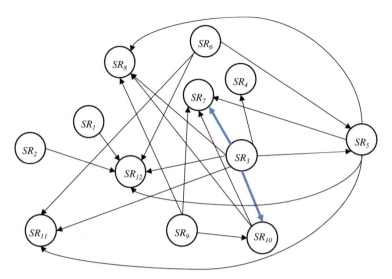

a. Relationship digraph from the proposed method

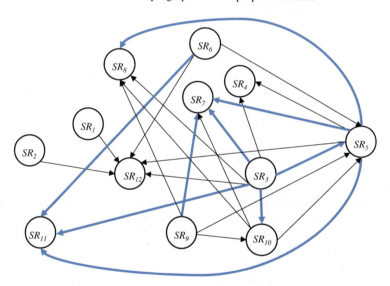

b. Relationship digraph from the crisp group DEMATEL

**Fig. 2.11** Relationship digraph for most influential relationships of PSS requirements (Song and Cao 2017)

there are two thick arrows representing higher influence relationships between PSS requirements, i.e., $SR_3$ (Wide scope of condition monitoring)-$SR_7$ (High availability of repair), $SR_3$ (Wide scope of condition monitoring)-$SR_{10}$ (Quick service response) with relation value greater than 0.25. However, in addition to $SR_3$–$SR_7$ and $SR_3$–$SR_{10}$, there are more higher influence relationships in Fig. 2.11b based on the crisp group DEMATEL, such as $SR_5$–$SR_7$, $SR_5$–$SR_8$, $SR_6$–$SR_{11}$, $SR_3$–$SR_5$, and $SR_3$–$SR_{11}$, etc. Focusing on requirement of $SR_6$ (Elevator operation training) in Fig. 2.11a, it could indirectly influence requirement of $SR_7$ (High availability of repair) through $SR_5$ (Reliable and timely maintenance). In Fig. 2.11b, $SR_9$ (Wide coverage of service center) could indirectly influence requirement of $SR_4$ (Accurate failure diagnosis), $SR_{11}$ (Safe and efficient operation), and $SR_{12}$ (Low energy consumption) through $SR_5$ (Reliable and timely maintenance).

The causal diagram in Fig. 2.12a based on the proposed method indicates that $SR_1$ (Professional procurement advice), $SR_2$ (Professional installation and commissioning), $SR_3$ (Wide scope of condition monitoring), $SR_6$ (Elevator operation training) and $SR_9$ (Wide coverage of service center) are influence dispatching requirements. The rest of elevator PSS requirements are influence receiving requirements, e.g., $SR_4$, $SR_5$, $SR_7$, $SR_8$, $SR_{10}$, $SR_{11}$, and $SR_{12}$. However, the crisp interaction evaluation method considers the $SR_4$, $SR_5$, and $SR_7$ as the influence dispatching requirements (see Fig. 2.12b). Although experts did not consider $SR_9$ and $SR_6$ (Elevator operation training) as a very important requirement of significance, this requirement directly or indirectly exerted more influence on other requirements (e.g., $SR_7$, $SR_8$, and $SR_{10}$) in both proposed and crisp methods.

The different judgment manipulating mechanism between the proposed method and the crisp DEMATEL is the main reason for the differences. The proposed method considers not only the individual judgment but also the judgment distribution among all the decision makers' judgments in the same category. For example, when evaluating $SR_7$ (High availability of repair)'s influence on $SR_{10}$(Quick service response), five decision makers provide their judgments as {3, 3, 4, 2, 4}. The rough approach converts this judgment set into {[2.667, 3.500], [2.667, 3.500], [3.200, 4.000], [2.000, 3.200], [3.200, 4.000]}, and aggregates the rough intervals into [2.747, 3.640] which considers the vagueness in group decision making process. On the contrary, the crisp group DEMATEL only aggregates the original scores to obtain the average crisp value 3.200 which does not consider the influence of judgment distribution and interaction on the whole decision making. Furthermore, the proposed method can identify and reveal the change of expert judgments on the interaction. For instance, when the original scores {3, 3, 4, 2, 4} are changed into {1, 3, 4, 4, 4}, the rough approach converts this judgment set into {[1.000, 3.200], [2.000, 3.750], [3.200, 4.000], [3.200, 4.000], [3.200, 4.000]}, and aggregates the rough intervals into [2.520, 3.790]. However, the crisp group DEMATEL still aggregates the original scores to obtain the average crisp value 3.200 without revealing decision makers' judgments changes. In this respect, the proposed method is more reasonable than the crisp group DEMATEL.

In summary, the features revealed by the proposed method for interaction evaluation of PSS requirement are listed as follows:

(1) This proposed method integrates strength of group DEMATEL in revealing interaction relationships and merit of rough set theory in dealing with subjective PSS requirement interaction judgments.

## 2.4 PSS Requirement Interaction Analysis

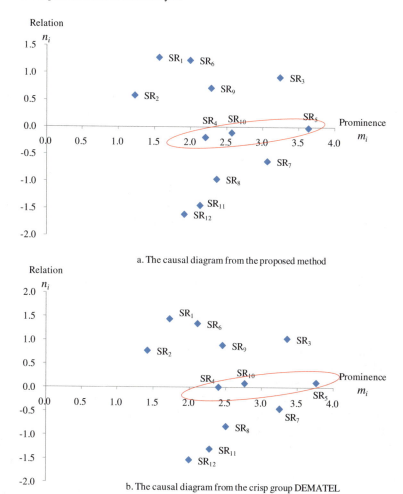

**Fig. 2.12** The causal diagram for the elevator PSS requirement relationships (Song and Cao 2017)

(2) The research successfully adapts DEMATEL in uncertain environment by using the flexible rough intervals which well reflects decision maker's subjective and vague judgments. In addition, the presented approach can discern the judgment changes in decision making of requirement interaction evaluation.

(3) Under vague environment, the proposed method can successfully determine the weight of each PSS requirement, and further obtain the causal and effect relationships among requirements. This helps the manager to identify the essential requirements to pertinently allocate resources for the PSS development project.

(4) The presented rough group DEMATEL method can be also applied in other fields where critical factors are needed to be identified among various influencing elements. Besides, it is applicable to systems facing problems that require to segment complex factors by group decision in a vague environment.

## 2.5 Customer Requirement Forecast

To well reflect the future state of customer requirement, Song et al. (2013b) integrate the strength of Kano model in customer requirement classification, the advantage of Grey theory in trends description and the merit of Markov chain in modeling local fluctuations of prediction. With forecasting results from the proposed method, companies can well know the complex and rapidly changing states of customer requirement in advance and design the right product/service at right stage to satisfy customer demand or even exceeding their expectation, thereby enhancing customer satisfaction and loyalty. Further, predicting the states of customer requirements with the approach in Song et al. (2013b) may also help companies to well understand the psychological and behavioral characteristics of each market segment, and develop precise and effective marketing strategies in early development phase.

### 2.5.1 The Method for Customer Requirements Forecast

Kano model is a useful tool to classify and prioritize customer requirements based on how they affect customer's satisfaction (Kano 1984; He et al. 2017). In practice, four types of design attributes are identified in Kano model: (1) must-be attributes are expected by the customers and they lead to extreme customer dissatisfaction if they are absent or poorly satisfied, (2) one-dimensional attributes are those for which better fulfillment leads to linear increment of customer satisfaction, (3) attractive attributes are usually unexpected by the customers and can result in great satisfaction if they are available, and (4) indifferent attributes are those that the customer is not interested in the level of their performance. Generally, customer requirements with different attributes (e.g. "attractive" and "indifferent") are not always reflected in the conventional customer requirements analysis and prediction. This would lead to some customer requirements being overestimated or underestimated. Furthermore, it is difficult to acquire a large amount of customer requirement data in engineering practice, which would make it difficult to forecast the evolution tends of future customer requirements. In addition, there are some fluctuations in the transforming process of customer requirement. Therefore, it is necessary to develop a new prediction method to manipulate those problems. Kano model is a good static requirement classification tool, but it can not handle the dynamic customer requirements transition. Forecast using Grey theory requires fewer data and it has higher accuracy. However, Grey theory is not efficient in processing sequence with fluctuations which always lead to poor prediction accuracy. On the contrary, Markov chain theory can well reflect random fluctuations with transition probability matrix. Hence, this work is expected to first use grey theory model GM (1, 1) to describe future trends of customer requirements states from the Kano model. And then, the Markov chain is used to predict the residual representing fluctuations in sequence of future customer requirements. Figure 2.13 shows the framework of the states prediction of customer requirement.

## 2.5 Customer Requirement Forecast

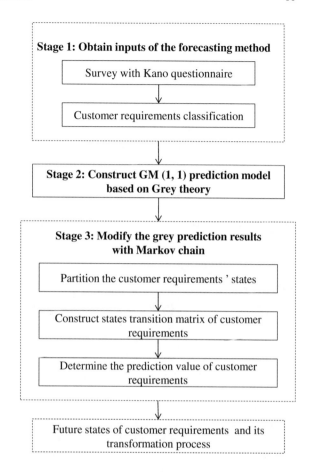

**Fig. 2.13** The framework of the states prediction of customer requirement (Song et al. 2013b)

### Phase 1. Obtain inputs of the forecasting method

Customer requirements distribution T (CRm, k) is first-hand information from Kano questionnaire analysis, which is input of the model. T (CRm, k) represents states value of the customer requirement 'm' at time 'k'. The following research is assumed to focus on certain selected customer segmentation (e.g. 18–25 years old, office workers), because focusing on certain customer segmentation would bring practical and specific guidance to industry. In this way, company can not only develop right products for right customer group, but also develop more precise marketing strategies.

First, Kano questionnaire is designed based on the customer requirement of a particular product. Kano questionnaire (see Table 2.14) includes questions both in functional form and dysfunctional form about customer requirements. For each part of the questions, customers are expected to select one of five alternative answers, which are described as "Like"; "Must-be"; "Neutral"; "Live-with"; and "Dislike". Then, select certain customer segmentation to conduct the survey.

**Table 2.14** Classic questions in Kano questionnaire (Fricker et al. 2010)

| Kano question | Answer |
|---|---|
| Functional form of the question (e.g. if the mobile phone has a screen of 7 inches, how do you feel?) | (1) I dislike it that way<br>(2) I can live with it that way<br>(3) I am neutral<br>(4) It must be that way<br>(5) I like it that way |
| Dysfunctional form of the question (e.g. if the mobile phone does not have has a screen of 7 inches, how do you feel?) | (1) I dislike it that way<br>(2) I can live with it that way<br>(3) I am neutral;<br>(4) It must be that way<br>(5) I like it that way |

**Table 2.15** Kano's classification scheme (Chen and Weng 2006)

| | | Functional form of the question | | | | |
|---|---|---|---|---|---|---|
| | | Like | Must-be | Neutral | Live with | Dislike |
| Dysfunctional form of the question | Like | O | A | A | A | O |
| | Must-be | R | I | I | I | M |
| | Neutral | R | I | I | I | M |
| | Live with | R | I | I | I | M |
| | Dislike | R | R | R | R | Q |

Note: *A* Attractive; *O* One-dimensional; *M* Must-be; *I* Indifference; *R* Reverse; *Q* Questionable

The second step is to analyze data acquired from survey and get customer requirements states distribution according to Kano classification scheme (see Table 2.15).

Thus, we can get the distribution of customer requirements' states T ($CR_m$, k), e.g., T ($CR_m$, k) = {9, 35, 60, 10, 5, 1}, and we know that this customer requirement is in state of 'Must-be' because 60 customers consider it as must be attribute.

According to characteristics of product, select suitable time interval for Kano survey, and repeat the above steps until the historical data is sufficient to forecast. Then, we get state distribution of different customer requirements in different past periods.

**Phase 2. Construct GM (1, 1) prediction model for customer requirements states**

Suppose the original non-negative data series is $X^{(0)} = \{x^{(0)}(1), x^{(0)}(2), ..., x^{(0)}(n)\}$, $n \geq 4$. Use accumulated generating operation (AGO) to form a new data series $X^{(1)} = \{x^{(1)}(1), x^{(1)}(2), ..., x^{(1)}(n)\}$, where $x^{(1)}(k) = \sum_{i=1}^{k} x^{(0)}(i)$, k = 2, 3, ..., n.

Then, the sequence of generated mean value of consecutive neighbors can be derived as $Z^{(1)} = \{z^{(1)}(2), z^{(1)}(3), ..., z^{(1)}(n)\}$, where $z^{(1)}(k) = \frac{1}{2}(x^{(1)}(k) + x^{(1)}(k-1))$, k = 2, 3, ..., n.

## 2.5 Customer Requirement Forecast

Then we get GM(1, 1) model, a grey differential equation, as follows.

$$x^{(0)}(k) + az^{(1)}(k) = u \qquad (2.47)$$

where $a$ and $u$ are grey parameters.

Since $X^{(1)}$ is monotonic increase sequence that is similar to the solution curve of first order linear ordinary differential equation. the solution curve of following differential equation could represent the approximation of $X^{(1)}$.

$$\frac{dx^{(1)}}{dt} + ax^{(1)} = u \qquad (2.48)$$

where $\frac{dx^{(1)}}{dt}$ is deformed to show the difference of the forward and the backward values, i.e., $\frac{dx^{(1)}}{dt} \rightarrow x^{(1)}(k+1) - x^{(1)}(k) = x^{(0)}(k+1)$, Eq. (2.48) is a differential equation to replace the source model $x^{(0)}(k) + az^{(1)}(k) = u$.

The model parameters $a$ and $u$ are

$$\begin{bmatrix} a \\ u \end{bmatrix} = (B^T B)^{-1} B^T y_n \qquad (2.49)$$

where B and $y_n$ are defined as follows

$$B = \begin{bmatrix} -\frac{X^{(1)}(1)+X^{(1)}(2)}{2} & 1 \\ -\frac{X^{(1)}(2)+X^{(1)}(3)}{2} & 1 \\ \vdots & \vdots \\ -\frac{X^{(1)}(k-1)+X^{(1)}(k)}{2} & 1 \end{bmatrix} \quad y_n = \begin{bmatrix} x^{(0)}(2) \\ \vdots \\ x^{(0)}(n) \end{bmatrix} \qquad (2.50)$$

Solve Eq. (2.49) together with initial condition $x^{(0)}(1) = x^{(1)}(1)$, and the particular solution is

$$\hat{x}^{(1)}(k) = (x^{(0)}(1) - \frac{u}{a})e^{-a(k-1)} + \frac{u}{a}, \quad (k = 2, 3, \ldots) \qquad (2.51)$$

where ^ represents Grey forecast value, and cumulative reduction is conducted as follows:

$$\hat{x}^{(0)}(k+1) = x^{(1)}(k+1) - x^{(1)}(k), \quad (k = 1, 2, \ldots \ldots n) \qquad (2.52)$$

Then GM (1, 1) prediction value $\hat{x}^{(0)}(k)$ is obtained as follows.

$$\begin{cases} \hat{x}^{(0)}(1) = x^{(0)}(1) \\ \hat{x}^{(0)}(k+1) = (x^{(0)}(1) - \frac{u}{a})(1-e^a)e^{-ak} \end{cases} \quad (k = 1, 2, \ldots n) \quad (2.53)$$

It is necessary to forecast each vector of customer requirements to obtain the future states distribution of customer requirements. Therefore, GM (1, 1) model is used similarly to predict trend of each vector, i.e. Must-be attribute (M), One-dimensional attribute (O), Attractive attribute (A), and Indifferent attribute (I). Mathematical expressions for prediction values of customer requirement in future are as follows:

$$(CR_m, k) = \left\{ \hat{x}_A^{(0)}(k), \hat{x}_O^{(0)}(k), \hat{x}_M^{(0)}(k), \hat{x}_I^{(0)}(k), \hat{x}_R^{(0)}(k) \right\}, \quad \text{where } k \geq n.$$

**Phase 3. Modify the grey prediction results with Markov chain**

Forecast based on the GM (1, 1) model is accurate in short term prediction with fewer fluctuations. However, the prediction accuracy is lower when there are big variations of data sequence. Therefore, GM (1, 1) model should be adjusted by Markov chain theory to obtain a more reasonable and reliable customer requirement prediction.

*Step 1: Partition the customer requirement' states*

Here, the authors only select one vector of the customer requirements' distribution to illustrate the proposed forecast method. The other vectors of customer requirements could be obtained in the same way. The original data sequence of customer requirements' distribution could be marked as $X^{(0)}(k)$.

$$X^{(0)}(k) = \left\{ X^{(0)}(1), X^{(0)}(2), \ldots, X^{(0)}(n) \right\}$$

And forecast sequence with GM (1, 1) model is noted as $\hat{X}^{(0)}(k)$:

$$\hat{X}^{(0)}(k) = \left\{ \hat{X}^{(0)}(1), \hat{X}^{(0)}(2), \ldots \hat{X}^{(0)}(n) \right\}$$

Therefore, the residual $\Delta r(k)$ is calculated as follows.

$$\Delta r(k) = X^{(0)}(k) - \hat{X}^{(0)}(k) \quad (2.54)$$

Then the residual sequence is partitioned into several states according to the mean $\bar{x}$ and standard deviation $s$ of the residual sequence. In general, the residual sequence could be divided into three states. State 1: $(-\infty, \bar{x} - 0.5s)$, State 2: $(\bar{x} - 0.5s, \bar{x} + 0.5s)$, and State 3: $(\bar{x} + 0.5s, +\infty)$.

## 2.5 Customer Requirement Forecast

*Step 2: Construct states transition matrix of customer requirement*

$M_{ij}(m)$ is number of samples that transfer from states $i$ to states $j$ by $m$ steps, $l$ is the number of states, and $M_i$ stands for number of primary samples in states $i$, then the probability of state transition $p_{ij}(m)$ can be get as follows.

$$p_{ij}(m) = \frac{M_{ij}(m)}{M_i}, \quad i = 1, 2, \ldots l;\ j = 1, 2, \ldots l \tag{2.55}$$

$$P(m) = \begin{bmatrix} p_{11}(m) & \cdots & p_{1l}(m) \\ \vdots & \vdots & \vdots \\ p_{l1}(m) & \cdots & p_{ll}(m) \end{bmatrix} \tag{2.56}$$

where $P(m)$ is probability matrix of state transition.

Residual state vector is defined as $S(k)$ in the $k$th period, and then the probability vector of residual state in the $(k+1)^{th}$ period is calculated as follows.

$$S(k+1) = S(k) \times P(m) \tag{2.57}$$

The state of the residuals in the $(k+1)^{th}$ period is the column where the largest attribute value stays.

$P^{(k)}$ is defined as the probability matrix of states transition for the $k$th step, and $P^{(k)} = [P(m)]^k$.

*Step 3: Determine the forecast value of customer requirement state*

Once the customer requirement states are determined, both point estimation and fluctuation interval are also determined, which would enhance the reliability and the accuracy of the prediction. Point estimation from the Grey-Markov chain method can be calculated as follows.

$$\overset{\cap}{x}^{(0)}(k) = \hat{x}^{(0)}(k) + \frac{1}{2}(\delta_1 + \delta_2) \tag{2.58}$$

$\delta_1, \delta_2$ are the upper and lower boundary values of residual with different states. $\overset{\cap}{x}^{(0)}(k)$ is the modified point estimation value from the Grey-Markov chain method, and $\hat{x}^{(0)}(k)$ is prediction value of the GM (1, 1) model, ($k = 2, \ldots, n$).

The fluctuation interval of the prediction value $(c, d)$ could also be determined as follows.

$$c = \hat{x}^{(0)}(k) + \delta_1,\ d = \hat{x}^{(0)}(k) + \delta_2 \tag{2.59}$$

## 2.5.2 Case Study: Customer Requirements Forecast for Mobile Phone

In this section, to demonstrate the application of the proposed approach, forecast of customer requirements states for a mobile phone is taken as an example. W Company is a manufacturer that designs mobile phone for the young people and trend-setters. Their customers are mainly commuters, who usually spend nearly 2–3 h/day on the road by public transportation. Therefore, they often pay attention to the functions of entertainment and reading of the mobile phone. Nowadays, lifecycle of mobile phone is getting shorter and shorter. In volatile cellular phone market, due to the customer sophistication and intense competition, it is critical for the W company to predict the dynamic customer requirements. The company expects to develop a new type of mobile phone with "larger screen of 7 inches" to capture the future customers' taste with lower cost.

**Phase 1. Obtain inputs of the forecasting method**

Kano surveys have been conducted in the past five quarters. $CR_1$ stands for customer requirement of "larger screen of 7 in.". Here, number of customers is converted into percentage form to simplify calculations. The distributions of customer requirements in the past five quarters are shown in Table 2.16.

Obviously, percentage of customers who choose $CR_1$ as "attractive" attribute declines with time, while percentage of customers who choose $CR_1$ as "one-dimensional" attribute witnesses a gradual increase. In fact, percentage of the "attractive" has exceeded percentage of "one-dimensional" in the fifth quarter. Therefore, $CR_1$ has transformed from the "attractive" customer requirement into a "one-dimensional" one.

**Phase 2. Construct GM (1, 1) prediction model for customer requirements states**

In the past five quarters, we firstly utilize the "Attractive" (A) sequence (shown in Table 2.17) to illustrate how to predict customer requirements states. Forecast for other customer requirements (i.e. O, M, I) can be obtained in the same way.

First, accumulate the historical date sequence to generate a new sequence (see Table 2.17).

**Table 2.16** Historical distribution of $CR_1$ "larger screen of 7 in." in the past five quarters (Song et al. 2013b)

| k | $CR_1$ "larger screen of 7 in." | | | |
|---|---|---|---|---|
| | A | O | M | I |
| 1 | 0.740 | 0.100 | 0.090 | 0.070 |
| 2 | 0.690 | 0.180 | 0.090 | 0.040 |
| 3 | 0.570 | 0.300 | 0.110 | 0.020 |
| 4 | 0.440 | 0.380 | 0.150 | 0.030 |
| 5 | 0.320 | 0.460 | 0.200 | 0.020 |

## 2.5 Customer Requirement Forecast

**Table 2.17** The initial "Attractive" (A) sequence, accumulated sequence and prediction sequence (Song et al. 2013b)

| k | 1 | 2 | 3 | 4 | 5 | 6 |
|---|---|---|---|---|---|---|
| $x^{(0)}(k)$ | 0.740 | 0.690 | 0.570 | 0.440 | 0.320 | |
| $x^{(1)}(k)$ | 0.740 | 1.430 | 2.000 | 2.440 | 2.760 | |
| $\hat{x}^{(0)}(k)$ | 0.740 | 0.699 | 0.549 | 0.431 | 0.338 | 0.265 |
| Residual | 0.000 | −0.009 | 0.021 | 0.009 | −0.018 | |
| Relative error | 0.000 | −0.013 | 0.0368 | 0.0205 | −0.056 | |

Second, the matrix B and data vector $y_n$ are constructed according to the formula (2.50):

$$B = \begin{bmatrix} -1.085 & 1 \\ -1.175 & 1 \\ -2.220 & 1 \\ -2.600 & 1 \end{bmatrix} \quad y_n = \begin{bmatrix} 0.69 \\ 0.57 \\ 0.44 \\ 0.32 \end{bmatrix}$$

Third, according to the Formula (2.49), grey parameters are obtained as follows. $a = 0.243$, $u = 0.967$.

Fourth, the value of $a$, $u$ and $x^{(0)}(1)$ are put into the Formula (2.53) to get the "Attractive" attribute prediction model for $CR_1$.

$$\hat{x}^{(0)}(k+1) = 0.891 e^{-0.243k}, \quad (k = 1, 2, \ldots\ldots 5) \tag{2.60}$$

Fifth, the prediction value, residual and relative error of "attractive" attribute of $CR_1$ are calculated according to the Eq. (2.60). The results are also shown in Table 2.17.

### Phase 3. Modify the grey prediction results with Markov chain

In order to obtain a more reasonable and reliable prediction of customer requirement, Markov chain is used to modify the results from GM (1, 1) model.

*Step 1: Partition the customer requirement' states*

Considering the boundary value of residuals, we can partition the residual series into three states to ensure the convenience of calculation. That is, State 1: $(-0.019, \bar{x} - 0.5\,s)$; State 2: $(\bar{x} - 0.5\,s, \bar{x} + 0.5\,s)$; State 3: $(\bar{x} + 0.5\,s, 0.022)$. And then, the mean $\bar{x}$ and standard deviation s of residuals sequence are substituted into the above interval respectively to obtain criteria for classification of customer requirement' state (see Table 2.18).

**Table 2.18** Criteria for classification of "attractive" customer requirement' states (Song et al. 2013b)

| States | Criteria for classification of customer requirement' state | Meaning |
|---|---|---|
| 1 | (−0.019, −0.006) | Overestimated |
| 2 | (−0.006, 0.007) | Normal |
| 3 | (0.007, 0.022) | Underestimated |

**Table 2.19** The actual residuals' states and the forecasted residual states in different quarters (Song et al. 2013b)

| k/quarter | 1 | 2 | 3 | 4 | 5 | 6 |
|---|---|---|---|---|---|---|
| The actual residual state | 2 | 1 | 3 | 3 | 1 | |
| The Forecasted residual state | – | 1 | 3 | 3 | 3 | 3 |

**Table 2.20** States' transferring frequency distribution for "attractive" customer requirement (Song et al. 2013b)

| | State 1 (Overestimated) | State 2 (Normal) | State 3 (Underestimated) | Total |
|---|---|---|---|---|
| State 1 (Overestimated) | 0 | 0 | 1 | 1 |
| State 2 (Normal) | 1 | 0 | 0 | 1 |
| State 3 (Underestimated) | 1 | 0 | 1 | 2 |

Thus, according to the criteria for classification of "attractive" customer requirement' state, the actual residuals' states distribution in the last five quarters can be obtained in Table 2.19.

*Step 2: Construct states transition matrix of customer requirement*

We can obtain the transferring frequency distribution of the states (see Table 2.20) according to the state of residual in Table 2.19.

Thus, we get the states transition matrix P according to the Formula (2.55).

$$P = \begin{bmatrix} 0 & 0 & 1 \\ 1 & 1 & 0 \\ 0.5 & 0 & 0.5 \end{bmatrix}$$

We can see from Table 2.19 that the residual is in states 2 (Normal) in the 1st quarter, and thus, the probability vector S (0) = (0, 1, 0). Then we can predict prob-

## 2.5 Customer Requirement Forecast

**Table 2.21** The modified point prediction value in different quarters (Song et al. 2013b)

| k | 1 | 2 | 3 | 4 | 5 | 6 |
|---|---|---|---|---|---|---|
| Actual value | 0.740 | 0.690 | 0.570 | 0.440 | 0.320 | |
| Modified prediction value | | 0.686 | 0.564 | 0.446 | 0.353 | 0.280 |
| Fitting error | | 0.004 | 0.006 | −0.006 | −0.033 | |

ability vector in the second quarter S (1) = S (0) × P = (1, 0, 0).Therefore, residual is in state 1 (Overestimated) in the 2nd quarter. Similarly, we can forecast residual states (see Table 2.19) in other quarters with the Formula (2.57).

*Step 3: Determine the forecast value of customer requirement*

Grey-Markov chain model predictions in different periods are calculated based on the data in Tables 2.17 and 2.18. For example, the residual is in states 1 (see Table 2.19) in the 2nd quarter, and its corresponding fluctuation interval is (−0.019, −0.006).Therefore, modified point prediction value of customer requirement could be obtained according to the Formula (2.58), e.g. modified point prediction value in the 2nd quarter is calculated as follows.

$$\overset{\frown}{x}^{(0)}(2) = \hat{x}^{(0)}(2) + \frac{1}{2}(\delta_1(2) + \delta_2(2)) = 0.699 + \frac{-0.019 - 0.006}{2} = 0.687$$

The modified point prediction values in other quarters are listed in Table 2.21.

Then, considering the reliability and reasonability of the prediction (forecast fluctuations), the form of interval prediction of customer requirement is conducted in the following steps.

First, the upper and lower limits of fluctuation interval of point prediction value can be respectively calculated in line with the Formula (2.59) and Table 2.18. For instance, when k = 6, $c = \hat{x}^{(0)}(6) + \delta_1(6) = 0.265 + 0.007 = 0.272$, $d = \hat{x}^{(0)}(6) + \delta_2(6) = 0.265 + 0.022 = 0.287$.

So the fluctuation interval form of the prediction is (0.272, 0.287).

Second, the actual probability vector in the 5th quarter is in state 1, and thus S (5) = (1, 0, 0), according to the Formula (2.57),

$$S(6) = S(5) \times P = (1, 0, 0) \times \begin{bmatrix} 0 & 0 & 1 \\ 1 & 1 & 0 \\ 0.5 & 0 & 0.5 \end{bmatrix} = (1, 0, 0),$$ So the probability of

prediction value' falling into interval of (0.272, 0.287) is 100%.

The proposed Grey Markov chain method does not take prediction fluctuations into account, but its future fluctuation rang. Besides, it also provides probability of prediction values' falling into the fluctuation range. Therefore, it is more reliable and reasonable than other single point prediction methods.

**Table 2.22** Point predictions for customer requirements states of A, O, M and I (Song et al. 2013b)

| k | Point predictions from Grey Markov chain method ||||
|---|---|---|---|---|
|   | A | O | M | I |
| 1 | – | – | – | – |
| 2 | 0.686 | 0.190 | 0.089 | 0.041 |
| 3 | 0.564 | 0.294 | 0.111 | 0.029 |
| 4 | 0.446 | 0.340 | 0.150 | 0.029 |
| 5 | 0.353 | 0.471 | 0.200 | 0.020 |
| 6 | 0.280 | 0.595 | 0.257 | 0.021 |

Similarly, we can obtain point predictions for other attributes of $CR_1$ (e.g. O, M, and I) in Table 2.22. Therefore, the states distribution vector of the customer requirement ("larger screen of 7 in.") in the 6th quarter T ($CR_1$, 6) is obtained as follows.

$$T(CR_1, 6) = \{0.280, 0.595, 0.257, 0.021\}.$$

Clearly, "larger screen of 7 in." is "one dimensional" customer requirement at the 6th quarter. Table 2.23 shows predictions in form of intervals and probability of the point estimations falling into prediction intervals.

## 2.5.3 Comparisons and Discussion

The actual value of "attractive attribute" of $CR_1$ is compared with the prediction value from the integrated method in Fig. 2.14. It is clear to be seen from Fig. 2.14 and Table 2.21 that the fitting errors of the proposed prediction approach is smaller, e.g. the fitting error in the 2nd quarter is only 0.004. The average fitting error (the 2nd quarter-the 5th quarter) is −0.007.

To reveal the advantages of the proposed method, we also compare it with forecast approach using only the Grey theory in Fig. 2.15.

As shown in Fig. 2.15, the prediction results from the proposed method are different from those of the GM (1, 1) method. The proposed prediction method based on Grey-Markov chain provides interval form of customer requirement forecast, which is more reasonable and reliable than the other point prediction methods (e.g. GM (1, 1) method). For example, the "One-dimensional" state of the customer requirement (larger screen of 7 in.) in the 6th quarter is predicted to be (0.584, 0.606), and the interval 0.022 is considered as the accuracy of the prediction, which would provide useful information for the company. However, the GM (1, 1) prediction method only presents single point result (0.616), irrespective of the uncertainties included in the forecasting process. This would lead to overestimated prediction. In fact, predicted

## 2.5 Customer Requirement Forecast

**Table 2.23** Prediction fluctuations range and states probability of forecast in the 6th quarter (Song et al. 2013b)

| k = 6 | Fluctuation range | Probability | States |
|---|---|---|---|
| A | (0.246, 0.259) | 0 | State 1 (Overestimated) |
|   | (0.259, 0.272) | 0 | State 2 (Normal) |
|   | (0.272, 0.287) | 100% | State 3 (Underestimated) |
| O | (0.584, 0.606) | 100% | State 1 (Overestimated) |
|   | (0.605, 0.626) | 0 | State 2 (Normal) |
|   | (0.626, 0.641) | 0 | State 3 (Underestimated) |
| M | (0.255, 0.259) | 100% | State 1 (Overestimated) |
|   | (0.259, 0.262) | 0 | State 2 (Normal) |
|   | (0.262, 0.265) | 0 | State 3 (Underestimated) |
| I | (0.006, 0.014) | 0 | State 1 (Overestimated) |
|   | (0.014, 0.019) | 0 | State 2 (Normal) |
|   | (0.019, 0.023) | 100% | State 3 (Underestimated) |

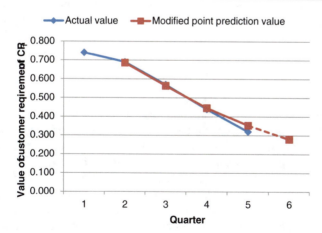

**Fig. 2.14** Actual value and modified point prediction value for "attractive attribute" of $CR_1$ (Song et al. 2013b)

values of customer requirement tend to fluctuate within a certain range due to the complex nature of factors. The interval form of prediction enhances the reliability and reasonability of the forecast.

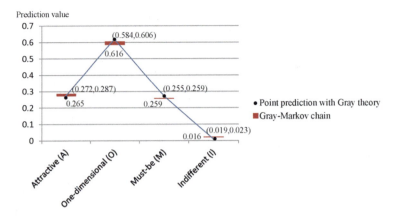

**Fig. 2.15** Comparison between Grey theory-based method and Grey-Markov chain in the 6th quarter (Song et al. 2013b)

As we can see from Fig. 2.16, $CR_1$ ("larger screen of 7 in.") is attractive attribute to customers from the 1st quarter to the 4th quarter. In fact, $CR_1$ is a delighter to targeted customers because there are fewer manufacturers introduced mobile phone with "larger screen of 7 in." especially for e-reading on mobile phone with the same price according to the company's survey. In addition, the targeted customers in the case study are young commuters who often spend 2–3 h on the public transportation every day, and they are loyal supporters of e-reading on mobile phone. Therefore, the bigger-screen mobile phone would give these targeted customers surprising experience of reading at the beginning of the market introduction. The $CR_1$ begins to shift from "One-dimensional" (O) to "Attractive" (A) attribute between the 4th quarter and the 5th quarter, because several major rivals of the company has launched competitive products (e.g. Pad with partial function of cellular phone) with the same price early in the 4th quarter in the light of the company's business intelligence, and $CR_1$ ("larger screen of 7 in.") could no longer bring customers much pleasant and surprising experience as before. In the 6th quarter, the percentage of people who select $CR_1$ ("larger screen of 7 in.") as "Must-be" requirement almost matched the percentage of people who choose $CR_1$ as "Attractive" requirement. Generally, the customer requirement ($CR_1$) in the 6th quarter is still "One-dimensional". W company should continue to invest resources to meet the demand of targeted customers so as to enhance customer satisfaction and loyalty. W company adopts alternative materials to reduce costs, and provides customers with cheaper screen that has the same function.

In summary, the features of the proposed Grey-Markov chain prediction method are listed as follows.

First, different from traditional prediction methods (e.g. time series-based methods), the proposed approach does not require much historical data to predict the future states of customer requirement, which would greatly reduce the workload and cost. For example, in the case study, customer requirement information of 5 quarters

## 2.5 Customer Requirement Forecast

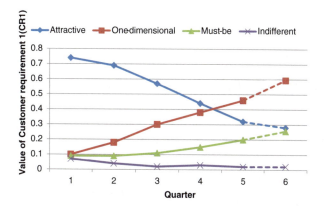

**Fig. 2.16** The trends of Customer requirement 1 ("larger screen of 7 in.") (Song et al. 2013b)

is sufficient to predict the state distribution of the next quarter. Second, the proposed prediction method not only adopts the strength of grey theory in describing the overall trend of customer requirements, but also takes the local fluctuations with Markov chain into account. This characteristic ensures the accuracy of the prediction. Third, with the help of the proposed method, manufacturing companies can well know the transition rule of different customer requirements to design the right product for the right customer at the right time. In addition, it also reduces the unnecessary design changes due to customer requirement variation and avoids undesirable delays in schedules. Fourth, the interval form of prediction from the proposed approach is more reliable and reasonable than that of other point estimation methods. For instance, the predicted one-dimensional state of the customer requirement in the 6th quarter is (0.584, 0.606) are more reasonable than the overestimated point prediction 0.616 due to it's considering the inherent uncertainty in the prediction. Fifth, in the proposed method, it is not necessary to assume as the traditional prediction methods that the data possess a known statistical distribution.

## References

Chen, L. H., & Weng, M. C. (2006). An evaluation approach to engineering design in QFD processes using fuzzy goal programming models. *Eur J Oper Res, 172*(1), 230–248.

Cohen, L. (1995). *Quality function deployment: how to make QFD work for you*. USA: Prentice Hall

De Bruijn, H., & Herder, P. M. (2009). System and actor perspectives on sociotechnical systems. *IEEE Transactions on systems, man, and cybernetics-part A: Systems and Humans, 39*(5), 981–992.

Forman, E., & Peniwati, K. (1998). Aggregating individual judgments and priorities with the analytic hierarchy process. *Eur J Oper Res, 108*(1), 165–169.

Fricker, S., Gorschek, T., Byman, C., & Schmidle, A. (2010). Handshaking with implementation proposals: Negotiating requirements understanding. *IEEE Software, 27*(2), 72.

He, L., Song, W., Wu, Z., Xu, Z., Zheng, M., & Ming, X. (2017). Quantification and integration of an improved Kano model into QFD based on multi-population adaptive genetic algorithm. *Comput Ind Eng, 114,* 183–194.

Jung, C. (2006). Anforderungsklärung in interdisziplinärer Entwicklungsumgebung (Doctoral dissertation, Technische Universität München)

Kano, N. (1984). Attractive quality and must-be quality. *Hinshitsu (Quality, The Journal of Japanese Society for Quality Control), 14,* 39–48.

Kruse, P. J. (1996). *Anforderungen in der Systementwicklung.* Düsseldorf: VDI-Verlag.

Kwong, C. K., & Bai, H. (2002). A fuzzy AHP approach to the determination of importance weights of customer requirements in quality function deployment. *Journal of Intelligent Manufacturing, 13*(5), 367–377.

Lin, R. J. (2013). Using fuzzy DEMATEL to evaluate the green supply chain management practices. *Journal of Cleaner Production, 40,* 32–39.

Saaty, T. L. (1977). A scaling method for priorities in hierarchical structures. *The Journal of Mathematical Psychology, 15*(3), 234–281.

Shen, X. X., Xie, M., & Tan, K. C. (2001). Listening to the future voice of the customer using fuzzy trend analysis in QFD. *Quality Engineering, 13*(3), 419–425.

Song, W., Ming, X., Han, Y., & Wu, Z. (2013a). A rough set approach for evaluating vague customer requirement of industrial product-service system. *International Journal of Production Research, 51*(22), 6681–6701.

Song, W. (2017). Requirement management for product-service systems: Status review and future trends. *Computers in Industry, 85,* 11–22.

Song, W., & Cao, J. (2017). A rough DEMATEL-based approach for evaluating interaction between requirements of product-service system. *Computers & Industrial Engineering, 110,* 353–363.

Song, W., Ming, X., & Xu, Z. (2013b). Integrating Kano model and grey–Markov chain to predict customer requirement states. *Proceedings of the Institution of Mechanical Engineers, Part B: Journal of Engineering Manufacture, 227*(8), 1232–1244.

Wu, H. H., Liao, A. Y. H., & Wang, P. C. (2005). Using grey theory in quality function deployment to analyse dynamic customer requirements. *The International Journal of Advanced Manufacturing Technology, 25*(11–12), 1241–1247.

Xu, Z., Ming, X., Song, W., Li, M., He, L., & Li, X. (2014). Towards a new framework: Understanding and managing the supply chain for product-service systems. *Proceedings of the Institution of Mechanical Engineers, Part B: Journal of Engineering Manufacture, 228*(12), 1642–1652.

Xu, Z., Song, W., Zhang, Q., Ming, X. G., He, L., & Liu, W. (2017). Product service demand forecasting in hierarchical service structure. *Procedia CIRP, 64,* 145–150.

Zhai, L. Y., Khoo, L. P., & Zhong, Z. W. (2009). Design concept evaluation in product development using rough sets and grey relation analysis. *Expert Syst Appl, 36*(3), 7072–7079.

# Chapter 3
# Requirements Specification for Customizable PSS

In this Chapter, the elicited PSS requirements are converted into technical attributes based on a rough QFD (Quality function deployment) approach developed by Song et al. (2014). The method includes two stages: determining importance of customer requirement and the prioritizing the technical attributes based on rough set theory and grey relational analysis (GRA). Then, the interactions and conflicts between technical attributes are identified with an integrated method proposed by Song and Sakao (2016), which is based on Service Function and Attribute Analysis (SFAA), group decision making with unbalanced linguistic label set and TRIZ methodology.

## 3.1 Specification of PSS Requirement

The requirements of customers expressed with their own language cannot be directly used in design of PSS. The customer requirements need to be converted into the form that PSS designer can understand (Mannweiler and Aurich 2011; Li and Song 2016). Conversion of the user requirements into specific product design requirements and service design requirements is illustrated in Fig. 3.1. Interactions between different kinds of requirement are also shown in Fig. 3.1.

After converting the PSS requirements into PSS technical characteristics, it is necessary to timely check whether there are conflicts between different PSS technical characteristics as well as the degree of conflict. Since enhancement of one technical characteristic may affect the performance of other technical characteristics of PSS, which will lead to the difficulty and cost increasing of PSS delivery, or even cause failure of PSS solution. Potential conflicts can lead to service failure or malfunction in delivery phase of PSS, and eventually lead to customer dissatisfaction. Blackhurst et al. (2008) believe that the conflict can degrade the overall performance of the system if they are not handled effectively. In this regard, conflict resolution is the key to successful implementation of PSS. Thus, the ability to discover conflicts would be a valuable asset, particularly if the discovery occurred proactively. Systematic

**Fig. 3.1** PSS requirement conversion process (Song 2017)

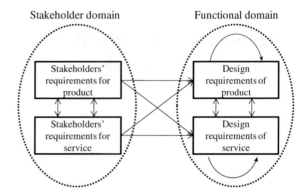

researches on PSS conflict resolution are still fewer. Most of previous researches have focused on domain of product conflict resolution, such as conflict resolution in collaborative product design and concurrent design (Hou et al. 2008).

## 3.2 PSS Requirement Conversion

Song et al. (2014) develop a rough QFD to achieve more rational PSS requirement conversion. The proposed method includes two stages of analysis: the importance calculation of customer requirement and the prioritizing the technical attributes using an integrated approach based on a rough set theory and grey relational analysis (GRA). The approach integrates the advantage of rough set theory in dealing with vagueness without requirement of extra priori information and the strength of GRA in establishing analytical framework and detecting necessary information of the data interactions.

### 3.2.1 Preliminaries

Pawlak (1982) first proposes the rough set theory (RST). It is an effective mathematical tool to manipulate subjectivity and vagueness even if the data set is small in size and its distribution is unknown. It merely depends on the original data without the need for auxiliary information. Pawlak (2012) uses a pair of precise concepts with the lower and upper approximations to represent each vague concept in RST (see Fig. 3.2). The lower approximation of set $S$ in Fig. 3.2 is the set of all elements certainly included in $S$, and the upper approximation of the set $S$ includes the elements which cannot be characterized with certainty as belong or not to $S$. Assume that $U$ is the universe containing all the objects, a boundary region of $S$ in $U$ is composed of the elements that can neither be ruled in nor ruled out as member of the

## 3.2 PSS Requirement Conversion

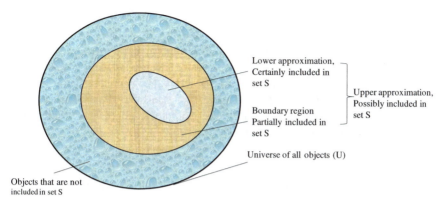

**Fig. 3.2** Basic notion of rough set theory (Song et al. 2014)

target set (Greco et al. 2001). The lower approximation, the upper approximation, and boundary region are defined in the rough set theory as follows (Khoo et al. 1999).

Assume that there is a set of $n$ classes of human judgments, $R = \{J_1, J_2, \ldots, J_n\}$, ordered in the manner of $J_1 < J_2 < \cdots < J_n$ and $Y$ is an arbitrary objects of $U$, then the lower approximation of $J_i$, the upper approximation of $J_i$, and boundary region are defined.

$$\text{Lower approximation}: \underline{Apr}(J_i) = \cup \{Y \in U/R(Y) \leq J_i\} \quad (3.1)$$

$$\text{Upper approximation}: \overline{Apr}(J_i) = \cup \{Y \in U/R(Y) \geq J_i\} \quad (3.2)$$

$$\text{Boundary region}: Bnd(J_i) = \cup \{Y \in U/R(Y) \neq J_i\}$$
$$= \{Y \in U/R(Y) > J_i\} \cup \{Y \in U/R(Y) < J_i\} \quad (3.3)$$

$J_i$, the greatest definable set contained in the concept is called the lower approximation of $J_i$. The least definable set containing concept $J_i$ is called the upper approximation of $J_i$. Elements belonging only to the upper approximation compose the boundary region.

Based on the definition of Khoo et al. (1999), Zhai et al. (2008) propose that the class, $J_i$, can be represented by a rough number which is defined by its lower limit $\underline{Lim}(J_i)$ and upper limit $\overline{Lim}(J_i)$. Lee et al. (2012) provide the calculation principle as follows.

$$\underline{Lim}(J_i) = \left[\prod_{k=1}^{N_L} R(Y) | Y \in \underline{Apr}(J_i)\right]^{1/N_L} \quad (3.4)$$

$$\overline{Lim}(J_i) = \left[\prod_{k=1}^{N_U} R(Y) | Y \in \overline{Apr}(J_i)\right]^{1/N_U} \quad (3.5)$$

$N_L$ and $N_U$ are the number of objects included in the lower approximation and upper approximation of $C_i$ respectively. The human judgments can be represented by rough numbers on the basis of lower limit ($\underline{Lim}(J_i)$) and upper limit ($\overline{Lim}(J_i)$) that are referred to as the mean of elements in the lower approximation and upper approximation respectively. In this regard, the interval of boundary region denotes the degree of preciseness. A rough number with a larger interval of boundary region is interpreted as vaguer or less precise one. The human judgment and interval of boundary region are expressed by following equations:

$$\text{Rough number}: RN(J_i) = \left[\overline{Lim}(J_i), \underline{Lim}(C_i)\right] \qquad (3.6)$$

$$\text{Interval of boundary region}: IBR(J_i) = \overline{Lim}(J_i) - \underline{Lim}(J_i) \qquad (3.7)$$

The arithmetic operations of interval analysis can also be applied to rough numbers as follows (Zhai et al. 2008; Lee et al. 2012).

$$RN_1 + RN_2 = (L_1, U_1) + (L_2, U_2) = (L_1 + L_2, U_1 + U_2) \qquad (3.8)$$

$$RN_1 \times k = (L_1, U_1) \times k = (kL_1, kU_1) \qquad (3.9)$$

$$RN_1 \times RN_2 = (L_1, U_1) \times (L_2, U_2) = (L_1 \times L_2, U_1 \times U_2) \qquad (3.10)$$

where $RN_1 = (L_1, U_1)$ and $RN_2 = (L_2, U_2)$ are two rough numbers and $k$ is a nonzero constant.

Grey theory is firstly proposed by Deng (1989). It is used to deal with uncertainties in small data samples with imprecise information. Grey relational analysis (GRA) is an evaluation model that measures the degree of similarity or difference between two sequences based on the grade of relation (Deng 1989; Chan and Tong 2007). It is based on finding relationships in both independent and interrelating data series. Utilizing GRA, the GRD (grey relational degree) can be used to evaluate the relationships between reference series and the series themselves. The steps of GRA are presented as follows:

Step 1: List the series of comparison $x_i(k)$. There are $m$ data series available for comparison: $x_i(k), i = 1, 2, \ldots, m; k = 1, 2, \ldots, n$.
Step 2: Normalization.

These series data can be pre-processed with normalization by maximum value, minimum value or objective value.

For the data of "the larger the better":

$$x_i^*(k) = \frac{x_i(k) - \min_k x_i(k)}{\max_k x_i(k) - \min_k x_i(k)} \qquad (3.11)$$

## 3.2 PSS Requirement Conversion

For the data of "the smaller the better":

$$x_i^*(k) = \frac{\max_k x_i(k) - x_i(k)}{\max_k x_i(k) - \min_k x_i(k)} \quad (3.12)$$

For the data of "the nominal the best":

$$x_i^*(k) = 1 - \frac{x_i(k) - x_{objectives}(k)}{\max\left\{\max_k x_i(k) - x_{objective}(k), x_{objective}(k) - \min_k x_i(k)\right\}} \quad (3.13)$$

where $\max_k x_i(k)$ and $\min_k x_i(k)$ are the maximum value and the minimum value of entity k. The $x_{objective}(k)$ is the target value of the entity k, $\min_k x_i(k) < x_{objective}(k) < \max_k x_i(k)$.

Step 3: Find the reference sequences in the grey relational space: $x_0(k)$, $k = 1, 2,\ldots, n$.

where $x_0(k) = \{x_0^*(1), x_0^*(2), \ldots, x_0^*(n)\}$

$$x_0^*(k) = \{\max_{i=1}^m \{x_i^*(k)\}\} \quad (3.14)$$

where $x_0^*(k)$ is the reference value with respect to the k-th criterion.

Step 4: Calculate the difference series $\Delta_{0i}(k)$.

Calculate the absolute value of the difference between referential $x_0(k)$ and $x_i(k)$,

$$\Delta_{0i}(k) = |x_0(k) - x_i(k)| \quad (3.15)$$

Step 5: Calculate the grey relational coefficient for each entity.

The grey relational coefficient between the comparative series $x_i(k)$ and the referential series $x_0(k)$ is defined as:

$$\gamma_{0i}(k) = \frac{\min_i \min_k \Delta_{0i}(k) + \xi \times \max_i \max_k \Delta_{0i}(k)}{\Delta_{0i}(k) + \xi \times \max_i \max_k \Delta_{0i}(k)} \quad (3.16)$$

The distinguishing coefficient $\zeta$ ($\zeta \in [0,1]$) is used to control the resolution between $\max_i \max_k \Delta_{0i}(k)$ and $\min_i \min_k \Delta_{0i}(k)$, and it is typically taken as 0.5 (Chang and Lin 1999). The smaller the values of $\xi$, the higher its distinguishability.

Step 6. Ranking grey relational coefficients $\Gamma_{0i}$.

Calculate the grey relational degree. A grey relational degree is a weighted sum of the grey relational coefficients given by the following equation:

$$\Gamma_{0i} = \sum_{k=1}^{n} w_i(k) \times \gamma_{0i}(k), \quad \sum_{k=1}^{n} w_i(k) = 1 \qquad (3.17)$$

where $w_i(k)$ is the weight of the $k$th criterion. $\Gamma_{0i}$ is the grey relational degree which denotes the magnitude of similarity measured between the compared $i$th sequence and the reference sequence. Therefore, with the grey relational degrees, the candidate sequences can be prioritized and the one with the highest degree of relation will be considered as the sequence that represents the best solution.

### 3.2.2 The Method of PSS Requirement Conversion

Prioritizing technical attributes in QFD can be regarded as a problem of group multi-attribute decision making (MADM) (see Fig. 3.3). Customer requirements (CRs) are considered as the evaluation criteria in the MADM structure, and the technical attributes (TAs) are the alternatives designed to satisfy the customer requirements. The relationship $r_{ij}$ can be regarded as the utility value of the technical attribute $j$ with respect to the customer requirements $i$.

Accurate QFD analysis process is mainly impeded by two problems. One of the problems is to handle vagueness, subjectivity and limited data available in QFD analysis process. If the vagueness is not appropriately manipulated, it will influence the accuracy of the QFD analysis results especially under the environment of limited available data. The other problem is to deal with the information discovered with limited data in QFD analysis. The final priority of technical attributes will also be affected by the inherent links between the CR-TA relationships. However, the QFD in previous researches cannot make full use of the given data to provide auxiliary information for product-service design decision making.

In order to deal with the problems, Song et al. (2014) propose a rough QFD approach. This novel method combines the strength of rough set theory in manipulating vagueness without extra information, and the merit of Grey Relational Analysis in structuring analytical framework and discovering necessary information of the data interactions. Two phases are included in the proposed method (see Fig. 3.4). The first phase is to determine customer requirement importance in the form of rough number. In this way, all the crisp judgments of customer requirement importance can be expressed by the rough numbers with boundary intervals denoting vagueness. In the second phase, the rough importance of each TA is determined by integrating the grey relational analysis and rough set theory. The crisp judgments of CR-TA relationship matrix in QFD are transformed into rough number form. Then, the QFD analysis can be regarded as a problem of multi-attribute decision making with rough number. Grey Relational Analysis procedure is adopted to solve this rough MADM problem to get grey relational degrees. Meanwhile, it helps to discover inherent links between the CR-TA relationships to provide auxiliary information for QFD analysis. After that, TAs can be ranked according to the grey relational degrees.

## 3.2 PSS Requirement Conversion

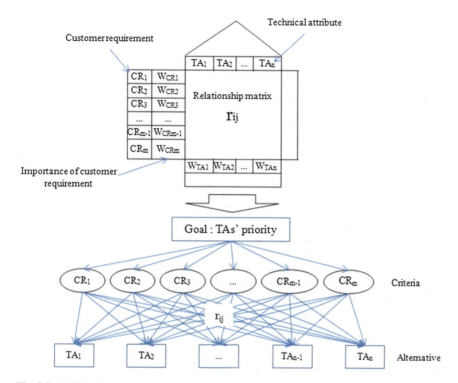

**Fig. 3.3** Multi-attribute decision making (MADM) view of QFD (Song et al. 2014)

### Phase 1: determine rough importance for customer requirement

The determination of rough importance of customer requirement is shown in following steps.

*Step 1: Evaluate customer requirement importance with crisp judgment*

After determining the customer requirement from the market survey and interview, the importance of customer requirement is judged with the 9-point scale assessment. Score of 1 means very low importance, while score of 9 indicates very high importance. The rest of scores 3, 5, 7 denote low, moderate, and high importance respectively. Thus, crisp evaluation value for each customer requirement importance can be acquired.

$$w_i = \left[w_i^1, w_i^2, \ldots, w_i^k, \ldots, w_i^l\right] \quad i = 1, 2, \ldots, m. \tag{3.18}$$

where $w_i^k$ represents the $k$th customer's evaluation on the importance of the customer requirement $i$. $l$ is the number of customer representatives.

82        3 Requirements Specification for Customizable PSS

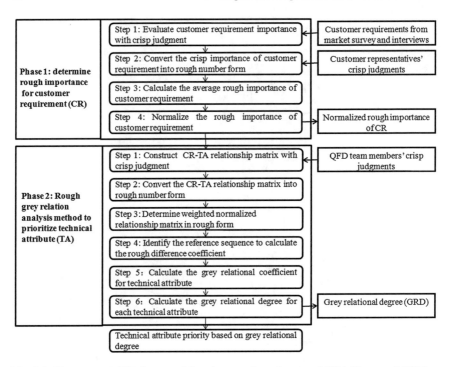

**Fig. 3.4** The proposed QFD framework based on rough set theory and GRA (Song et al. 2014)

*Step 2: Convert the crisp importance value of CR into rough number form*

The crisp importance of CR is converted into rough number form with Formulas (3.1)–(3.6). The rough interval form of CR's importance $w_i^k$ can be obtained as follows.

$$RN(w_i^k) = \left[w_i^{kL}, w_i^{kU}\right] \quad (3.19)$$

where $w_i^{kL}$ and $w_i^{kU}$ are the lower limit and upper limit of rough number $RN(w_i^k)$. The boundary interval of the rough number denotes vagueness of each individual judgment.

*Step 3: Aggregate individual rough importance to generate group importance of CR*

The rough group importance of $i$th customer requirement $\overline{RN(w_i)}$ is aggregated as follows.

$$w_i^L = \left(\prod_{k=1}^{l} w_i^{kL}\right)^{1/l} \quad (3.20)$$

## 3.2 PSS Requirement Conversion

$$w_i^U = \left(\prod_{k=1}^{l} w_i^{kU}\right)^{1/l} \quad (3.21)$$

$i = 1, 2, \ldots, m$, $w_i^L$ and $w_i^U$ are lower limit and upper limit of rough weight $\overline{RN(w_i)}$ respectively. Aggregating individual judgments (AIJ) is appropriate for group members that act together as a unit. The aggregated importance of customer requirement in rough number form is considered the key input of the rough group QFD.

*Step 4: Normalize the rough importance of customer requirement*

Normalize the rough importance of customer requirement as follows:

$$w_i^{'L} = \frac{w_i^L}{\max_{i=1}^{m}\{\max[w_i^L, w_i^U]\}}, \quad w_i^{'U} = \frac{w_i^U}{\max_{i=1}^{m}\{\max[w_i^L, w_i^U]\}} \quad (3.22)$$

$w_i^{'L}$ and $w_i^{'U}$ are lower limit and upper limit of normalized form for the rough weight $\overline{RN(w_i)}$, respectively.

**Phase 2: calculate the technical attribute importance with rough group GRA**

*Step 1: Construct CR-TA relationship matrix with crisp judgment*

In this step, design experts are firstly invited to transform the customer requirements of product or service into technical attributes. And then, the experts are required to judge the relationships between customer requirement and technical attribute with the crisp 9-point scale assessment. Score of 1 indicates very low relevance, while score of 9 reveals very high relevance. The rest of scores 3, 5, 7 denote low, moderate, and high relevance respectively. Thus, crisp evaluation value for relationships between customer requirement and technical attribute can be obtained. The CR-TA relationship matrix describes the influence degree of each technical attribute on the different customer requirements.

The $k$th expert crisp relationship matrix $R_k$ can be expressed as:

$$R_k = \begin{bmatrix} r_{11}^k & r_{12}^k & \cdots & r_{1n}^k \\ r_{21}^k & r_{22}^k & \cdots & r_{2n}^k \\ \vdots & \vdots & \ddots & \vdots \\ r_{m1}^k & r_{m2}^k & \cdots & r_{mn}^k \end{bmatrix} \quad (3.23)$$

where $r_{ij}^k$ is the $k$th expert's crisp judgment value for the relationship between the $i$th customer requirement and the $j$th technical attribute. For each TA, the larger the relation score, the greater the impact of the TA is on the CR. The TA with higher relation scores is more critical to the final customer satisfaction. Thus, in this research, the relation scores are considered as the TA performance values that are used in the

GRA calculations when the CRs are considered as the evaluation criteria, because the higher relation scores indicate stronger relationships and more importance.

*Step 2: Convert the CR-TA relationship matrix into rough number form*

The crisp value of relationship is converted into rough number form with Formulas (3.1)–(3.6). The rough interval form of $r_{ij}^k$ can be obtained as follows.

$$\text{RN}(r_{ij}^k) = [r_{ij}^{kL}, r_{ij}^{kU}] \tag{3.24}$$

where $r_{ij}^{kL}$ and $r_{ij}^{kU}$ are the lower limit and upper limit of rough interval $\text{RN}(r_{ij}^k)$.

Individual rough judgments on the relationship between customer requirement and technical attribute are aggregated to generate group judgments as follows.

$$r_{ij}^L = \left(\prod_{k=1}^{h} r_{ij}^{kL}\right)^{1/h} \tag{3.25}$$

$$r_{ij}^U = \left(\prod_{k=1}^{h} r_{ij}^{kU}\right)^{1/h} \tag{3.26}$$

$i = 1, 2,\ldots, m, j = 1, 2,\ldots, n$, $r_{ij}^L$ and $r_{ij}^U$ are lower limit and upper limit of rough group interval $\overline{RN(r_{ij})}$ respectively, and $h$ is the number of experts.

Therefore, a new rough relationship matrix M at the group level is developed based on the individual judgments. In this way, different experts' judgments are considered and subjectivity can be well manipulated.

$$M = \begin{bmatrix} [r_{11}^L, r_{11}^U] & [r_{12}^L, r_{12}^U] & \cdots & [r_{1n}^L, r_{1n}^U] \\ [r_{21}^L, r_{21}^U] & [r_{22}^L, r_{22}^U] & \cdots & [r_{2n}^L, r_{2n}^U] \\ \vdots & \vdots & \ddots & \vdots \\ [r_{m1}^L, r_{m1}^U] & [r_{m2}^L, r_{m2}^U] & \cdots & [r_{mn}^L, r_{mn}^U] \end{bmatrix} \tag{3.27}$$

The above rough group relationship matrix M indicates that there are $n$ technical attributes to meet the $m$ customer requirements. Each column of matrix M denotes the relevance sequence of each technical attribute with respect to different customer requirements.

*Step 3: Determine weighted normalized relationship matrix in rough number form.*

To transform TAs' relevance value with respect to each CR into a comparable scale, the normalization method is conducted as follows:

$$r_{ij}^{'L} = \frac{r_{ij}^L}{\max_{i=1}^{n}\{\max[r_{ij}^L, r_{ij}^U]\}}, \quad r_{ij}^{'U} = \frac{r_{ij}^U}{\max_{i=1}^{n}\{\max[r_{ij}^L, r_{ij}^U]\}} \tag{3.28}$$

## 3.2 PSS Requirement Conversion

$r_{ij}^{'L}$ and $r_{ij}^{'U}$ denotes the lower and upper limits of normalized from of interval $[r_{ij}^{L}, r_{ij}^{U}]$, respectively. The normalization method mentioned above is to preserve the property that the ranges of normalized interval numbers belong to [0, 1]. Then the weighted normalized rough relationship matrix can be calculated as follows.

$$v_{ij}^{L} = w_{i}^{'L} \times r_{ij}^{'L}, \quad i = 1, 2, \ldots, m, \quad j = 1, 2, \ldots, n. \quad (3.29)$$
$$v_{ij}^{U} = w_{i}^{'U} \times r_{ij}^{'U}, \quad i = 1, 2, \ldots, m, \quad j = 1, 2, \ldots, n. \quad (3.30)$$

where $w_{i}^{'L}$ and $w_{i}^{'U}$ represents the lower and upper limits of customer requirement's weight in rough number form respectively.

Then, the weighted normalized relationship matrix $M'$ can be obtained as follows:

$$M' = \begin{bmatrix} [v_{11}^{L}, v_{11}^{U}] & [v_{12}^{L}, v_{12}^{U}] & \cdots & [v_{1n}^{L}, v_{1n}^{U}] \\ [v_{21}^{L}, v_{21}^{U}] & [v_{22}^{L}, v_{22}^{U}] & \cdots & [v_{2n}^{L}, v_{2n}^{U}] \\ \vdots & \vdots & \ddots & \vdots \\ [v_{m1}^{L}, v_{m1}^{U}] & [v_{m2}^{L}, v_{m2}^{U}] & \cdots & [v_{mn}^{L}, v_{mn}^{U}] \end{bmatrix} \quad (3.31)$$

*Step 4: Identify the reference sequence to calculate the rough difference coefficient*

Generate the reference sequence based on the characteristic of each customer requirement. Obviously, for each customer requirement, the ideal relevance value (in interval form) of technical attribute is the largest value that it may take. The larger the relevance value of technical attribute, the stronger capability to meet the customer requirement it has. Thus, the ideal reference value is selected as follows.

$$v^{0}(i) = \{\max_{j=1}^{n}(v_{ij}^{U}), i=1, 2, \ldots, m.\}. \quad (3.32)$$

where $v^{0}(i)$ is the maximum of upper limits of ideal reference value of relationship with respect to customer requirement $i$.

Hence, the reference sequence is

$$V^{0}(i) = \{v^{0}(1), v^{0}(2), \ldots, v^{0}(m)\} \quad (3.33)$$

Calculate the deviation coefficient based on each customer requirement. The deviation coefficient $d_{ij}$ is essentially a measure to depict the distance between a relevance value of technical attribute and its ideal reference value. It is defined as follows.

$$d_{ij} = \max\{v^{0}(i) - v_{ij}^{L}\}, \quad i = 1, 2, \ldots, m; \quad j = 1, 2, \ldots, n \quad (3.34)$$

Next, the deviation coefficient matrix $d^{+}$ can be established as follows:

$$d^+ = \begin{bmatrix} d_{11} & d_{12} & \cdots & d_{1n} \\ d_{21} & d_{22} & \cdots & d_{2n} \\ \vdots & \vdots & \ddots & \vdots \\ d_{m1} & d_{m2} & \cdots & d_{mn} \end{bmatrix} \quad (3.35)$$

*Step 5: Calculate the grey relational coefficient for technical attribute*

The grey relational coefficient $\gamma_{ij}$ for technical attribute is calculated as follows:

$$\gamma_{ij} = \frac{\min_{i=1}^{m} \min_{j=1}^{n} d_{ij} + \xi \times \max_{i=1}^{m} \max_{j=1}^{n} d_{ij}}{d_{ij} + \xi \times \max_{i=1}^{m} \max_{j=1}^{n} d_{ij}} \quad (3.36)$$

where $\xi$ ($0 \leq \xi \leq 1$) is known as the distinguishing coefficient. The smaller the value of $\xi$, the higher its distinguish ability. In most situations, $\xi$ takes the value of 0.5, because this value usually offers moderate distinguishing effects and good stability (Chang and Lin 1999).

*Step 6: Calculate the grey relational degree for each technical attributes*

A grey relational degree $\Gamma_j$ for the $j$th technical attribute is the mean of the grey relational coefficients provided by the following formula:

$$\Gamma_j = \frac{\sum_{i=1}^{m} \gamma_{ij}}{m}, \quad j = 1, 2, \ldots, n. \quad (3.37)$$

The grey relational degree for the technical attribute is defined to indicate the similarity of a TA's relevance value sequence from its reference value. A technical attribute with a larger $\Gamma_j$ is probably closer to the ideal reference value and has higher priority.

### 3.2.3 Case Study: Conversion of Compressor Rotor Service Requirement

In this section, the proposed methodology is applied to rotor service design for air compressor in Company I. Company I is an air compressor industry leader who has been in business for over 20 years. It has a national sales and service network. Company I's products range from complete compressed air systems, tools to spare parts. It also provides industrial service to enhance productivity of air compressor. The rotor is the most important components of air compressor, and it has impact on the air discharge capability of compressor. If the rotor is not provided with timely maintenance and repair service, it would often lead to vibrations and other failure modes of the air compressor. Better quality of the maintenance and repair service can reduce unnecessary wear of gears and bearings, extend the service life of rotor, and

## 3.2 PSS Requirement Conversion

**Table 3.1** Crisp ratings for CRs' importance (Song et al. 2014)

| Customer requirement | $C_1$ | $C_2$ | $C_3$ | $C_4$ | $C_5$ | $C_6$ |
|---|---|---|---|---|---|---|
| $CR_1$:availability | 9 | 9 | 7 | 9 | 9 | 7 |
| $CR_2$:safety | 7 | 9 | 7 | 5 | 9 | 9 |
| $CR_3$:easy to maintain | 7 | 7 | 3 | 5 | 7 | 1 |
| $CR_4$:economical | 9 | 7 | 9 | 7 | 7 | 9 |
| $CR_5$:energy saving | 7 | 7 | 5 | 5 | 7 | 7 |
| $CR_6$:lower operation noise | 3 | 5 | 5 | 7 | 5 | 3 |

*Note* Part of the customer requirements are listed in Table 3.1 due to space limitations and privacy regulation

optimize the operation of rotor. Six key customer requirements are identified with questionnaire, focus group and interviews. They are better availability (lower failure rate) ($CR_1$), safety ($CR_2$), easy to maintain ($CR_3$), economical ($CR_4$), energy saving ($CR_5$), and lower operation noise ($CR_6$).

**Phase 1: Determine rough importance for customer requirement**

*Step 1: Evaluate customer requirement importance with crisp judgment*

After determination of the customer requirements of the rotor service, subjective evaluations of six industrial customer representatives ($C_1$–$C_6$) in crisp variables are used to determine the importance of CR (shown in Table 3.1).

*Step 2: Convert the crisp importance value of CR into rough number form*

The crisp importance ratings of customer requirement in Table 3.1 are converted into rough number form with Formulas (3.1)–(3.6). For instance, the six industrial customer representatives' crisp ratings for "$CR_1$:availability" are {9,9,7,9,9,7}. According to Formulas (3.1)–(3.6),

$$\underline{Lim}(7) = \sqrt[2]{7 \times 7} = 7 \quad \overline{Lim}(7) = \sqrt[6]{7 \times 7 \times 9 \times 9 \times 9 \times 9} = 8.277$$
$$\underline{Lim}(9) = \sqrt[6]{9 \times 9 \times 9 \times 9 \times 7 \times 7} = 8.277 \quad \overline{Lim}(9) = \sqrt[4]{9 \times 9 \times 9 \times 9} = 9$$

The rough interval form of crisp importance of "$CR_1$:availability" can be obtained as follows.

$$RN(w_1^1) = RN(w_1^2) = RN(w_1^4) = RN(w_1^5) = RN(9) = [8.277, 9]$$
$$RN(w_1^3) = RN(w_1^6) = RN(7) = [7, 8.277]$$

**Table 3.2** The rough group importance and normalized importance for CRs (Song et al. 2014)

| Customer requirement | Rough group importance | Normalized rough importance |
|---|---|---|
| CR$_1$ | [7.827, 8.752] | [0.894, 1.000] |
| CR$_2$ | [6.601, 8.444] | [0.754, 0.965] |
| CR$_3$ | [2.596, 6.083] | [0.297, 0.695] |
| CR$_4$ | [7.454, 8.452] | [0.852, 0.966] |
| CR$_5$ | [5.807, 6.743] | [0.663, 0.770] |
| CR$_6$ | [3.736, 5.310] | [0.427, 0.607] |

*Step 3: Aggregate individual rough importance to generate group importance of CR*

According to Eqs. (3.20)–(3.21), the rough group importance of the 1st customer requirement is $\overline{RN(w_1)} = [7.827, 8.752]$. Similarly, rough group interval for other customer requirements can be obtained in Table 3.2.

*Step 4: Normalize the rough group importance of customer requirement*

According to Formula (3.22), the normalized form of rough group importance of customer requirement are also show in Table 3.2.

**Phase 1: Rank the technical attribute with rough group GRA-based QFD**

*Step 1: Construct CR-TA relationship matrix with crisp judgment*

In this step, five domain experts are requested to convert the customer requirements into technical attributes of service. They get eleven technical attributes for the rotor service as follows: TA$_1$ "obtaining failure information timely", TA$_2$ "failure diagnosis with high accuracy", TA$_3$ "rapid feedback of diagnostic results", TA$_4$ "quickly response to repair", TA$_5$ "lower repair cost", TA$_6$ "accurate supply of spare parts", TA$_7$ "supply of spare parts with lower cost", TA$_8$ "carbon mud cleaning timely and professionally", TA$_9$ "professional installation and commissioning of rotor", TA$_{10}$ "timely lubrication", and TA$_{11}$ "parts clearance adjustment".

After the determination of the technical attributes for the rotor service, the experts judge the relationships between customer requirement and technical attribute with the crisp 9-point scale assessment (shown in Table 3.3).

*Step 2: Convert the CR-TA relationship matrix into rough number form*

The crisp value of relationship between CRs and TAs (Table 3.3) is converted into rough number form using Formulas (3.24)–(3.27), and thus the rough interval evaluations of relationship can be obtained in Table 3.4.

## 3.2 PSS Requirement Conversion

**Table 3.3** Crisp ratings for relationships between CRs and TAs of rotor service (Song et al. 2014)

| CR | Technical attributes (TA) | | | | | | | |
|---|---|---|---|---|---|---|---|---|
| | $TA_1$ | $TA_2$ | $TA_3$ | $TA_4$ | ... | $TA_9$ | $TA_{10}$ | $TA_{11}$ |
| $CR_1$ | 7, 9, 5, 9, 7 | 9, 9, 7, 7, 9 | 7, 9, 7, 5, 9 | 9, 7, 9, 9, 9 | ... | 3, 5, 3, 3, 5 | 5, 5, 3, 5, 3 | 5, 3, 3, 3, 3 |
| $CR_2$ | 5, 5, 5, 3, 5 | 7, 9, 7, 7, 7 | 5, 3, 3, 3, 5 | 7, 5, 7, 5, 7 | ... | 5, 5, 5, 3, 5 | 7, 9, 7, 9, 9 | 5, 3, 5, 5, 3 |
| $CR_3$ | 5, 3, 5, 5, 3 | 5, 3, 3, 3, 3 | 7, 9, 7, 7, 9 | 5, 5, 7, 3, 5 | ... | 5, 5, 3, 5, 3 | 9, 9, 7, 9, 7 | 7, 9, 7, 9, 7 |
| $CR_4$ | | | | | ... | | 3, 3, 3, 5, 3 | 3, 3, 3, 3, 1 |
| $CR_5$ | | | | | ... | 5, 5, 3, 5, 3 | 5, 5, 3, 5, 5 | |
| $CR_6$ | | | | | ... | 3, 3, 3, 5, 3 | 7, 9, 7, 7, 7 | 9, 9, 9, 9, 7 |

*Note* Only a part of crisp ratings is listed in Table 3.3 due to space limitations

**Table 3.4** The rough evaluation matrix for relationships between CRs and TAs (Song et al. 2014)

| CR | Technical attributes (TA) | | | | | | |
|---|---|---|---|---|---|---|---|
| | $TA_1$ | $TA_2$ | $TA_3$ | $TA_4$ | ... | $TA_{10}$ | $TA_{11}$ |
| $CR_1$ | [6.341, 8.194] | [7.663, 8.645] | [6.341, 8.194] | [8.221, 8.910] | ... | [3.606, 4.608] | [3.062, 3.606] |
| $CR_2$ | [4.160, 4.899] | [7.071, 7.663] | [3.255, 4.160] | [5.644, 6.633] | ... | [7.663, 8.645] | [3.606, 4.608] |
| $CR_3$ | [3.601, 4.608] | [3.062, 3.606] | [7.287, 8.221] | [4.152, 5.586] | ... | [7.663, 8.645] | [7.287, 8.221] |
| $CR_4$ | | | | | ... | [3.062, 3.606] | [2.065, 2.871] |
| $CR_5$ | | | | | ... | [4.160, 4.899] | |
| $CR_6$ | | | | | ... | [7.071, 7.663] | [8.221, 8.910] |

*Note* Part of rough evaluations is listed in Table 3.4 due to space limitations

*Step 3: Determine weighted normalized relationship matrix in rough number form.*

Determine weighted normalized relationship matrix in rough number form. Normalize the rough evaluation matrix for relationships in Table 3.4 according to Formula (3.28), and then calculate the weighted normalized rough relationship matrix using the Eqs. (3.29)–(3.30). The rough weighted normalized matrix is shown in Table 3.5.

**Table 3.5** The rough weighted normalized matrix of relationships between CRs and TAs (Song et al. 2014)

| CR | Technical attributes (TA) | | | | | | |
|---|---|---|---|---|---|---|---|
| | TA$_1$ | TA$_2$ | TA$_3$ | TA$_4$ | ... | TA$_{10}$ | TA$_{11}$ |
| CR$_1$ | [0.636, 0.920] | [0.769, 0.970] | [0.636, 0.920] | [0.825, 1.000] | ... | [0.362, 0.517] | [0.307, 0.405] |
| CR$_2$ | [0.363, 0.547] | [0.617, 0.855] | [0.284, 0.464] | [0.492, 0.740] | ... | [0.669, 0.965] | [0.315, 0.514] |
| CR$_3$ | [0.124, 0.370] | [0.105, 0.290] | [0.250, 0.661] | [0.142, 0.449] | ... | [0.263, 0.695] | [0.250, 0.661] |
| CR$_4$ | | | | | ... | [0.293, 0.391] | [0.197, 0.311] |
| CR$_5$ | | | | | ... | [0.360, 0.493] | |
| CR$_6$ | | | | | ... | [0.339, 0.522] | [0.394, 0.607] |

*Note* Part of rough evaluations is listed in Table 3.4 due to space limitations

*Step 4: Identify the reference sequence to calculate the rough difference coefficient*

Identify the reference sequence with Formulas (3.32) and (3.33). The reference sequence $v^0(i) = \{1.000, 0.965, 0.695, 0.966, 0.770, 0.607\}$.

According to Formulas (3.34) and (3.35), the deviation coefficients between relevance value of technical attribute and ideal reference value are obtained in Table 3.6.

*Step 5: Calculate the grey relational coefficient for technical attribute*

The grey relational coefficient for each technical attribute is calculated with Eq. (3.36), and the distinguishing coefficient $\xi$ in Eq. (3.36) takes the value of 0.5 to provide moderate distinguishing effects and good stability. All the grey relational coefficients are shown in Table 3.7.

*Step 6: Calculate the grey relational degree for each technical attribute*

Grey relational degrees (also see Table 3.7) are obtained with Formula (3.37), and weights and priority of TAs are listed in Table 3.7. It can be clearly seen from Table 3.7 that the rank of technical attributes is: TA$_{10}$, TA$_8$, TA$_2$, TA$_4$, TA$_{11}$, TA$_9$, TA$_3$, TA$_6$, TA$_5$, TA$_1$, and TA$_7$. Apparently, TA$_{10}$ (timely lubrication), TA$_8$ (carbon mud cleaning timely and professionally), TA$_2$ (parts clearance adjustment) are top 3 technical attributes with higher priorities. The least important technical attribute is TA$_7$ (supply of spare parts with lower cost).

## 3.2 PSS Requirement Conversion

**Table 3.6** The deviation coefficient matrix (Song et al. 2014)

| CR | Technical attributes (TA) | | | | | | | | | | |
|---|---|---|---|---|---|---|---|---|---|---|---|
| | $TA_1$ | $TA_2$ | $TA_3$ | $TA_4$ | $TA_5$ | $TA_6$ | $TA_7$ | $TA_8$ | $TA_9$ | $TA_{10}$ | $TA_{11}$ |
| $CR_1$ | 0.364 | 0.231 | 0.364 | 0.175 | 1.000 | 0.231 | 1.000 | 0.638 | 0.673 | 0.638 | 0.693 |
| $CR_2$ | 0.602 | 0.348 | 0.681 | 0.472 | 0.965 | 0.861 | 0.965 | 0.329 | 0.602 | 0.296 | 0.650 |
| $CR_3$ | 0.571 | 0.590 | 0.445 | 0.553 | 0.626 | 0.553 | 0.626 | 0.445 | 0.571 | 0.432 | 0.445 |
| $CR_4$ | 0.966 | 0.966 | 0.966 | 0.966 | 0.180 | 0.966 | 0.233 | 0.966 | 0.966 | 0.673 | 0.768 |
| $CR_5$ | 0.770 | 0.770 | 0.770 | 0.770 | 0.770 | 0.770 | 0.770 | 0.158 | 0.458 | 0.410 | 0.770 |
| $CR_6$ | 0.607 | 0.607 | 0.607 | 0.607 | 0.607 | 0.607 | 0.607 | 0.607 | 0.460 | 0.268 | 0.213 |

**Table 3.7** The grey relational coefficient and grey relational degree (Song et al. 2014)

| TA | Grey relational coefficient ||||||  Grey relational degree $\Gamma_j$ | Rank |
|---|---|---|---|---|---|---|---|---|
|  | $CR_1$ | $CR_2$ | $CR_3$ | $CR_4$ | $CR_5$ | $CR_6$ |  |  |
| $TA_1$ | 0.762 | 0.597 | 0.614 | 0.449 | 0.518 | 0.595 | 0.589 | 10 |
| $TA_2$ | 0.901 | 0.776 | 0.604 | 0.449 | 0.518 | 0.595 | 0.641 | 3 |
| $TA_3$ | 0.762 | 0.557 | 0.697 | 0.449 | 0.518 | 0.595 | 0.596 | 7 |
| $TA_4$ | 0.975 | 0.677 | 0.625 | 0.449 | 0.518 | 0.595 | 0.640 | 4 |
| $TA_5$ | 0.439 | 0.449 | 0.585 | 0.968 | 0.518 | 0.595 | 0.592 | 9 |
| $TA_6$ | 0.901 | 0.484 | 0.625 | 0.449 | 0.518 | 0.595 | 0.595 | 8 |
| $TA_7$ | 0.439 | 0.449 | 0.585 | 0.898 | 0.518 | 0.595 | 0.581 | 11 |
| $TA_8$ | 0.578 | 0.794 | 0.697 | 0.449 | 1 | 0.595 | 0.685 | 2 |
| $TA_9$ | 0.561 | 0.597 | 0.614 | 0.449 | 0.687 | 0.686 | 0.599 | 6 |
| $TA_{10}$ | 0.578 | 0.827 | 0.706 | 0.561 | 0.723 | 0.857 | 0.709 | 1 |
| $TA_{11}$ | 0.552 | 0.572 | 0.697 | 0.519 | 0.518 | 0.923 | 0.630 | 5 |

**Table 3.8** Ranking of TAs in the fuzzy QFD, conventional QFD and rough QFD (Song et al. 2014)

| TA | Conventional QFD || Fuzzy QFD ($\xi = 0.5$) || Rough QFD ($\xi = 0.5$) ||
|---|---|---|---|---|---|---|
|  | $W_{TAj}$ | Ranking | $\Gamma_j$ | Ranking | $\Gamma_j$ | Ranking |
| $TA_1$ | 0.078 | 7 | 0.698 | 8 | 0.589 | 10 |
| $TA_2$ | 0.097 | 4 | 0.730 | 5 | 0.641 | 3 |
| $TA_3$ | 0.085 | 6 | 0.720 | 6 | 0.596 | 7 |
| $TA_4$ | 0.097 | 4 | 0.733 | 4 | 0.640 | 4 |
| $TA_5$ | 0.055 | 9 | 0.681 | 10 | 0.592 | 9 |
| $TA_6$ | 0.067 | 8 | 0.690 | 9 | 0.595 | 8 |
| $TA_7$ | 0.053 | 10 | 0.676 | 11 | 0.581 | 11 |
| $TA_8$ | 0.120 | 2 | 0.782 | 2 | 0.685 | 2 |
| $TA_9$ | 0.086 | 5 | 0.700 | 7 | 0.599 | 6 |
| $TA_{10}$ | 0.157 | 1 | 0.822 | 1 | 0.709 | 1 |
| $TA_{11}$ | 0.105 | 3 | 0.744 | 3 | 0.630 | 5 |

### 3.2.4 Comparisons and Discussion

To reveal the effectiveness of the proposed QFD method, both the conventional QFD (using crisp ratings) and QFD based on fuzzy GRA (using symmetrical triangular fuzzy number) are also applied in the same case study (see Table 3.8).

From Table 3.8, it can be clearly seen that the ranks of $TA_4$ (rank is 4), $TA_8$ (rank is 2), and $TA_{10}$ (rank is 1) are the same in the three types of QFD approaches. In addition, the ranks from the rough QFD and fuzzy QFD are basically consistent with each other except for several TAs. Almost half of rank results (e.g. $TA_1$, $TA_2$, $TA_7$ and $TA_9$) from the conventional QFD are different with fuzzy QFD and rough QFD.

## 3.2 PSS Requirement Conversion

In the conventional QFD, $TA_2$ and $TA_4$ have the same rank of 5. However, the grey relational degrees and ranks in the rough QFD are different with each other. In this respect, the rough GRA-based QFD used in the case study has higher distinguishing ability.

The rank differences between the rough QFD and fuzzy QFD mainly derive from their different mechanisms of subjectivity and vagueness manipulation. In fact, the rough QFD can fully consider the subjectivity and preference of decision makers. Although QFD using fuzzy numbers provides a rational way to deal with the priorities of technical attributes, it has limitations of subjective and pre-set fuzzy membership function. In addition, the fuzzy intervals indicating the degree of evaluation uncertainty is fixed, which is determined by the types of membership functions. For example, in fuzzy QFD, the crisp ratings of $CR_1$-$TA_2$ relationship are 9,9,7,7 and 9, and they are presented as the symmetrical triangular fuzzy number [8,10], [8,10], [6,8], [6,8]and [8,10] with fixed interval of 2 respectively. The aggregated group fuzzy interval is [6.4, 8.4]. This is not true in reality, because the boundary interval indicating estimation range varies across QFD team members with different knowledge, experience and expertise. On the contrary, in rough QFD approach, the ratings of 9,9,7,7 and 9 are presented with the flexible and smaller interval form ([7.000,8.139], [7.000,8.139], [8.139,9.000], [8.139,9.000], and [8.139,9.000] respectively). The aggregated group rough interval is [7.663, 8.645] which is smaller than the aggregated group fuzzy interval [6.4, 8.4].

The customer requirement importance is critical input of QFD which influences the final priority accuracy of technical attributes. Thus, the vagueness manipulating mechanisms of customer requirement importance in fuzzy QFD, rough QFD and crisp QFD are compared in Fig. 3.5. It can be seen clearly from Fig. 3.5 that the three methods produce different forms of CR's importance. The conventional QFD analysis approach only presents crisp weights for criteria without considering the subjectivity and vagueness. On the contrary, both the fuzzy QFD and the rough QFD provide interval boundary indicating the confidence level for the CRs' importance degrees. But the rough importance and fuzzy importance have different interval boundaries denoting different level of uncertainty. Compared with the fuzzy method, the rough method can well reflect subjectivity change in the light of the inherent vagueness of decision makers' judgments. For instance, the judgments on the importance of $CR_6$ are 3,5,5,7,5, and 3 respectively. Those ratings can be holistically converted into rough number form as [3.000, 4.460], [3.75, 4.729], [3.75, 4.729], [4.460, 7.000] and [3.75, 4.729]. They can also transformed into fuzzy number [2,4], [4,6], [4,6], [6,8] and [4,6]. Once the decision makers change their judgments on the importance of $CR_6$ to be 3,3,5,5, and 5, the rough importance is [3.000,4.217], [3.000,4.217], [4.217,5.000], [4.217,5.000] and [4.217,5.000], and the fuzzy importance is [2,4], [2,4], [4,6], [4,6], and [4,6]. Apparently, the rough number forms of importance can adjust their intervals according to the general distribution of judgments. However, the fuzzy number forms of importance provide fixed and static interval (2) due to the preset membership function.

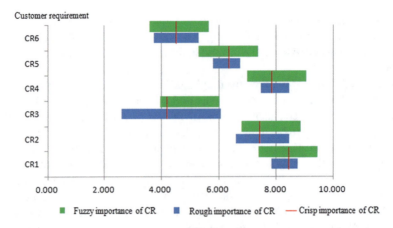

**Fig. 3.5** Different vagueness manipulations for judgments on CR's importance (Song et al. 2014)

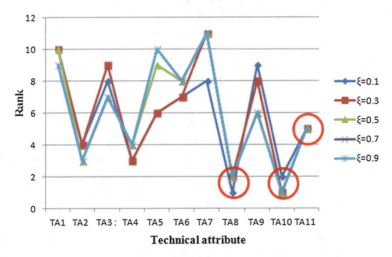

**Fig. 3.6** The impact of distinguishing coefficient on the TAs' priorities from rough QFD (Song et al. 2014)

In addition, this research also analyzes the impact of distinguishing coefficient on TAs' priorities from QFD based on the rough group GRA. The TAs' ranks with different distinguishing coefficient (0.1, 0.3, 0.5, 0.7, and 0.9) are shown in Fig. 3.6.

Figure 3.6 demonstrates that the impact of the distinguishing coefficient on the technical attributes' priorities from rough QFD is small. For example, for all tested distinguishing coefficients, $TA_{11}$ is always ranked the 5th. $TA_{10}$ and $TA_8$ are often ranked the 1st and the 2nd, respectively.

3.2 PSS Requirement Conversion

**Table 3.9** Comparisons between the conventional QFD, fuzzy QFD and rough QFD (Song et al. 2014)

| Method | Distinguishing ability of TA's priority | Flexibility in reflecting vagueness | Need for priori information or assumption | Consideration of ratings' distribution | Information discovering ability |
|---|---|---|---|---|---|
| Conventional QFD | Medium | None | Partial | No | None |
| Fuzzy QFD | High | Medium | Yes | Yes | Medium |
| Rough QFD | Higher | Higher | No | Yes | Higher |

In sum, a simple and effective mechanism for QFD analysis approach considering uncertainty is provided in this research, and the proposed rough grey relational analysis based-QFD does not require much data and priori information as fuzzy method does. Comparisons between the conventional QFD, fuzzy QFD and rough QFD are summarized in Table 3.9.

In conclusion, the proposed method reveals the following features: To avoid customer requirements and CR-TA relationship from being underestimated or overestimated, rough intervals are used to manipulate the vagueness in the QFD analysis process. The rough GRA provides an analytical framework to discover necessary information of the data interactions among the vague CR-TA relationships. QFD based on the rough-GRA can be conducted without much priori information (e.g. pre-set membership functions in fuzzy methods) and large amount of data. Rough interval with flexible boundary can well reflect decision maker's subjective judgment and preference, and therefore reduce the information lost in QFD process to achieve accurate results.

## 3.3 PSS Design Conflict Identification and Resolution

Many manufacturers today are striving to provide their customers with high value-added PSS. PSS has heterogonous structure and various requirements, which may lead to conflicts of technical attributes during the design process. The conflicts will lead to the difficulty of concept generation, increase in service delivery failure, and ultimately the decrease of customer satisfaction. However, the conflicts in PSS design areas are more intangible and harder to formulate. Besides, those conflicts are often resolved with trial and error methods in ad hoc processes, which largely depend on the designer's intuition. Thus, Song and Sakao (2016) propose a systematic method to identify PSS design conflicts and resolve them. The proposed method is based on the approach of Service Function and Attribute Analysis (SFAA), group decision making with unbalanced linguistic label set and TRIZ methodology.

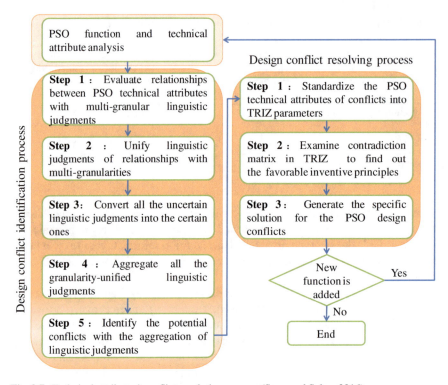

**Fig. 3.7** Technical attributes' conflict resolution process (Song and Sakao 2016)

### 3.3.1 The Method for Identifying and Resolving PSS Design Conflicts

The method proposed by Song and Sakao (2016) consists of three phases, i.e., PSS function and technical attribute analysis, PSS design conflict identification, and PSS design conflict resolution (see Fig. 3.7). Firstly, based on the analysis of interactions among product, stakeholders and external environments, an approach of Service Function and Attribute Analysis (SFAA) is proposed to present the service attributes of the PSS. Secondly, to identify potential conflicts between different PSS technical attributes, a method of group decision making based on unbalanced linguistic label set is utilized. Thirdly, the contradiction matrix and inventive principles in TRIZ methodology is then introduced to resolve the identified design conflicts of PSS. After resolving conflicts, designers will analyze whether the solution of PSS design conflicts bring new functions or not. If yes, they will implement again the process from stage 1 to stage 3. If not, the whole process is end. The proposed method provides a standard reference process for the conflict identification and resolution of PSS.

3.3 PSS Design Conflict Identification and Resolution

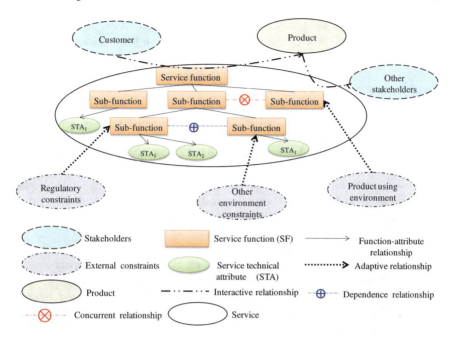

**Fig. 3.8** Service Function and Attribute Analysis (SFAA) (Song and Sakao 2016)

**Phase 1: Service function and attribute analysis**

To analyze the PSS function and technical attribute, this section develops a method called Service Function and Attribute Analysis (SFAA) (Fig. 3.8) based on the graph of interactors (Maussang et al. 2009) and function hierarchical structure. Unlike the method in Maussang et al. (2009), SFAA consider the function decomposition based on function hierarchical structure. In SFAA, PSS can be broken down into some sub-functions, each of which can be described by its name and certain service technical attributes. Besides, SFAA considers both hierarchical and horizontal relationships between functions, which helps to comprehensively elicit specific service technical attributes. The function decomposition is also a process of interaction between customers and the service provider which can facilitate the subsequent PSS design, because it helps designers to know more about the customers' task and contributes to accurately expressing the service technical attributes. Moreover, unlike the modeling scheme proposed by Arai and Shimomura (2004) and further developed by Sakao et al. (2009), interrelations (e.g. dependence relationship and concurrent relationship) between functions are also considered. In this regard, SFAA is a richer presentation tool for PSS, and it is also a tool for describing the attributes of the service functions. The designers can define the PSS with a series of service functions and technical attributes, e.g. service availability, service cost, and response time, etc.

SFAA process allows designers to analyze the interactions among product, stakeholders and external environment. Based on this, service functions and service attributes can be acquired. SFAA also reveals the relationships between service functions and technical attributes. As can be seen from Fig. 3.8, customers and other stakeholders interact with each other through the product to perform certain service functions. In order to meet customer requirement of effective and efficient use of product in the whole product lifecycle, stakeholders interact with each other to perform certain service functions. For instance, in order to provide customers with reliable and stable compressed air, the compressor manufacture, spare part supplier, and customers should keep interactions to deliver the service performance of "failure warning and diagnosis". Besides, constrained by the external environment, PSS should also provide certain service functions to adapt to the environment (production environment, ecological environment, and regulatory environment, etc.), such as energy-saving and noise controlling. For instance, installation and commissioning service need to take into account the layout, lighting, humidity and temperature and other environmental conditions of workshop..

Requirements of stakeholders and external environment can then be converted to the specific service functions and technical attributes. Service designers can use service technical attributes to describe certain service function based on some qualitative or quantitative features. For instance, "quickly access of failure information of product" and "high reliability of failure diagnosis" can be used to describe the service function of product failure diagnosis. With the method of SFAA, the PSS technical attributes can well be defined.

In SFAA, concurrent or dependence relationships between functions will be also identified. Concurrent relationship refers to the relationship between two or more service activities which must be simultaneously implemented. Only all the service activities in parallel are completed, the service function supported by the concurrent service activities can be considered to be performed. Dependence relationship refers to the relationship between two or more service activities which must be executed sequentially. The complementation of the previous service activity is the premise of the next service activity.

**Phase 2: Service conflict identification in PSS design**

Conflict identification is the critical step of conflict management. There are generally three types of correlations between the technical attributes, namely, positive correlation, irrelevant correlation and negative correlation. Positive correlation indicates that the two technical attributes are mutually reinforcing, and negative correlation indicates that the two technical attributes are mutually conflicting. Each technical attribute needs to be examined to see whether or not it contradicts with some other technical attributes. The concurrent or dependence relationships between functions will help the experts to explore the possible conflicts. Competition for limited service resources or even the same resource may lead to conflicts between service activities with concurrent relationships. Conflicts may also exist between the service activities with dependence relationships, because lack of necessary previous service output will cause the next service activity waiting for inputs.

With the presented relationships between functions in SFAA, the experts can describe and share preliminary judgments on the type of conflict. If there is a

## 3.3 PSS Design Conflict Identification and Resolution

concurrent relationship between two service functions, conflict identification team would mainly check whether there are resource competitions between technical attributes of the concurrent functions, i.e. resource-based conflict. While dependence relationships exists between two service functions, the team would mainly check whether there are chronological contradiction or information lacking between technical attributes of the dependent functions, i.e. process-based conflict. Using SFAA in this manner, early conflict identification is more supported and documented. In industry, conflict identification of PSS technical attributes is essentially conducted as group decision making. Various experts tend to choose linguistic terms with different granularities in judging on the potential conflicts. In fact, in the process of group decision-making, decision-makers prefer to use linguistic terms with different granularities to present their judgments (Malakooti 2012). Some inexperienced experts may even use the uncertain linguistic terms with intervals to evaluate the potential conflicts. Therefore, to use linguistic terms to identify the potential design conflicts of PSS, it is necessary to unify the linguistic terms with multi-granularity into uniform granularity-based linguistic judgments, and aggregate the linguistic judgments to obtain the comprehensive judgment on the potential conflict. The granularity here refers to the number of linguistic terms in a linguistic label set. For instance, to assess a service performance, decision-maker A prefer to use the linguistic label set with granularity of 3{−1 = *extremely poor*, 0 = *medium*, 1 = *extremely good*}, and decision-maker B use the linguistic label set with granularity of 9 {−4 = *extremely poor*, −2 = *very poor*, −1 = *poor*, −0.4 = *slightly poor*, 0 = *fair*, 0.4 = *slightly good*, 1 = *good*, 2 = *very good*, 4 = *extremely good*}. Although both decision-makers A and B provide score of 1 for the service performance, their meanings are different (A considers that the service is *extremely good*, while B considers that the service is *good*). Therefore, it is necessary to unify the linguistic terms to avoid unnecessary loss of information.

The conflict identification process of PSS is described as follows:

**Step 1**: the relationship between different technical attributes $TA_j$ ($j = 1, 2, \ldots, n$) is firstly evaluated based on unbalanced linguistic label set $S^{(k)}$ (Xu 2009).

$$S^{(k)} = \left\{ S_\beta^{(k)} | \beta = 1-k, 2(2-k)/3, 2(3-k)/4, \ldots, 0, \ldots, 2(k-3)/4, 2(k-2)/3, k-1 \right\} \tag{3.38}$$

In Eq. 3.38, $k$ is a positive integer to be used to calculate linguistic label in the linguistic label set. From Eq. (3.38), we can see that the number of linguistic variables in the linguistic label set $S^{(k)}$ is $2k − 1$. The larger the value of $k$ is, the more linguistic terms in the linguistic label set. $S_\beta^{(k)}$ is the linguistic judgment on relationship between PSS technical attributes. $S_{1-k}^{(k)}$ and $S_{k-1}^{(k)}$ represent the upper and lower boundaries of the linguistic label set, respectively. $\beta$ represents the degree of conflict or cooperation relationships between PSS technical attributes; $k$ is an integer which is greater than zero. Different linguistic label sets with different granularities can be acquired by setting different values for $k$. For example, when $k = 4$, the granularity of the linguistic label set is 7. Thus, $S^{(4)} = \{ S_{-3}^{(4)}$ = "strong conflict", $S_{-4/3}^{(4)}$ = "medium conflict", $S_{-1/2}^{(4)}$

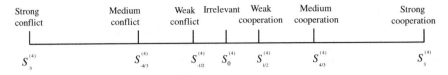

**Fig. 3.9** Linguistic label set $S^{(4)}$ with granularity of 7 (Song and Sakao 2016)

= "weak conflict", $S_0^{(4)}$ = "irrelevant", $S_{1/2}^{(4)}$ = "weak cooperation", $S_{4/3}^{(4)}$ = "medium cooperation" $S_3^{(4)}$ = "strong cooperation"} (see Fig. 3.9), then $\beta = -3, -4/3, -1/2, 0, 1/2, 4/3$ and 3, respectively.

In the design process of PSS, experienced professionals tend to use crisp value to judge the relationships between different technical attributes, while inexperienced design team members tend to use the uncertain linguistic variables with intervals. Thereby, the initial linguistic judgment matrix $M_{cq}$ can be obtained as follows:

$$M_{cq} = (c_{ijq})_{n \times n} (q = 1, 2, \ldots, l).$$

$c_{ijq}$ denotes the $q$th expert's judgment on the relationship between the $i$th technical attributes and the $j$th technical attributes, and $l$ is the number of experts in the design team.

For any linguistic judgment $S_{\beta1}^{(k)}, S_{\beta2}^{(k)}$, if $\lambda, \lambda_1, \lambda_2 \in [0,1]$, their operation rules (Wu and Chen 2007) are as follows:

$$S_{\beta1}^{(k)} \oplus S_{\beta2}^{(k)} = S_{\beta2}^{(k)} \oplus S_{\beta1}^{(k)} = S_{\beta1+\beta2}^{(k)} \tag{3.39}$$

$$\lambda S_{\beta}^{(k)} = S_{\lambda\beta}^{(k)} \tag{3.40}$$

$$\left(S_{\beta}^{(k)}\right)^{\lambda} = S_{\beta\lambda}^{(k)} \tag{3.41}$$

$$\lambda\left(S_{\beta1}^{(k)} \oplus S_{\beta2}^{(k)}\right) = \lambda S_{\beta2}^{(k)} \oplus \lambda S_{\beta1}^{(k)} = S_{\lambda(\beta1+\beta2)}^{(k)} \tag{3.42}$$

$$(\lambda_1 + \lambda_2) S_{\beta}^{(k)} = \lambda_1 S_{\beta}^{(k)} + \lambda_2 S_{\beta}^{(k)} \tag{3.43}$$

**Step 2**: the experts' linguistic judgments come from the different unbalanced linguistic label sets with different granularities. In order to make the linguistic labels uniform without losing decision information, it is necessary to unify them into the linguistic judgments with the same granularity. Besides, the linguistic judgments with the same granularity will facilitate judgments aggregation in decision making of the conflict degree. Then, we firstly introduce the granularity transformation functions in Xu (2009) to unify different unbalanced linguistic label sets with different granularities in a unique linguistic label set.

Assume that $\bar{S}^{(k_1)} = \{S_{\beta}^{(k_1)} | \beta \in [1 - k_1, k_1 - 1]\}$, $\bar{S}^{(k_2)} = \{S_{\gamma}^{(k_2)} | \gamma \in [1 - k_2, k_2 - 1]\}$ are two linguistic label sets with different granularities, respec-

## 3.3 PSS Design Conflict Identification and Resolution

tively, then they can be converted to be each other in accordance with the following formula (Xu 2009):

$$F_{k_1}^{k_2} : S_{[1-k_1,k_1-1]}^{(k_1)} \rightarrow S_{[1-k_2,k_2-1]}^{(k_2)} \quad (3.44)$$

$$\gamma = F(\beta) = \frac{\beta(k_2 - 1)}{k_1 - 1} \quad (3.45)$$

For example, we can use the equation $\gamma = \frac{\beta(4-1)}{3-1} = \frac{3}{2}\beta$, to convert the linguistic label set $S^{(3)}$ into $S^{(4)}$. That is, $S_{-2}^{(3)} \rightarrow S_{-3}^{(4)}$, $S_{-2/3}^{(3)} \rightarrow S_{-1}^{(4)}$ and the like.
Similarly,

$$F_{k_2}^{k_1} : S_{[1-k_2,k_2-1]}^{(k_2)} \rightarrow S_{[1-k_1,k_1-1]}^{(k_1)} \quad (3.46)$$

$$\beta = \frac{\gamma(k_1 - 1)}{k_2 - 1} \quad (3.47)$$

Then the linguistic label set $S^b$ utilized by most of experts is considered to be the basic reference linguistic label set. Other linguistic label sets with different granularities can be unified into the reference linguistic label set $S^b$ according to Formulas (3.44)–(3.47). Then, all the linguistic judgments $c_{ijq}$ in the initial linguistic judgment matrix $M_{cq}$ ($q = 1, 2,..., l$) can be unified. Direct calculation of the linguistic judgments of technical attributes' relationships is expected to reduce unnecessary loss of information in the decision making process.

From Step 3 to Step 5, we consider uncertain linguistic judgments of conflicts for the first time, and convert them into crisp judgments to get the aggregated value of individual judgments which denote the conflict degree or cooperation degree, which doesn't appear in past researches.

**Step 3**: all the uncertain linguistic judgments in the linguistic judgment matrix are converted into the certain ones. For any linguistic judgments with intervals ($\widetilde{c_{ijq}} = [c_{ijq}^L, c_{ijq}^U]$), the coefficient ξ (0<ξ<1) is introduced, then the uncertain linguistic judgments can be converted into crisp ones is as follows:

$$c_{ijq} = (1 - \xi) \times c_{ijq}^L + \xi \times c_{ijq}^U \quad (3.48)$$

where $c_{ijq}$ denotes the $q$th expert's judgment on the relationship between the $i$th technical attribute and the $j$th technical attribute; $c_{ijq}^L$ and $c_{ijq}^U$ represent the upper boundary and lower boundary of the uncertain linguistic judgment $c_{ijq}$; ξ represents expert's preference towards the upper boundary and lower boundary, and the value of ξ is generally set as 0.5 to keep a neutral preference.

Then, according to Eq. (3.48), all the elements in the linguistic judgment matrix have been converted to the crisp linguistic judgments with uniform granularities. The new linguistic judgment matrix is denoted as $M_{cq}^a = \left(c_{ijq}^a\right)_{n \times n}$ ($q = 1, 2,..., l$).

**Step 4**: all the granularity-unified linguistic judgments ($c_{ijq}^a$) of different experts are aggregated to get the decision value ($c_{ij}^a$) of the conflict as follows:

$$c_{ij}^a = \left[\sum_1^l c_{ijq}^a\right]/l \tag{3.49}$$

where $l$ is the number of decision makers; $i, j = 1, 2,\ldots, n$, $q = 1, 2,\ldots, l$.

**Step 5**: the potential conflicts are identified with the decision value ($c_{ij}^a$). If the subscript of $c_{ij}^a$ is smaller than 0, there is a conflict between the $i$th PSO technical attribute and the $j$th PSO technical attribute. The conflict with lager absolute value of the subscript should be given priority to be resolved.

Because the conflicts only exist between PSS technical attributes that are negatively correlated, the technical attributes that are judged to be positively correlated should not be considered in the aggregation process. This way simplifies the design conflict identification process.

**Phase 3: Service conflict resolution in PSS design**

In order to resolve the identified conflict, this section proposes a PSS conflict resolution process based on technical contradiction matrix leveraged from TRIZ. Details of PSS design conflict resolution process are described as follows:

**Step 1**: the corresponding TRIZ parameters are identified for the PSS technical attributes.

Typical PSS technical attributes include service response, service flexibility, service reliability, service quality, service availability, service efficiency, service resource, service time and service cost, etc. These PSS technical attributes cannot be directly used in TRIZ. Therefore, it is necessary to firstly refine and standardize the conflicted PSS technical attributes into TRIZ parameters. The conflicting PSS technical attributes are matched with corresponding TRIZ parameters in the light of their similar connotations. For instance, the PSS technical attribute "quick service response " means that the service provider responses to customer service requests with relatively high speed, and therefore, this PSS technical attribute can be represented by the TRIZ parameter "9. Speed" (The velocity of an object; the rate of a process or action in time). Similarly, other PSS technical attributes can also be represented by the corresponding TRIZ parameters.

**Step 2**: the TRIZ contradiction matrix is examined to find out the corresponding favorable inventive principles.

Designers can use the contradiction matrix in TRIZ to solve the identified conflicts. Firstly, it is necessary to detect the TRIZ parameter which is "feature to improve" in the columns and "undesired result" in the rows. Then, the conflict of PSO technical attribute is resolved by using the recommend inventive principles that are listed in the intersection of the improving and worsening TRIZ parameters. The inventive

3.3 PSS Design Conflict Identification and Resolution    103

principles are used to inspire the possible conflict resolutions. Some appropriate re-explanations of the traditional 40 TRIZ inventive principles is necessary, because it will make the 40 TRIZ inventive principles adapt to the conflict resolving problems in the field of product service offerings. For instance, the invention principle 2 "Extraction (Extracting, Retrieving, Removing)" in the TRIZ is as follows:

a. Extract the "disturbing" part or property from an object.
b. Extract only the necessary part or property from an object.

Based on hints from the "Extraction", design experts can re-explain and adjust the invention principle 2 "Extraction" as follows:

a. Extract the "disturbing" process or task from a product-service offering (e.g. outsourcing).
b. Extract only the key process or task from a product-service offering.

Similarly, other inventive principles can be also well re-explained and adjusted to adapt to its use in domain of PSS.

**Step 3**: the specific solution for the PSS design conflicts is generated.

Following the recommended principles and suggested ways, design experts can make possible conflict resolutions.

## 3.3.2 Case Study: Design Conflict Resolution for Elevator PSS

To demonstrate how the proposed method of conflict resolution works, we applied it to an actual PSS design case in elevator manufacturing Company M. Elevator Company M is a leading manufacturer providing different types of elevators including passenger/freight elevator, hospital elevator, escalator, and elevator monitoring system, etc. In addition, the Company also offers elevator services including installation, maintenance, repair, remote monitoring, elevator upgrading and spare parts supply, etc. Company M wants to enhance its competitiveness in the elevator service market by improving its service design efficiency.

**Phase 1: Elevator service function and attribute analysis**

Taking into account the external environment and stakeholders' interactions, method of SFAA proposed in Sect. 3.1 was used to describe the elevator service functions and technical attributes (see Fig. 3.10). Table 3.10 lists the technical attributes of elevator service.

**Phase 2: Conflict identification for elevator service technical attribute**

Five design experts made judgments on the relationships between different technical attributes of elevator service by using unbalanced linguistic label set with different

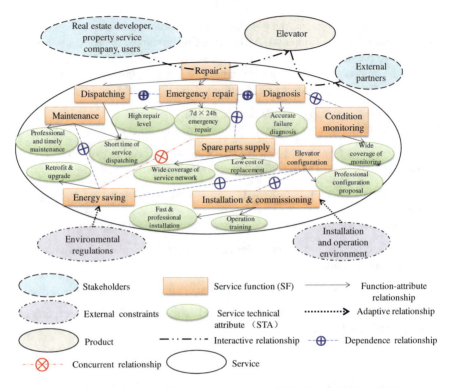

**Fig. 3.10** Service function and attribute analysis of elevator PSS (Song and Sakao 2016)

**Table 3.10** Technical attributes of elevator service (Song and Sakao 2016)

| No. | Technical attributes | No. | Technical attributes |
| --- | --- | --- | --- |
| $TA_1$ | Professional configuration proposal | $TA_7$ | Repair level |
| $TA_2$ | Fast & professional installation | $TA_8$ | Cost of spare parts replacement |
| $TA_3$ | Coverage of condition monitoring | $TA_9$ | Coverage of service network |
| $TA_4$ | Accuracy of failure diagnosis | $TA_{10}$ | Short time of service dispatching |
| $TA_5$ | Professional and timely maintenance | $TA_{11}$ | Availability of 7d × 24 h emergency repair |
| $TA_6$ | Elevator operation training | $TA_{12}$ | Retrofit and upgrade |

granularity of 7, 9, and 5. The 1st expert and the 4th experts used uncertain linguistic judgments with intervals to evaluate the relationships between technical attributes, because they lack some experience in elevator service design. The team considered only the pair of technical attributes existing at least one linguistic judgment of negative correlation (see Table 3.11), because the collective value of judgments may be negative which finally denotes conflicts between technical attributes.

3.3 PSS Design Conflict Identification and Resolution

**Table 3.11** The linguistic judgments on the relationships between TAs of elevator service (Song and Sakao 2016)

| Pair of technical attributes | Expert 1 | Expert 2 | Expert 3 | Expert 4 | Expert 5 |
|---|---|---|---|---|---|
| TA$_1$–TA$_2$ | $\left[s_{-1/2}^{(4)}, s_0^{(4)}\right]$ | $s_3^{(4)}$ | $s_{-1}^{(5)}$ | $\left[s_{-2}^{(3)}, s_0^{(3)}\right]$ | $s_{1/2}^{(4)}$ |
| TA$_3$–TA$_4$ | $\left[s_{-4/3}^{(4)}, s_{-1/2}^{(4)}\right]$ | $s_{-3}^{(4)}$ | $s_{-2}^{(5)}$ | $\left[s_{-2/3}^{(3)}, s_0^{(3)}\right]$ | $s_{-4/3}^{(4)}$ |
| TA$_9$–TA$_{10}$ | $\left[s_{-4/3}^{(4)}, s_0^{(4)}\right]$ | $s_{-3}^{(4)}$ | $s_{-2}^{(5)}$ | $\left[s_{-2}^{(3)}, s_{-2/3}^{(3)}\right]$ | $s_{-4/3}^{(4)}$ |

**Table 3.12** The unified linguistic judgments on the relationships between TAs (Song and Sakao 2016)

| Pair of technical attributes | Expert 1 | Expert 2 | Expert 3 | Expert 4 | Expert 5 |
|---|---|---|---|---|---|
| TA$_1$–TA$_2$ | $\left[s_{-1/2}^{(4)}, s_0^{(4)}\right]$ | $s_3^{(4)}$ | $s_{-3/4}^{(4)}$ | $\left[s_{-3}^{(4)}, s_0^{(4)}\right]$ | $s_{1/2}^{(4)}$ |
| TA$_3$–TA$_4$ | $\left[s_{-4/3}^{(4)}, s_{-1/2}^{(4)}\right]$ | $s_{-3}^{(4)}$ | $s_{-3/2}^{(4)}$ | $\left[s_{-1}^{(4)}, s_0^{(4)}\right]$ | $s_{-4/3}^{(4)}$ |
| TA$_9$–TA$_{10}$ | $\left[s_{-4/3}^{(4)}, s_0^{(4)}\right]$ | $s_{-3}^{(4)}$ | $s_{-3/2}^{(4)}$ | $\left[s_{-3}^{(4)}, s_{-1}^{(4)}\right]$ | $s_{-4/3}^{(4)}$ |

According to Formulas (3.44)–(3.47), the linguistic judgments are unified in Table 3.11 into the linguistic judgments with the same granularity. The linguistic label set $S^{(4)}$ was considered to be the basic reference linguistic label set, because it was utilized by most of experts in the design team. The linguistic judgments with uniform granularity of 7 can be seen in Table 3.12.

Then, the uncertain linguistic judgments are converted into the certain ones according to Formula (3.48) ($\xi = 0.5$). After that, aggregate all the granularity-unified linguistic judgments of different experts to get the indication value of the conflict in the light of (3.49).

It is clear to be seen from the Table 3.13 that the indication values of conflict hold the following relation: $S_{-1.7}^4 < S_{-1.45}^{(4)} < S_0^{(4)} < S_{0.2}^{(4)}$. Thus, we can know that TA$_9$ (Wide coverage of service network) conflicts with TA$_{10}$ (Short time of service dispatching) and TA$_3$ (Wide coverage of condition monitoring) conflicts with TA$_4$ (Accurate failure diagnosis).

**Phase 3: Conflict resolution of elevator service technical attribute**

**Step 1**: the corresponding TRIZ parameters were identified for the corresponding service technical attributes TA$_3$ (Wide coverage of condition monitoring), TA$_4$ (Accurate failure diagnosis), TA$_9$ (Wide coverage of service network) and TA$_{10}$ (Short time of service dispatching).

**Table 3.13** The unified linguistic judgments and indication value of conflict (Song and Sakao 2016)

| Pair of technical attributes | Expert 1 | Expert 2 | Expert 3 | Expert 4 | Expert 5 | Indication value of conflict |
|---|---|---|---|---|---|---|
| TA$_1$–TA$_2$ | $S^{(4)}_{-1/4}$ | $S^{(4)}_{3}$ | $S^{(4)}_{-3/4}$ | $S^{(4)}_{-3/2}$ | $S^{(4)}_{1/2}$ | $S^{(4)}_{0.2}$ |
| TA$_3$–TA$_4$ | $S^{(4)}_{-0.917}$ | $S^{(4)}_{-3}$ | $S^{(4)}_{-3/2}$ | $S^{(4)}_{-0.5}$ | $S^{(4)}_{-4/3}$ | $S^{(4)}_{-1.45}$ |
| TA$_9$–TA$_{10}$ | $S^{(4)}_{-2/3}$ | $S^{(4)}_{-3}$ | $S^{(4)}_{-3/2}$ | $S^{(4)}_{-2}$ | $S^{(4)}_{-4/3}$ | $S^{4}_{-1.7}$ |

TA$_3$ (Wide coverage of condition monitoring) was represented by the TRIZ parameter "37. Difficulty of detecting and measuring" (Measuring or monitoring systems that are complex, costly, require much time and labor to set up and use, or that have complex relationships between components or components that interfere with each other all demonstrate "difficulty of detecting and measuring." Increasing cost of measuring to a satisfactory error is also a sign of increased difficulty of measuring).

TA$_4$ (Accurate failure diagnosis) was represented by the TRIZ parameter "28. Measurement accuracy" (The closeness of the measured value to the actual value of a property of a system. Reducing the error in a measurement increases the accuracy of the measurement).

TA$_9$ (Wide coverage of service network) was represented by the TRIZ parameter "33. Ease of operation" (Simplicity: The process is NOT easy if it requires a large number of people, large number of steps in the operation, needs special tools, etc. "Hard" processes have low yield and "easy" process have high yield; they are easy to do right).

TA$_{10}$ (Short time of service dispatching) was represented by the TRIZ parameter "25. Loss of time" (Time is the duration of an activity. Improving the loss of time means reducing the time that is taken for the activity).

**Step 2**: the TRIZ contradiction matrix was examined to find out the corresponding favorable inventive principles.

Firstly, the TRIZ parameter "37. Difficulty of detecting and measuring" and "33. Ease of operation" were detected as "improving parameter" in the columns, while "28. Measurement accuracy" and "25. Loss of time" were detected as "worsening parameter" in the rows. Then, search through the intersection of the improving and worsening TRIZ parameters in contradiction matrix for the recommend inventive principles. The number of recommend inventive principles for resolving conflict between TA$_3$ (Wide coverage of condition monitoring) and TA$_4$ (Accurate failure diagnosis) is 24, 26, 28, and 32, respectively. The number of recommend inventive principles for resolving conflict between TA$_9$ (Wide coverage of service network) and TA$_{10}$ (Short time of service dispatching) is 4, 10, 28, and 34, respectively.

## 3.3 PSS Design Conflict Identification and Resolution

**Table 3.14** The recommended principles for resolving TA' conflicts of elevator service (Song and Sakao 2016)

| Improving parameter | Worsening parameter | The recommend inventive principles |
|---|---|---|
| "37. Difficulty of detecting and measuring" ($TA_3$-Wide coverage of condition monitoring) | "28. Measurement accuracy" ($TA_4$ -Accurate failure diagnosis) | Principle 24: Intermediary/Mediator<br>Principle 26: Copying<br>Principle 28: Replacement of mechanical system<br>Principle 32: Colour change |
| "33. Ease of operation" ($TA_9$ Wide coverage of service network) | "25. Loss of time" ($TA_{10}$ -Short time of service dispatching) | Principle 4: Asymmetry<br>Principle 10: Prior action<br>Principle 28: Replacement of mechanical system<br>Principle 34: Discarding and Recovering |

The appropriate re-explanations of the recommend inventive principles are shown in Table 3.14 to make them adapt to the problems in the field of product service offerings.

**Step 3**: the specific solution for the PSS design conflicts was generated.

Following the recommended principles and suggested ways, design experts can make possible conflict resolutions.

Elevator service designers considered that "Principle 24: Intermediary/Mediator" and "Principle 26: Copying" were suitable to solve the conflict between $TA_3$ (Wide coverage of condition monitoring) and $TA_4$ (Accurate failure diagnosis). Referring to the sub-principle "Use an intermediary carrier article or intermediary process" in "Principle 24: Intermediary/Mediator" and "Replace unavailable, expensive or fragile object with available or inexpensive copies" in "Principle 26: Copying", there was a hint for designers to make full use of an computer-aided service system to replace the human service, and remote service to replace the field service to improve the diagnosis efficiency. Therefore, elevator service design team proposed a case-based reasoning diagnosis to solve the conflict between $TA_3$ and $TA_4$. The solution is described as follows: First, sensors on the periphery of elevator collected information of floor, running speed, status of door opening and closing, failure of squatting, failure of hoisting, and maintenance status, etc. Then, the information is transmitted to the platform of elevator operation management by communication module of General Packet Radio Service (GPRS). After that, the elevator operation management platform can obtain the different features of elevator failures through data mining of failure information. The failure feature information is stored in a case library of elevator failure. Once a new problems arises, the elevator operation management platform can quickly search the failure case library to find a similar problem with possible solutions based on the matching of failure features. This is expected to enhance the efficiency and accuracy of failure diagnosis.

The elevator design team decided to choose inventive principle 10 (Preliminary action) to solve the identified conflict. According to the sub-principle of the inventive principle 10 (Preliminary action) "Pre-arrange objects such that they can come into action from the most convenient place and without losing time for their delivery," it was necessary to provide service skill training for works in advance, and keep the service facilities in good condition. More importantly, it is recommended that service scheduling should be optimized to reduce customer waiting time. Here, the core problem is to reduce PSS delivery time without affecting the coverage of service network. If the designers interpreted the principle 10 (Preliminary action) into a preventive maintenance, or improved elevator reliability, it cannot essentially resolve the targeted conflict between TA9 (Wide coverage of service network) and TA10 (Short time of service dispatching). This is because preventive maintenance, or improving elevator reliability contribute less to solving the core problem (reducing PSS *delivery* time without affecting the coverage of service network) even if they may keep the elevator in good condition. Based on these analysis and suggestions of '10. Preliminary action', elevator service design team proposed a precise dispatching method to solve the conflict between **TA$_9$** (Wide coverage of service network) and **TA$_{10}$** (Short time of service dispatching). The precise dispatching method is described as follows: The CRM (customer relationship management) system, information system of repair and maintenance, call centre, GIS-based positioning system are recommended to be integrated together. The dispatching system in the call center calculates the optimal service path based on elevator's geographic information, suitable service engineers on duty, and service requirements, etc. Then the service engineer is assigned to go to the filed following the optimal service path. A service work order sheet created by the call centre platform is automatically sent to CRM system. The CRM system will automatically send short messages with voice prompts to the service engineer dispatched. After receiving the dispatching message, the service engineer must respond to it within three minutes, otherwise, this dispatching message will be directly sent to the manager of service centre. If the manager of service centre does not respond within three minutes, it will be automatically reported to service director of company. If the service engineer cannot accept the service work order due to reasonable reasons, he or she must immediately click the "delegate to others" in the hand-held terminal. Once the service assignment is completed, customers will receive a reminder message from the call centre platform so that they can supervise and prepare for the entire service process. In this way, the time of service dispatching can be shortened on the basis of service route and resources optimization in advance.

After finding the solutions to resolve the conflict, designers analyzed the solutions to decide whether they bring new functions or not. To simplify the description yet maintaining the essence for the method verification, the cycle repeats are not described here.

### 3.3.3 Discussion

The proposed method with SFAA provides a more specific representation of a structure of PSS functions and design attributes. Compared with the graph of interactors (Maussang et al. 2009), SFAA can help to decompose a service function hierarchically into its sub-functions or its underlying functions. Interrelations between functions are also considered. In SFAA, both hierarchical and horizontal relationships between PSS functions can be presented, which helps to comprehensively elicit specific service technical attributes. In this regard, the description with SFAA helps to share the intention and motivation of service functions. This will provide critical inputs for the following process of conflict identification of technical attributes. This also means that application areas of TRIZ-based conflict solving methods are expanded to include PSS.

The case study shows conflict identification results, which illustrate that the group decision making approach with multi-granular uncertain linguistic information is efficient and reliable for identifying conflicts under imprecise and vague environments. The method enables the service design experts to freely and fully express their judgments, which better reflects group-oriented features of conflict identification. It will improve decision-making in PSS conflict identification. This research provides one of the first articles that introduce such a group decision making method based on unbalanced linguistic label set to identification of PSS design conflicts under vague judgment environment.

Another contribution of the method is that it develops a systematic and integrative process to identify and resolve PSS design conflicts, which is useful for practitioners in industry. In previous literature, other researches sporadically focus on conflict identification or resolution, for instance, in Chai et al. (2005), the researchers only provide conflict resolving method directly based on TRIZ without specific conflict analysis and identification method and process. On the contrary, this research not only presents a systematic process but also provides supporting methods including SFAA, group-oriented conflict identification, and conflict resolving approaches. In addition, the proposed method also considers practice in industry for example of conflict identification, and thus has high potential for usage by industry.

### References

Arai, T., & Shimomura, Y. (2004). Proposal of service CAD system-a tool for service engineering. *CIRP Annals-Manufacturing Technology, 53*(1), 397–400.

Blackhurst, J., Wu, T. T., & Craighead, C. W. (2008). A systematic approach for supply chain conflict detection with a hierarchical Petri Net extension. *Omega, 36*(5), 680–696.

Chai, K. H., Zhang, J., & Tan, K. C. (2005). A TRIZ-based method for new service design. *Journal of Service Research, 8*(1), 48–66.

Chan, J. W., & Tong, T. K. (2007). Multi-criteria material selections and end-of-life product strategy: Grey relational analysis approach. *Materials and Design, 28*(5), 1539–1546.

Chang, T. C., & Lin, S. J. (1999). Grey relation analysis of carbon dioxide emissions from industrial production and energy uses in Taiwan. *Journal of Environmental Management, 56*(4), 247–257.

Deng, J. (1989). Introduction to grey system theory. *The Journal of grey system, 1*(1), 1–24.

Greco, S., Matarazzo, B., & Slowinski, R. (2001). Rough sets theory for multicriteria decision analysis. *European Journal of Operational Research, 129*(1), 1–47.

Hou, J., Su, C., Tang, L., & Wang, W. (2008, September). Conflict resolution for collaborative design. In Automation and Logistics, 2008. ICAL 2008. IEEE International Conference on (pp. 875–880). IEEE.

Khoo, L. P., Tor, S. B., & Zhai, L. Y. (1999). A rough-set-based approach for classification and rule induction. *The International Journal of Advanced Manufacturing Technology, 15*(6), 438–444.

Lee, C., Lee, H., Seol, H., & Park, Y. (2012). Evaluation of new service concepts using rough set theory and group analytic hierarchy process. *Expert Systems with Applications, 39*(3), 3404–3412.

Li, X., & Song, W. (2016). A rough VIKOR-based QFD for prioritizing design attributes of product-related service. Mathematical Problems in Engineering, 2016.

Malakooti, B. (2012). Decision making process: Typology, intelligence, and optimization. *Journal of Intelligent Manufacturing, 23*(3), 733–746.

Mannweiler, C., & Aurich, J. C. (2011). Customer oriented configuration of product-service systems. In Functional Thinking for Value Creation (pp. 81–86). Berlin: Springer.

Maussang, N., Zwolinski, P., & Brissaud, D. (2009). Product-service system design methodology: From the PSS architecture design to the products specifications. *Journal of Engineering Design, 20*(4), 349–366.

Pawlak, Z. (1982). Rough sets. *International Journal of Computer and Information Sciences, 11*(5), 341–356.

Pawlak, Z. (2012). Rough sets: Theoretical aspects of reasoning about data (Vol. 9). Berlin: Springer Science & Business Media.

Sakao, T., Shimomura, Y., Sundin, E., & Comstock, M. (2009). Modeling design objects in CAD system for service/product engineering. *Computer Aided Design, 41*(3), 197–213.

Song, W. (2017). Requirement management for product-service systems: Status review and future trends. *Computers in Industry, 85,* 11–22.

Song, W., & Sakao, T. (2016). Service conflict identification and resolution for design of product–service offerings. *Computer and Industrial Engineering, 98,* 91–101.

Song, W., Ming, X., & Han, Y. (2014). Prioritising technical attributes in QFD under vague environment: A rough-grey relational analysis approach. *International Journal of Production Research, 52*(18), 5528–5545.

Wu, Z., & Chen, Y. (2007). The maximizing deviation method for group multiple attribute decision making under linguistic environment. *Fuzzy Sets and Systems, 158*(14), 1608–1617.

Xu, Z. (2009). An interactive approach to multiple attribute group decision making with multigranular uncertain linguistic information. *Group Decision and Negotiation, 18*(2), 119–145.

Zhai, L. Y., Khoo, L. P., & Zhong, Z. W. (2008). A rough set enhanced fuzzy approach to quality function deployment. *The International Journal of Advanced Manufacturing Technology, 37*(5–6), 613–624.

# Chapter 4
# Modularization of PSS

PSS is high-value service solution (e.g. repair, maintenance, and energy management) based on product to help manufacturers to achieve sustainable growth and profitability. Modularization can help to realize customization, increase in flexibility, reusability of service modules, and simplification of complex PSS systems, etc. However, compared with tangible product, the modularization of PSS has rarely been handled, despite its potential benefits (Sakao et al. 2017). More specifically, how to identify service components and partition modules in the practical context remains to be an unexplored subject. Therefore, to enhance the efficiency and flexibility of PSS design, Song et al. (2015) propose a PSS modularization approach based on PSS blueprint and fuzzy graph. The proposed PSS blueprint is used to present the whole PSS scenario and identify all the service components. Then, the fuzzy graph theory is used to cluster service components into modules. The proposed method graphically helps the designers to build PSS modules, which is the basis for the module-based PSS configuration in Chap. 5.

## 4.1 PSS Modularization

Unlike products, PSS includes various intangible service processes, activities and service resources, etc. When the external environment (e.g. customer requirements) changes dramatically, the manufacturing service providers have to re-arrange service processes and resources, and even to redesign the whole PSS to adapt to the changed demands. This may not only lead to increase of the service response time and service delivery time, but also cause unnecessary waste of design resources. Modular thinking is a good way to solve this problem, because modularization has been suggested to have many benefits ranging from development to production, such as economies of scale, increased feasibility of change, increased variety, ease of design and testing, decreased lead-times, and easier diagnosis and maintenance (Gershenson et al. 2003; Wang 2009). Therefore, the introduction of the concept of modularization to

**Table 4.1** The differences between service module and product module (Song et al. 2015)

| Module category | Element | Module interface | Module feature | Manifestation |
|---|---|---|---|---|
| Product module | Parts, components, and assemblies, etc. | Interface between physical components; interface between hardware and technology | Control product performance by adjusting the design parameters | Product design drawing |
| Service module | Service object, resources, processes, and activities, etc. | Function interface specified by service contract or agreement; process interface specified by service plan | Control the service level with service capacity planning and service contact mode | Service flow chart |

PSS seems to be a promising approach to tackle the current need for efficient service customization.

To provide a basis for further methods development of PSS modularization, this section briefly introduces and defines the main terms of service component and service module.

**Definition 4.1: Service Component**

Service component is the basic element of which a PSS is made or assembled. A service component can be considered as a service activity (such as failure diagnosis) or service resource (e.g. human resources, physical resources and information) that leads to a partial function of the overall PSS. In general, it is defined by a set of processes, operations, people or other objects. Different service components constitute service modules with different functions.

There are interdependencies between service components, which indicate that service component influences one another. Interdependencies exist, when a change on one aspect of a service component requires a change on another service component. The interdependencies between service components can have different strengths.

**Definition 4.2: Service Module**

Service module integrates service components with strong interdependencies among each other. Service components of different modules have little interdependencies, which gives service modules a high degree of independence among each other facilitating exchangeability. A service module can integrate different service components. In fact, a service module is a set of service components for performing a service function. The differences between service module and physical product module are provided in Table 4.1.

These definitions provide a foundation for modularizing PSS. Based on the above definitions, we can define the modularization of PSS as follows.

## 4.1 PSS Modularization

**Definition 4.3: PSS modularization**

PSS modularization is the action of decomposing a PSS into service components, analyzing interdependencies between the service components and clustering them into service modules to achieve simplification, standardization, customization, flexibility, and reusability.

Modularity allows changes within one service module without requiring changes on other service modules. Only a small part of the PSS would have to be redesigned allowing economies of scale for all carry-over modules.

## 4.2 The Method for Modularizing PSS

### 4.2.1 Preliminaries

This Section introduces the terminology of graph theory which is the basis of service module partition method presented in this section.

Graph G can be expressed as an ordered triple $(A(G), E(G), \mu_G)$, where $A(G)$ is the set of all vertices of the graph G, and $A(G) = (v_1, v_2, \ldots, v)$. $E(G)$ is the set of all edges of the graph G, and $E(G) = \{e_1, e_2, \ldots, e_n\}$. Each edge connects a pair of vertices $\mu_G$ is the correlation function of the graph G, and it ensures the corresponding relations between the edges and its vertices in graph G. For any edge in graph G, there exist unique vertex $v_i$ and vertex $v_j$ to ensure $\mu_G(e) = v_i v_j$.

If vertex $v_i$ and vertex $v_j$ are disordered, the graph G is an undirected graph. On the contrary, the graph G is a directed graph (Bondy and Murty 1976). For graph $G_1$ and $G_2$, If $A(G_1) \subseteq A(G_2)$ and $E(G_1) \subseteq E(G_2)$, then $G_1$ is sub-graph of $G_2$; If $A(G_1) = A(G_2)$ and $E(G_1) \subseteq E(G_2)$, then $G_1$ is spanning sub-graph of $G_2$. If any two vertices $(a_i, a_j)$ in graph G are connected, the graph G is called as a connected graph.

If there isn't any loop existing in a connected graph, the connected graph is called as tree graph denoted as T. If the Tree graph T is sub-graph of the connected graph G, and number of vertices in T is equal to that in the connected graph G, then the tree graph T is called as spanning tree of the connected graph G.

Fuzzy graph $\tilde{G}$ (Rosenfeld 1975) is an ordered triple $(G, \sigma, w)$, where $G = (A(G), E(G), \mu_G)$, and graph G is undirected finite graph. $\sigma$ and $w$ are the mappings of vertices set $A(G)$ in graph G and the edge set $A(G)$ in graph G to interval (0,1), respectively. For the edge $e \in E(G)$, $w(e) \leq \sigma(v_i) \wedge \sigma(v_j)$, where $v_i$ and $v_j$ are the endpoints of edge $e$, and the graph G is the basic graph of fuzzy graph $\tilde{G}$.

For any spanning tree $\tilde{T}^* = (T^*, \sigma, w)$ of fuzzy graph $\tilde{G}$, if it satisfies the following equation:

$$\sum_{e \in E(T^*)} w(e) \leq \sum_{e \in E(T)} w(e) \qquad (4.1)$$

where $\tilde{T} = (T, \sigma, w)$ is a spanning tree of fuzzy graph $\tilde{G}$.

Then the spanning tree $\tilde{T}$ is considered as the maximum spanning tree of the fuzzy graph $\tilde{G}$, and it depicts the fuzzy equivalence between vertices in the graph. The spanning tree $\tilde{T}$ can be used to define a fuzzy classification (Hu 2010).

### 4.2.2 Service Components Identification

To build service module for PSS, designers must firstly decompose the target PSS into the basic service components (service, activities, resources, and other objects). However, service decomposition is more complicated in practice, because it is difficult to achieve accurate service description and representation in PSS design. Quantifiable design elements of product (such as product specifications and tolerances) can rarely be used in PSS design due to intangibility of service. In addition, complex interrelationship between service components also makes it difficult to describe and represent the PSS.

Therefore, this section provides a service component identification tool named modified service blueprint. The modified service blueprint is used to fully represent PSS operation and reveal the complex relationships between the service elements. Modified service blueprint covers all relevant service elements and shows an overall view of the service system, thus facilitate the designers to identify service components in PSS.

In general, modified service blueprint consists of three main domains, that is, the domain of product-related activities, the domain of service activities and the domain of resources supporting these activities. The domain of product-related activities is implemented to realize the expected target and function of product. It includes the product using activities and product management activities. The domain of service activities is set to achieve the purpose and function of service, and it consists of a set of visualized service activities and invisible service activities. The domain of resources is the basis of the domain of product-related activities and the domain of service activities, because it provides the underlying services resource to achieve expected product and service results. Partition representation and description of PSS with modified service blueprint will help designers clearly obtain structure of PSS.

As is shown in Fig. 4.1, modified service blueprint has four boundaries, and they are boundary between product and service, boundary between activity and resource, boundary of using and boundary of visualization. The four boundary lines divide the whole PSS into five different functional areas, namely product using domain, product management domain, visualized service domain (foreground), invisible service domain (background) and resources domain. All service elements have been represented with unified and standardized symbols (see Fig. 4.1). Modified service blueprint reflects the interactions between actors, product and service.

First, the boundary between product and service divides the PSS into product activity domain and service activity domain, which mainly describe the interaction between the use of product and service. Product activity domain includes activi-

## 4.2 The Method for Modularizing PSS

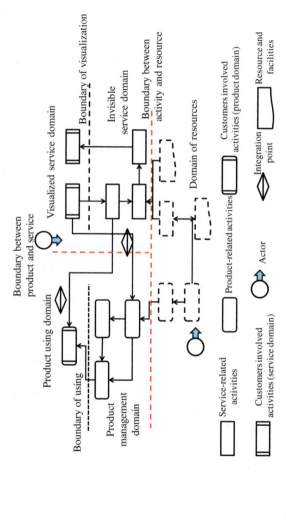

**Fig. 4.1** General structure modeling for modified service blueprint (Song et al. 2015)

ties related to product using and management, the service activity domain includes foreground and background service activities. Second, the product activity domain is divided into product using domain and product management domain by the boundary of using. Interactions between product using and supporting activities are described in this way. Product using domain includes core activities to realize product functions, and product management domain includes activities such as debugging, status monitoring and other management activities completed with software. Third, to describe perceivable and imperceptible service activities, the boundary of visualization divides the service activity domain into visualized domain and non-visualized domain, respectively. Among them, the visualized service domain includes perceivable and visualized service activities which customers can be involved. However, the non-visualized domain includes imperceptible service activities that customers cannot be involved. Interactions between various activities in service domain can be transmission of material, information, knowledge or skill. Fourth, the overall PSS is divided into activity domain and resource domain by boundary between activity and resource. Resource domain includes key resources to support the implementation and delivery of PSS, such as service tools, service personnel, and related software, etc. The activity domain consists of all the activities related with product using, product management, foreground service and background service that supported by the resources in resource domain.

With the modified service blueprint, service designers can identify service components (activities, resources, and roles, etc.) and visually show the interactions between components. Different boxes in Fig. 4.1 represent service components to be identified. Modified service blueprint provides a method of partitioning representation for PSS, and it also describes the specific processes in each domain. Therefore, modified service blueprint can effectively help definers to identify the various types of service components, and lay the foundation for creation of service module.

### 4.2.3 Correlation Analysis for Service Components

From the Sect. 4.1, we can know that a number of components contained in PSS, and interactions between them are complex. To create the service module, it is necessary to analyze the interdependencies between those service components, because they influence the way service components bundled into modules.

**Phase 1: Evaluation Criteria for Interdependencies Between Service Components**

In the process of PSS modularization, in addition to the specific service processes, it is necessary to consider both the service function (output) and service resource (input). Thus, in order to describe interactions between service components, it needs to consider their interdependencies from the perspective of process, function and resource.

## 4.2 The Method for Modularizing PSS

**Table 4.2** Evaluation criteria for function-based interdependency of service components (Song et al. 2015)

| Description | Value |
|---|---|
| Function-based interdependency are very strong | 1 |
| Function-based interdependency are strong | 0.8 |
| Function-based interdependency are medium | 0.6 |
| Function-based interdependency are weak | 0.4 |
| Function-based interdependency are very weak | 0.2 |
| No function-based interdependency | 0 |

**Table 4.3** Evaluation criteria for service flow-based interdependency of service components (Song et al. 2015)

| Description | Value |
|---|---|
| Service flow-based interdependency are very strong | 1 |
| Service flow-based interdependency are strong | 0.8 |
| Service flow-based interdependency are medium | 0.6 |
| Service flow-based interdependency are weak | 0.4 |
| Service flow-based interdependency are very weak | 0.2 |
| No service flow-based interdependency | 0 |

Function-based interdependency

To enhance the functional dependency of service module, it is necessary to bundle together the service components with similar or relevant function to form a service module. Function-based interdependency refers to relevance between functions of two service components. Table 4.2 provides the evaluation criteria for function-based interdependency of service components. For example, activity of failure diagnosis and failure diagnosis system are both indispensable to realizing the service function of diagnosis, so the value indicating the interdependency strength between them can be determined as 1.

(2) Service flow-based interdependency

In PSS, the interactions of service components are mainly reflected in transmission of material and information, conversion of knowledge or skill between service actors. The transfer of material, information and knowledge constitute the service flows in PSS. If output of one service component is used as input by another service component, the two service components are considered to be service flow-based interdependent. The evaluation criteria for service flow-based interdependency are shown in Table 4.3.

**Table 4.4** Evaluation criteria for resource-based interdependency (Song et al. 2015)

| Description | Value |
|---|---|
| Resource-based interdependency are very strong | 1 |
| Resource-based interdependency are strong | 0.8 |
| Resource-based interdependency are medium | 0.6 |
| Resource-based interdependency are weak | 0.4 |
| Resource-based interdependency are very weak | 0.2 |
| No resource-based interdependency | 0 |

(3) Resource-based interdependency

If two service components share the same service resources, they are resource-based interdependent. For example, multi-skilled worker is a kind of human resource shared by both product repair and spare parts test. Therefore, product repair and spare parts test can be considered as resource-based interdependent. The service resource here mainly refers to the key elements to realize service functions. There are always three types of service resource, that is, software systems (such as failure diagnosis system), hardware (such as maintenance tool), and human resources (such as maintenance engineer). The evaluation criteria for resource-based interdependency are shown in Table 4.4.

**Phase 2: Evaluation of interdependencies between service components**

Pair-wise comparison method (Saaty 2008) can be used to determine the weights of evaluation criteria for service component interdependency. The weights need to meet the constraints as follows.

$$w_f + w_p + w_r = 1 \quad (4.2)$$

where $w_f$ is weight of function-based interdependency, $w_p$ is weight of service flow-based interdependency, and $w_r$ is weight of resource-based interdependency.

The comprehensive strength of interdependency $R(i, j)$ can be obtained as follows:

$$R(i, j) = \begin{cases} w_f R^f(i, j) + w_p R^p(i, j) + w_r R^r(i, j), & i \neq j \\ 1, & i = j \end{cases} \quad (4.3)$$

where $i, j \in \{1, 2, \ldots, n\}$, n indicates the number of service components, $R^f(i, j)$ is the strength of function-based interdependency, $R^p(i, j)$ is the strength of service flow-based interdependency, $R^r(i, j)$ is the strength of resource-based interdependency.

Thus, a comprehensive strength matrix of interdependency R for all service components can be obtained as follows.

4.2 The Method for Modularizing PSS

$$R = \begin{bmatrix} R(1,1) & R(1,2) & R(1,3) & \cdots & R(1,n) \\ R(2,1) & R(2,2) & R(2,3) & \cdots & R(2,n) \\ R(3,1) & R(3,2) & R(3,3) & \cdots & R(3,n) \\ \vdots & \vdots & \vdots & \ddots & \vdots \\ R(n,1) & R(n,2) & R(n,3) & \cdots & R(n,n) \end{bmatrix} \begin{matrix} c_1 \\ c_2 \\ c_3 \\ \vdots \\ c_n \end{matrix} \quad (4.4)$$

(with column labels $c_1\ c_2\ c_3\ \cdots\ c_n$)

where, $c_1, c_2, \ldots, c_n$ are the service components. The comprehensive strength matrix of interdependency $R = [R(i, j)]_{n \times n}$ needs to meet the following conditions:

(1) $R(i, j) > 0$, $i, j = 1, 2, \ldots n$;
(2) $R(i, j) = R(j, i)$, $i, j = 1, 2, \ldots n$;
(3) $R(i, i) = 1$, $i = 1, 2, \ldots n$.

### 4.2.4 PSS Module Partition Based on Fuzzy Graph

After analyzing the dependencies between service components, fuzzy graph method is applied in service module partition process. Different geometric structures or graphs can be used to impose a structure on a PSS. The nodes are the service components and the edges represent the relation between these nodes. Service module partition based on fuzzy graph can simplify the representation of complex interactions between service components, because it can visually express these intangible service interactions in a tree graph, which helps the designers to identify the possible modules.

PSS modularization process is described as follows:

(1) Each service component is considered as the graph node, and thus n vertices can be obtained which is denoted by $C_i$ ($1 \leq i \leq n$).
(2) For any comprehensive strength of interdependency $R(i, j)$ between service component $C_i$ and service component $C_j$, when $R(i, j) \neq 0$, the node corresponding to service component $C_i$ is connected with the node corresponding to service component $C_j$ to form an edge $C_iC_j$.
(3) Prioritize all $R(i, j)$ ($1 \leq i, j \leq n$) with a descending order. Then, we can get $R_1(i, j) > R_2(i, j) > \cdots > R_k(i, j) > \cdots > R_h(i, j)$, where $R_k(i, j)$ (k = 1, 2, ..., h) is the kth comprehensive strength of interdependency between two service components, and h is the number of R(i, j) with different values.
(4) Connect the two nodes of $R_1(i, j)$ (the largest comprehensive strength of interdependency) to form an edge, and mark the corresponding comprehensive strength of interdependency ($R_1(i, j)$) on the edge. If loops appear in process of node connecting of two service components, the two service components should not be connected.

**Fig. 4.2** Exploded drawing view of rotor of screw air compressor (Song et al. 2015)

(5) Repeat the previous step(4) for the rest of comprehensive strengths of interdependency $R_2(i, j)$, $R_3(i, j)$, ..., $R_h(i, j)$ ($t \leq h$) respectively until all service components connected. Then we can get the maximum spanning tree T.

(6) Set different thresholds $\lambda$ according to marked values $R_k(i, j)$ on edges of the maximum spanning tree T. Cut off all the edges whose marked values are smaller than $\lambda$ to obtain sub-trees that represent clustered service modules. Different $\lambda$ may lead to different sub-trees partition. Then, the service modularization scheme under different threshold $\lambda$ can be acquired. In practice, $\lambda$ often takes value on the edge (dependency strength) of the graph. In fact, $\lambda$ is the coefficient indicating the module partition granularity. The bigger $\lambda$ is, the finer the partition granularity. The smaller $\lambda$ is, the more coarse the partition granularity.

## 4.3 Case Study: Modularizing Maintenance Service for Rotor of Compressor

In this section, to validate the feasibility and effectiveness of the proposed modularization method for PSS, it is applied into the maintenance service design of compressor rotor in company I, which mainly provides both compressor and the related industrial service. Rotor is an important component for the screw air compressor (see Fig. 4.2), and it directly determines the operation condition of the air compressor. Untimely rotor maintenance will lead to the air compressor vibration, compressor's inability to run at full speed. In the long run, the user of compressor has to replace the rotor with very high cost. In general, rotor maintenance can effectively prevent the failure caused by wear of gear and bearing, and keep the air compressor maintaining good running state. In this regard, maintenance can extend the service life of the rotor. However, the design of customized maintenance service for each individual customer takes higher cost and energy. So company I intends to adopt the modularization method of PSS to lower the design cost and enhance the design flexibility.

4.3 Case Study: Modularizing Maintenance Service for Rotor of Compressor   121

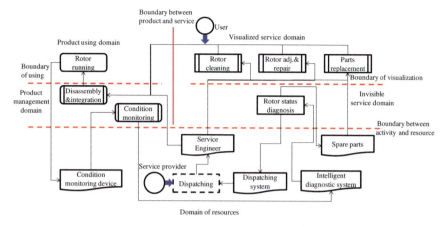

**Fig. 4.3** PSS blueprint for rotor maintenance service (Song et al. 2015)

## 4.3.1 Identification of Rotor Maintenance Service Components

Taking into account the company I's existing service processes and resources, the PSS blueprint is used to represent the whole scenario of rotor maintenance in Fig. 4.3. There are three types of customers-involved activities in the visualized service domain, i.e. rotor cleaning, rotor adjustment and repair, and parts replacement, all of which rely on a dispatching system to realize the service task assignment. The non-visualized service domain includes diagnosis of rotor operation status, which is mainly completed by an intelligent diagnostic system. The activity of rotor running in products using domain is mainly to achieve normal production of customer. Product management domain includes two types of service activities, i.e. rotor disassembly and integration test, and rotor condition monitoring. All the activities in both product domain and service domain require supports from resource domain. With the PSS blueprint, all the service components of the rotor maintenance can be identified, as shown in Table 4.5.

## 4.3.2 Correlation Analysis for Rotor Maintenance Service Components

The pair-wise comparison method is used to determine the weights of evaluation criteria for service components interdependency, which is not the focus of this Chapter. Thus, we do not discuss much about it here. Weight of function-based interdependency, weight of service flow-based interdependency and weight of resource-based interdependency are all shown in Table 4.6.

**Table 4.5** Service components of compressor rotor maintenance (Song et al. 2015)

| No. | Service component name | Type | Domain |
|---|---|---|---|
| C1 | Rotor cleaning | Activity | Visualized service domain |
| C2 | Rotor adjustment & repair | Activity | Visualized service domain |
| C3 | Parts replacement | Activity | Visualized service domain |
| C4 | Rotor status diagnosis | Activity | Invisible service domain |
| C5 | Rotor running | Activity | Product using domain |
| C6 | Disassembly & integration | Activity | Product management domain |
| C7 | Condition monitoring | Activity | Product management domain |
| C8 | Service engineer | Resource | Domain of resources |
| C9 | Spare parts | Resource | Domain of resources |
| C10 | Condition monitoring device | Resource | Domain of resources |
| C11 | Dispatching | Activity | Domain of resources |
| C12 | Intelligent diagnostic system | Resource | Domain of resources |
| C13 | Dispatching system | Resource | Domain of resources |

**Table 4.6** Pair-wise comparison matrix and weights of evaluation criteria (Song et al. 2015)

| | Function-based interdependency | Service flow-based interdependency | Resource-based interdependency | Weight |
|---|---|---|---|---|
| Function-based interdependency | 1 | 5 | 3 | $w_f = 0.637$ |
| Service flow-based interdependency | 0.2 | 1 | 0.333 | $w_p = 0.105$ |
| Resource-based interdependency | 0.333 | 3 | 1 | $w_r = 0.258$ |

Consistency ratio of pair-wise comparison matrix $CR = 0.03 < 0.1$, so it doesn't need to re-adjust the pair-wise comparison matrix.

According to the Tables 4.2, 4.3, and 4.4, the interdependencies of service components can be measured with the value of 0, 0.2, 0.4, 0.8 and 1, which are as shown in Tables 4.7, 4.8, and 4.9.

Comprehensive strength of interdependency of rotor service components is calculated based on the Formula (4.3) and the Formula (4.4). In this way, a comprehensive strength matrix of interdependency can be obtained (see Table 4.10).

4.3 Case Study: Modularizing Maintenance Service for Rotor of Compressor 123

Table 4.7 Strength matrix of function-based interdependency for rotor service components (Song et al. 2015)

|     | C1 | C2 | C3 | C4 | C5  | C6 | C7  | C8 | C9 | C10 | C11 | C12 | C13 |
|-----|----|----|----|----|-----|----|-----|----|----|-----|-----|-----|-----|
| C1  | 1  |    |    | 1  |     | 1  | 0.8 | 1  |    | 0.6 | 1   | 0.6 | 0.6 |
| C2  |    | 1  |    | 1  |     | 1  | 0.8 | 1  |    | 0.6 | 1   | 0.6 | 0.6 |
| C3  |    |    | 1  | 1  |     | 1  | 0.8 | 1  | 1  | 0.6 | 1   | 0.6 | 0.6 |
| C4  |    |    |    | 1  | 0.6 |    | 0.8 |    |    | 0.6 |     | 0.8 |     |
| C5  |    |    |    |    | 1   |    | 0.6 |    |    | 1   |     |     |     |
| C6  |    |    |    |    |     | 1  |     | 1  |    |     |     |     |     |
| C7  |    |    |    |    |     |    | 1   |    |    | 1   |     | 0.8 | 1   |
| C8  |    |    |    |    |     |    |     | 1  |    |     | 1   |     |     |
| C9  |    |    |    |    |     |    |     |    | 1  |     |     |     |     |
| C10 |    |    |    |    |     |    |     |    |    | 1   |     | 0.6 |     |
| C11 |    |    |    |    |     |    |     |    |    |     | 1   | 0.6 | 1   |
| C12 |    |    |    |    |     |    |     |    |    |     |     | 1   |     |
| C13 |    |    |    |    |     |    |     |    |    |     |     |     | 1   |

**Table 4.8** Strength matrix of service flow-based interdependency for service components (Song et al. 2015)

|     | C1 | C2 | C3 | C4 | C5 | C6  | C7 | C8 | C9  | C10 | C11 | C12 | C13 |
|-----|----|----|----|----|----|-----|----|----|-----|-----|-----|-----|-----|
| C1  | 1  |    |    |    |    | 1   |    | 1  |     |     |     |     |     |
| C2  |    | 1  |    |    |    | 1   |    | 1  |     |     |     |     |     |
| C3  |    |    | 1  |    |    | 1   |    | 1  | 1   |     |     |     |     |
| C4  |    |    |    | 1  |    |     |    |    | 0.8 |     |     | 1   | 0.6 |
| C5  |    |    |    |    | 1  | 0.8 | 1  |    |     | 1   |     |     |     |
| C6  |    |    |    |    |    | 1   |    | 1  |     | 1   |     |     |     |
| C7  |    |    |    |    |    |     | 1  |    |     |     |     | 1   |     |
| C8  |    |    |    |    |    |     |    | 1  | 1   |     | 1   |     |     |
| C9  |    |    |    |    |    |     |    |    |     |     |     |     |     |
| C10 |    |    |    |    |    |     |    |    |     |     |     | 1   |     |
| C11 |    |    |    |    |    |     |    |    |     |     | 1   |     | 1   |
| C12 |    |    |    |    |    |     |    |    |     |     |     | 1   |     |
| C13 |    |    |    |    |    |     |    |    |     |     |     |     | 1   |

4.3 Case Study: Modularizing Maintenance Service for Rotor of Compressor    125

Table 4.9 Strength matrix of resource-based interdependency for rotor service components (Song et al. 2015)

|     | C1 | C2 | C3 | C4 | C5 | C6  | C7 | C8 | C9 | C10 | C11 | C12 | C13 |
|-----|----|----|----|----|----|-----|----|----|----|-----|-----|-----|-----|
| C1  | 1  | 1  | 1  |    |    | 1   |    |    |    |     |     |     |     |
| C2  |    | 1  | 1  |    |    | 1   |    |    |    |     |     |     |     |
| C3  |    |    | 1  |    |    | 1   |    |    |    |     |     |     | 0.6 |
| C4  |    |    |    | 1  |    |     |    | 1  |    |     |     |     |     |
| C5  |    |    |    |    | 1  | 0.6 |    |    |    |     |     |     |     |
| C6  |    |    |    |    |    | 1   |    |    |    |     |     |     |     |
| C7  |    |    |    |    |    |     | 1  |    |    |     |     |     |     |
| C8  |    |    |    |    |    |     |    | 1  |    |     |     |     |     |
| C9  |    |    |    |    |    |     |    |    | 1  |     |     |     | 1   |
| C10 |    |    |    |    |    |     |    |    |    | 1   |     |     |     |
| C11 |    |    |    |    |    |     |    |    |    |     | 1   |     |     |
| C12 |    |    |    |    |    |     |    |    |    |     |     | 1   |     |
| C13 |    |    |    |    |    |     |    |    |    |     |     |     | 1   |

Table 4.10 Comprehensive strength matrix of interdependency of rotor service components (Song et al. 2015)

| | C1 | C2 | C3 | C4 | C5 | ... | C9 | C10 | C11 | C12 | C13 |
|---|---|---|---|---|---|---|---|---|---|---|---|
| C1 | 1.000 | 0.258 | 0.258 | 0.637 | | ... | | 0.382 | 0.637 | 0.382 | 0.382 |
| C2 | | 1.000 | 0.258 | 0.637 | | ... | | 0.382 | 0.637 | 0.382 | 0.382 |
| C3 | | | 1.000 | 0.637 | | ... | 0.742 | 0.382 | 0.637 | 0.382 | 0.382 |
| C4 | | | | 1.000 | 0.382 | ... | 0.084 | 0.382 | | 0.614 | 0.218 |
| C5 | | | | | 1.000 | ... | | 0.742 | | | |
| C6 | | | | | | ... | | | | | |
| C7 | | | | | | ... | | 0.742 | | 0.614 | |
| C8 | | | | | | ... | | | 0.742 | 0.000 | 0.637 |
| C9 | | | | | | ... | 1.000 | | | 0.382 | 0.258 |
| C10 | | | | | | ... | | 1.000 | | 0.487 | |
| C11 | | | | | | ... | | | 1.000 | | 0.742 |
| C12 | | | | | | ... | | | | 1.000 | |
| C13 | | | | | | ... | | | | | 1.000 |

### 4.3.3 Module Partition of Rotor Maintenance Service

Based on comprehensive strength matrix of interdependency, maximum spanning tree (as shown in Fig. 4.4) is obtained with the service module partition method proposed in Sect. 4.2.4.

Nodes in Fig. 4.4 are connected with undirected edge. The marked value on the edge is comprehensive strength matrix of interdependency between two service components. Different thresholds $\lambda$ are selected to truncate the edges of the maximum spanning tree in Fig. 4.4. Cut off all the edges whose marked values are smaller than $\lambda$ to obtain sub-trees representing different rotor service modules (see Table 4.11).

The designers can select the best service modularization scheme with some multi-criteria decision-making (MCDM) methods [e.g. concept selection method in Ayağ (2005) and Song et al. (2013)], which is not the focus of this research. So we don't discuss much about it here. Considering service flexibility, module cohesion, configuration complexity and module cost, the designers consider the modularization scheme 2 as the best rotor service partition scheme. That is, when the threshold $\lambda = 0.742$, {C1, C2, C3, C6, C8, C9, C11, C13}, {C5, C7, C10}, {C4}, {C12} is the best rotor service partition scheme (see Fig. 4.5).

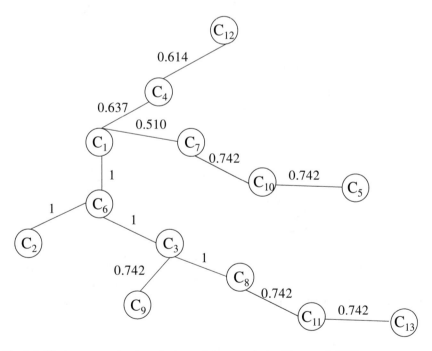

**Fig. 4.4** Maximum spanning tree of rotor maintenance service (Song et al. 2015)

**Table 4.11** Rotor service modularization scheme under different threshold of λ (Song et al. 2015)

| Service modularization scheme | | Modularization scheme 1 | Modularization scheme 2 | Modularization scheme 3 | Modularization scheme 4 |
|---|---|---|---|---|---|
| | | $\lambda = 1$ | $\lambda = 0.742$ | $\lambda = 0.637$ | $\lambda = 0.614$ |
| Service component distribution | Module 1 | C1, C2, C3, C6, C8 | C1, C2, C3, C6, C8, C9, C11, C13 | C1, C2, C3, C4, C6, C8, C9, C11, C13 | C1, C2, C3, C4, C6, C8, C9, C11, C12, C13 |
| | Module 2 | C4 | C5, C7, C10 | C5, C7, C10 | C5, C7, C10 |
| | Module 3 | C5 | C4 | C12 | / |
| | Module 4 | C7 | C12 | / | / |
| | Module 5 | C9 | / | / | / |
| | Module 6 | C10 | / | / | / |
| | Module 7 | C11 | / | / | / |
| | Module 8 | C12 | / | / | / |
| | Module 9 | C13 | / | / | / |

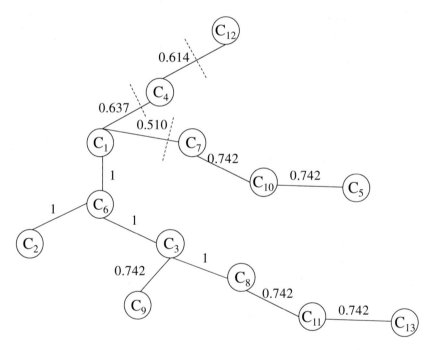

**Fig. 4.5** Best service modularization scheme for rotor service module (Song et al. 2015)

4.4 Comparisons and Discussion

**Table 4.12** Comparison between modified service blueprint and conventional service blueprint (Song et al. 2015)

| Method | Components of blueprints | Interaction presentation | Application scope |
|---|---|---|---|
| Conventional service blueprint | Customer actions, onstage/visible contact employee actions, backstage/invisible contact employee actions, support processes and physical evidence | It focuses on service operations and considers less about the special characteristics of product-service interaction | Traditional consumer services and other pure services, such as banking services, supermarkets services |
| Modified service blueprint | Product using activities, product management activities, visualized service activities, invisible service activities, and services resource | It integrates cooperation partners into the blueprint, and fully describes the complex interactions between various actors. It also charts interactions between users and manufacturer when simultaneously performing interactive tasks | Product extension services, such as repair, maintenance, overhaul, and spare parts, etc. |

## 4.4 Comparisons and Discussion

Compared with conventional service blueprint, modified service blueprint is more suitable for presenting structure of PSS. It can reflect the complex interactions (e.g. function-based interdependency and resource-based interdependency) between service components (see Table 4.12). PSS is an integrated offering including products, services, and infrastructures, not a single product or service. Although the conventional service blueprint provide the effective way to the conventional service representation, it is necessary to modify it to clearly represent the PSS. This is because the components of PSS are different from traditional offerings, many different actors exist, and the roles of products or services are different, etc.

Module partition based on maximum spanning tree is a graphical method which can visually show interdependency strengths between various service components. Therefore, it is easy to be used to modularize the PSS. Modular partition is the basis to realize the development of customized PSS. It enhances the ability of manufacturer to adapt to changes of requirement and reduce design costs. When failure happens in service delivery, modular PSS design facilitates manufacturer to quickly find the problematic service module. It is not necessary for the manufacturer check the whole service process, and thus it can help to take remedial measures timely to minimize potential losses.

In fact, the key to PSS modular design is module partition by clustering the service components. In the proposed PSS module partition approach based on fuzzy graph, $\lambda$ is introduced to partition the graph. The smaller $\lambda$ is, the more independencies are considered. Then the number of PSS modules is smaller and the number of service component in obtained PSS module is larger. The larger $\lambda$ is, the fewer independencies are considered. Then the number of PSS modules is bigger and the number of service component in module is smaller. For example, when $\lambda = 0.614$, the rotor maintenance service in the case is partitioned into 2 modules, that is, Module 1 {C1, C2, C3, C4, C6, C8, C9, C11, C12, C13} and Module 2 {C5, C7, C10}. However, when $\lambda = 1$, the whole rotor service in the case is partitioned into 9 modules, that is, Module 1 {C1, C2, C3, C6, C8}, Module 2{C4}, Module 3{C5}, Module 4{C7}, Module 5{C9}, Module 6{C10}, Module 7{C11}, Module 8{C12}, and Module 9{C13}. In this respect, $\lambda$ is the coefficient indicating the module partition granularity. The bigger $\lambda$ is, the finer the partition granularity. The smaller $\lambda$ is, the more coarse the partition granularity.

The PSS modularization approach has revealed the following advantages.

The proposed modified service blueprint considers interactions between physical product using behavior and other service operations. It can visually represent operations of the PSS and reveal the complex relationships between the service elements. This helps the designers to fully identify service components in PSS.

Correlation analysis for service components based on function, service flow and resource provides a new perspective to quantify interdependency between service components, which doesn't appear in previous literature. This is critical to PSS modularization, because it influnces the way service components bundled into modules.

Service module partition based on fuzzy graph can visually represent intangible service interactions in a tree graph, and simplify the representation of complex interactions between service components, thereby helping the designers to identify the possible modules.

# References

Ayağ, Z. (2005). A fuzzy AHP-based simulation approach to concept evaluation in a NPD environment. *IIE Transactions, 37*(9), 827–842.
Bondy, J. A., & Murty, U. S. R. (1976). *Graph theory with applications*. London: Macmillan.
Gershenson, J. K., Prasad, G. J., & Zhang, Y. (2003). Product modularity: Definitions and benefits. *Journal of Engineering Design, 14*(3), 295–313.
Hu, B. (2010). *Foundation of fuzzy theory*. Wuhan: Press of Wuhan University.
Rosenfeld, A. (1975). Fuzzy graphs. In *Fuzzy sets and their applications to cognitive and decision processes* (pp. 77–95).
Saaty, T. L. (2008). Decision making with the analytic hierarchy process. *International Journal of Services Sciences, 1*(1), 83–98.

# References

Sakao, T., Song, W., & Matschewsky, J. (2017). Creating service modules for customising product/service systems by extending DSM. *CIRP Ann, 66*(1), 21–24.

Song, W., Ming, X., & Wu, Z. (2013). An integrated rough number-based approach to design concept evaluation under subjective environments. *Journal of Engineering Design, 24*(5), 320–341.

Song, W., Wu, Z., Li, X., & Xu, Z. (2015). Modularizing product extension services: An approach based on modified service blueprint and fuzzy graph. *Computers & Industrial Engineering, 85,* 186–195.

Wang, C. S. (2009). Web-based modular interface geometries with constraints in assembly models. *Computers & Industrial Engineering, 56*(4), 1675–1686.

# Chapter 5
# Modular Configuration for Customizable PSS

Configuration is an efficient method for rapid PSS customization. However, the previous service configuration methods may produce a large number of feasible solutions, especially when there are more module instances or fewer configuration constraints. This will increase the burden of service solution screening and reduce the efficiency of service delivery. To solve this problem, Song and Chan (2015) develop a multi-objective optimization model for configuration of the PSS. The optimization model considers service performance, service cost and response time at the same time, and it is solved with non-dominated sorting genetic algorithm II (NSGA II) to obtain a set of optimal configuration solutions. In this way, the manufacturer can flexibly satisfy customer needs with a module-based PSS at lower cost. The PSS configuration optimization model is expected to enhance the customization ability of the service provider, because it can respond to customer requirements timely by providing the customized PSS. The rough TOPSIS approach developed by Song et al. (2013b) can then be used to evaluate and select the proper PSS concept from the configured PSS set.

## 5.1 Problem Formulation of PSS Configuration Optimization

The objective of PSS configuration is to find the suitable service portfolios based on various module instances that meet customer requirements (Shen et al. 2012). In this respect, the PSS configuration can be considered as a service module instantiation process driven by customer requirements. The modular configuration of PSS helps service providers to achieve customized service deliveries and timely responses to the market.

A service module is an independent service unit with standard interfaces. The service module includes different service components (e.g. service resources and

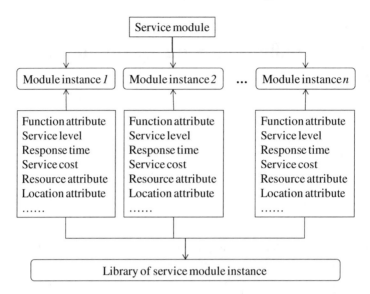

**Fig. 5.1** Relationship between service module, module instance and module attribute (Song and Chan 2015)

processes) arranged according to certain connection rules (Moon et al. 2010). The service module also has attributes to describe itself. The attributes consist of service level, service response, and service time, etc. Thus, these attributes can be used to identify and describe the service module. Different service module instances can be acquired by setting values for these attributes. For example, response time, diagnosis mode, and feedback mode comprise the attributes of a failure diagnosis service module. Different module instances can be obtained by setting values for the three attributes, that is, the remote failure diagnosis service module {response in half-hour, diagnose with intelligent system, online feedback} and the on-site failure diagnosis service module {response in 1 h, diagnose by experts, on-site feedback}. Figure 5.1 shows the connections among the service module, module instances and attributes. The service module can be categorized into mandatory service module (function modules to achieve an essential service) and optional service module (additional module to meet special customer requirements). Modular PSS configuration refers to the selection of appropriate service module instances to combine into complete PSS solutions under certain constraints (see Fig. 5.2).

Therefore, problem of service configuration optimization can be considered as the combinatorial optimization of service modules to fulfill the customer requirements. In this respect, PSS configuration can be regarded as the process of finding an optimal portfolio of module instance that satisfies pre-set constraints and targets. This is a typical problem of multi-objective combinatorial optimization. Based on the technical attributes derived from customer requirements, suitable service module instances are selected from the existing set of module instances. Combinatorial optimization of service module instances is then conduceted to obtain different optimized service solutions satisfying diverse customer's needs.

## 5.2 Methodology for PSS Configuration Optimization

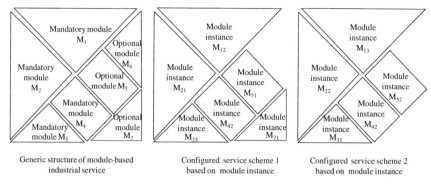

**Fig. 5.2** Schematic view of configuration for PSS (Song and Chan 2015)

## 5.2 Methodology for PSS Configuration Optimization

As shown in Fig. 5.3, in the PSS configuration, the service design team uses certain tools to elicit customer requirements of PSS, e.g. I-CAC analysis (industrial customer activity cycle analysis) (Song et al. 2013a), and they evaluate the relationships between customer requirements and service attributes. Then, they establish mappings between technical attributes and service module instances. A modular service solution set can then be obtained by retrieving appropriate module instances according to certain rules and constraints.

The specific steps for optimizing the service configuration are described as follows:

First, some tools such as service QFD (Song et al. 2014) are used to convert customer requirements into service attributes. This is because most customers do not have the professional knowledge and experience of PSS configuration. Thus, they may not be able to effectively choose the suitable service modules that meet their own needs.

Secondly, quantify the relationship between each service attribute and service module instance. Scores of 9, 3, 1, 0 are used to represent very strong, strong and weak and no correlation (Nilsson 1990) between service attributes and service module instances. Therefore, service attributes that represent customer requirement can be converted into configuration requirements of the service module instance.

Finally, construct PSS configuration optimization model based on service cost, service response time and module compatibility constraints. The optimized service solution should have the best service performance, shortest response time and lowest service cost.

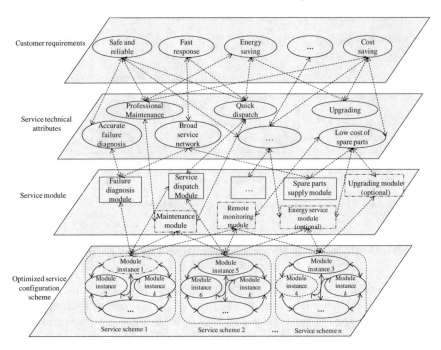

**Fig. 5.3** Relationship between different levels of configuration for PSS (Song and Chan 2015)

## 5.2.1 Modeling for PSS Configuration Optimization

**Step 1. Optimization objective of configured service performance**

Assume the customer requirement vector is $CR = [CR_1, CR_2, \ldots, CR_n]$, where $CR_i$ is the $i$th customer requirement ($i = 1, 2, \ldots, n$), $n$ is the number of customer requirements. Assume the weight vector of customer requirement $W_{CR} = [W_{cR1}, W_{cR2}, \ldots, W_{cRn}]$. The service attribute vector can be obtained as $TA = [TA_1, TA_2, \ldots, TA_P]$, the weight vector of the service attribute is denoted by $W_{TA}$, $W_{TA} = [W_{TA1}, W_{TA2}, \ldots, W_{TAP}]$, where $TA_l$ indicates the $l$th service attribute ($l = 1, 2, \ldots, p$), $p$ is the number of service attributes. The weight determination for customer requirements and service attributes is not the focus of this chapter, so it is not discussed here.

Assume there are totally $M_1$ mandatory service modules in the modular service scheme, and $C_{1j}$ indicates the number of module instances in the $j$th mandatory module ($j = 1, 2, \ldots, M_1$), and $M_{1jk}$ represents the $k$th instance of the $j$th module in mandatory service module. Then, the total number of module instances in the mandatory module is $\sum_{j=1}^{M_1} C_{1j}$. Assume there are totally $M_2$ optional service modules in the modular service scheme, and $C_{2j}$ indicates the number of module instances in the $j$th optional module ($j = 1, 2, \ldots, M_2$), $M_{2jk}$ represents the $k$th instance of the $j$th module in optional service module. Then, the total number of module instances in optional module is $\sum_{j=1}^{M_2} C_{2j}$.

## 5.2 Methodology for PSS Configuration Optimization

Based on the analysis above, the problem of modular configuration of PSS can be described as follows: select a module instance for each module in the $M_1$ mandatory service modules. After that, select $N$ ($N \leq M_2$) modules in the $M_2$ optional service modules, and then select an instance for each of the $N$ modules. Then all the module instances that constitute then PSS scheme can be obtained. Obviously, the total number of service module instances in PSS scheme is $M_1 + N$.

Therefore, the configured service can be represented as follows:

$$S = \{[I_{11}, I_{12}, \ldots, I_{1M_1}], [I_{21}, I_{22}, \ldots, I_{2N}]\}, \tag{5.1}$$

where $S$ is the configured service scheme; $I_{1k}$ are the $k$th instance of mandatory service module ($k = 1, 2, \ldots, M_1$); $I_{2k}$ are the $k$th instance of optional service module ($k = 1, 2, \ldots, N$).

The matrix of correlation between the service attributes and the service module instances can be represented as follows:

$$M_{I-TA} = \begin{bmatrix} M_{1,I-TA} \\ M_{2,I-TA} \end{bmatrix}_{\left(\sum_{i=1}^{2} \sum_{j=1}^{M_i} C_{ij}\right) \times p}, \tag{5.2}$$

where $M_{1,I-TA}$ is the matrix of correlation between the service attributes and the mandatory service module instances, and $M_{2,I-TA}$ is the matrix of correlation between the service attributes and the optional service module instances. Both of them are respectively represented as follows:

$$M_{1,I-TA} = \begin{bmatrix} \gamma_{1111} & \gamma_{1112} & \cdots & \gamma_{111p} \\ \gamma_{1121} & \gamma_{1122} & \cdots & \gamma_{112p} \\ \vdots & \vdots & \ddots & \vdots \\ \gamma_{11C_{11}1} & \gamma_{11C_{11}2} & \cdots & \gamma_{11C_{11}p} \\ \vdots & \vdots & \ddots & \vdots \\ \gamma_{1jC_{1j}1} & \gamma_{1jC_{1j}2} & \cdots & \gamma_{1jC_{1j}p} \\ \vdots & \vdots & \ddots & \vdots \\ \gamma_{1M_1C_{1M_1}1} & \gamma_{1M_1C_{1M_1}2} & \cdots & \gamma_{1M_1C_{1M_1}p} \end{bmatrix}_{\left(\sum_{j=1}^{M_1} C_{1j}\right) \times p}, \tag{5.3}$$

where $\gamma_{1jC_{1j}l}$ indicates the correlation between the $l$th service attribute and the $C_{1j}$th module instance of the $j$th module in the mandatory type of service module. $\gamma_{1jC_{1j}l}$ is judged by configuration engineers with rich experience and knowledge.

$$M_{2,I-TA} = \begin{bmatrix} \gamma_{2111} & \gamma_{2112} & \cdots & \gamma_{211p} \\ \gamma_{2121} & \gamma_{2122} & \cdots & \gamma_{212p} \\ \vdots & \vdots & \ddots & \vdots \\ \gamma_{21C_{21}1} & \gamma_{21C_{21}2} & \cdots & \gamma_{21C_{21}p} \\ \vdots & \vdots & \ddots & \vdots \\ \gamma_{2jC_{2j}1} & \gamma_{2jC_{2j}2} & \cdots & \gamma_{2jC_{2j}p} \\ \vdots & \vdots & \ddots & \vdots \\ \gamma_{2M_2C_{2M_2}1} & \gamma_{2M_2C_{2M_2}2} & \cdots & \gamma_{2M_2C_{2M_2}p} \end{bmatrix}_{\left(\sum_{j=1}^{M_2} C_{2j}\right) \times p}, \quad (5.4)$$

where $\gamma_{2jC_{2j}l}$ indicates the correlation between the $l$th service attribute and the $C_{2j}$th module instance of the $j$th module in the optional type of service module. $\gamma_{2jC_{2j}l}$ is also judged by configuration engineers with rich experience and knowledge.

Taking into account the weights of service attributes, the correlations between the service module instances and the service attributes can be expressed as follows:

$$D = M_{I-TA} \times W_{TA}$$
$$= \left( \sum_{l=1}^{p} (\gamma_{111l} w_{TA_l}), \sum_{l=1}^{p} (\gamma_{112l} w_{TA_l}), \ldots, \sum_{l=1}^{p} (\gamma_{ijkl} w_{TA_l}), \ldots, \sum_{l=1}^{p} (\gamma_{2M_2C_{2M_2}l} w_{TA_l}) \right), \quad (5.5)$$

where $\sum_{l=1}^{p} (\gamma_{ijkl} w_{TA_l})$ indicates comprehensive correlation between the service module instance $M_{ijk}$ and the vector of service attribute $TA$. It represents the service module instance's ability to meet the service attribute; $W_{TA}$ is the weight vector of the service attributes.

$\varepsilon_{ijk}$ is the binary decision variable that indicates the existence of service module instances in the process of optimizing service configuration. When $\varepsilon_{ijk} = 1$, the $k$th instance of the $j$th module in the $i$th type of services module (mandatory or optional) is selected; conversely, when $\varepsilon_{ijk} = 0$, the $k$th instance of the $j$th module in the $i$th type of services module (mandatory or optional) is not selected. Considering the correlation between the service module instance and the service attribute, and the existence of the service module instance in configuration, the optimization objective of comprehensive performance of the configured service can be expressed as

$$\max TAC = \sum_{i=1}^{2} \sum_{j=1}^{M_i} \sum_{k=1}^{C_{ij}} [\varepsilon_{ijk} \sum_{l=1}^{p} (\gamma_{ijkl} w_{TA_l})]. \quad (5.6)$$

The comprehensive performance of the configured service $TAC$ indicates the combination of the module instance's ability to meet the service attribute. The higher the value of $TAC$, the better the overall performance of the configured service.

## 5.2 Methodology for PSS Configuration Optimization

**Step 2. Optimization objectives of service cost and response time**

Construct cost matrix of PSS as follows:

$$Cost = (Cost_{111}, Cost_{112}, \ldots, Cost_{ijk}, \ldots, Cost_{2M_2C_{2M_2}}), \quad (5.7)$$

where $Cost_{ijk}$ indicates the service cost of the $k$th module instance of the $j$th module in the $i$th type of service module (mandatory or optional). Service cost is derived from the previous service operation data. The total cost of the configured service $Cost_s$ should be as small as possible. So optimization objectives of service cost can be obtained as follows:

$$\min Cost_S = \sum_{i=1}^{2} \sum_{j=1}^{M_i} \sum_{k=1}^{C_{ij}} (\varepsilon_{ijk} Cost_{ijk}). \quad (5.8)$$

Construct the response time matrix of the PSS as follows:

$$T = (T_{111}, T_{112}, \ldots, T_{ijk}, \ldots, T_{2M_2C_{2M_2}}), \quad (5.9)$$

where $T_{ijk}$ indicates the service response time of the $k$th module instance of the $j$th module in the $i$th type of service module (mandatory or optional). The total response time of the configured service $T_s$ should be as small as possible. So optimization objectives of service response time can be obtained as follows:

$$\min T_S = \sum_{i=1}^{2} \sum_{j=1}^{M_i} \sum_{k=1}^{C_{ij}} (\varepsilon_{ijk} T_{ijk}). \quad (5.10)$$

**Step 3. Constraints of service configuration optimization**

Service configuration based on modules needs to satisfy the following constraints:

$$\sum_{j=1}^{M_1} \varepsilon_{1jk} = M_1, \sum_{k=1}^{C_{ij}} \varepsilon_{ijk} = 1, i = 1 \quad (5.11)$$

$$\sum_{j=1}^{M_2} \varepsilon_{2jk} \leq M_2, \sum_{k=1}^{C_{ij}} \varepsilon_{ijk} \leq 1, i = 12 \quad (5.12)$$

The former part of constraint (5.11) ($\sum_{j=1}^{M_1} \varepsilon_{1jk} = M_1$) indicates that each of $M_1$ mandatory service modules must be selected in the configuration process, and the latter part of constraint (5.11) ($\sum_{k=1}^{C_{ij}} \varepsilon_{ijk} = 1, i = 1$) reveals that only one module instance can be chosen for the selected mandatory service module. The former part of constraint (5.12) ($\sum_{j=1}^{M_2} \varepsilon_{2jk} \leq M_2$) indicates that all the $M_2$ optional service modules are not necessarily to be selected in the configuration process, and the latter part of constraint (5.12) ($\sum_{k=1}^{C_{ij}} \varepsilon_{ijk} \leq 1$, $i = 2$) reveals that one instance can be selected at most for the optional service module.

Weight constraints of the service attributes can be expressed as follows:

$$\sum_{l=1}^{p} w_{TA_l} = 1, w_{TA_l} > 0. \tag{5.13}$$

Although some service contracts may be agreed based on strategic reasons, accepting the possibility of a loss, the total cost of the configured PSS is often expected to be less than the highest price that customer can afford in most cases. Then the customer may be willing to pay for the service, so the cost should satisfy the following constraint.

$$Cost_S(1+\alpha) \leq P_m, \tag{5.14}$$

where $Cost_S$ is cost of the configured service; $\alpha$ is pre-set expected profit margin by service provider; $P_m$ is the highest price of PSS that the customers can afford.

Besides, the total response time of the configured PSS must be less than the highest response time that customer can endure. So the service response time should satisfy the following constraint:

$$T_S \leq T_m, \tag{5.15}$$

where $T_S$ is response time of the configured service; $T_m$ is the highest response time that customer can endure.

In addition, not all of combinations of modules are rational in service configuration process, and there may be problem of mismatch. Therefore, the configuration of the PSS module should also satisfy certain combination rules as follows.

(a) Mutually inclusive: if the service module instance $M_{ijk}$ and service module instance $M_{i'j'k'}$ are mutually inclusive, and $M_{ijk}$ is not selected, then $M_{i'j'k'}$ cannot be selected for configuration either, and vice versa.

(b) Mutually exclusive: if the service module instance $M_{ijk}$ and service module instance $M_{i'j'k'}$ are mutually exclusive, then the configuration engineer can select $M_{ijk}$ but cannot choose $M_{i'j'k'}$, and vice versa; that is, the configuration engineer can only choose one of the two module instances.

## 5.2 Methodology for PSS Configuration Optimization

Configuration rules are mainly used to check the compatibility between modules in configuration process. Define a variable $Q_{ijk-i'j'k'}$ as follows:

$$Q_{ijk-i'j'k'} = \begin{cases} 1 & M_{ijk} \text{ and } M_{i'j'k'}, \text{ mutually inclusive} \\ -1 & M_{ijk} \text{ and } M_{i'j'k'}, \text{ mutually exclusive} \\ 0 & otherwise \end{cases} \quad (5.16)$$

where $i = 1, 2, j = 1, 2, \ldots, M_i, k = 1, 2, \ldots, C_{ij}$; $i' = 1, 2, j' = 1, 2, \ldots, M_i, k' = 1, 2, \ldots, C'_{ij}$. Then

$$\sum_{i'=1}^{2} \sum_{j'=1}^{M_i} \sum_{k'=1}^{C'_{ij}} Q_{ijk-i'j'k'} \varepsilon_{i'j'k'} = \begin{cases} 0 & \varepsilon_{ijk} = 0, Q_{ijk-i'j'k'} = 1 \\ 0 & \varepsilon_{ijk} = 1, Q_{ijk-i'j'k'} = -1 \end{cases}. \quad (5.17)$$

In the light of the above constraint, if a module instance is not selected ($\varepsilon_{ijk} = 0$), none of its mutually inclusive ($Q_{ijk-i'j'k'} = 1$) module instance should be selected. If a module instance is selected ($\varepsilon_{ijk} = 1$), its mutually exclusive ($Q_{ijk-i'j'k'} = -1$) module instance cannot be selected. These constraints are the basis of penalty in the evolutionary algorithm.

**Step 4. Generic model of PSS configuration optimization**

Service configuration optimization is a problem of multi-objective combinatorial optimization under multiple constraints. So it can be expressed with the following general model:

$$\begin{aligned} F(X) &= (TAC(X), Cost_s(X), T_s(X)), \\ \text{s.t. } g_a(X) &\geq 0, \quad a = 1, 2, \ldots, u; \\ h_b(X) &= 0, \quad b = 1, 2, \ldots, v; \\ X &= (\varepsilon_{111}, \varepsilon_{112}, \ldots, \varepsilon_{ijk}), \end{aligned} \quad (5.18)$$

where $TAC(X)$ is the benefit-based objective function for the efficiency, the larger the better, and $Cost_s(X)$ and $T_s(X)$ are cost-based objective functions, the smaller the better. $g_a(X)$ and $u$ are inequality constraints and the number of inequality constraints respectively, $h_b(X)$ and $v$ are equality constraints and the number of equality constraints respectively, $\varepsilon_{ijk}$ is 0–1 variable hat indicates whether the service module instance is selected or not.

According to the description above, the proposed configuration optimization model for PSS can be expressed as follows:

$$\begin{cases} F(X) = \{\max \sum_{i=1}^{2} \sum_{j=1}^{M_i} \sum_{k=1}^{C_{ij}} [\varepsilon_{ijk} \sum_{l=1}^{p} (\gamma_{ijkl} w_{TA_l})], \min \sum_{i=1}^{2} \sum_{j=1}^{M_i} \sum_{k=1}^{C_{ij}} (\varepsilon_{ijk} Cost_{ijk}), \min \sum_{i=1}^{2} \sum_{j=1}^{M_i} \sum_{k=1}^{C_{ij}} (\varepsilon_{ijk} T_{ijk})\} \\ s.t.\ Cost_S(1+\alpha) = P_m,\ T_S = T_m; \\ \sum_{j=1}^{M_1} \varepsilon_{1jk} = M_1, \sum_{j=1}^{M_2} \varepsilon_{2jk} = M_2; \\ \sum_{k=1}^{C_{ij}} \varepsilon_{ijk} = 1, i = 1; \sum_{k=1}^{C_{ij}} \varepsilon_{ijk} = 1, i = 2; \\ \sum_{l=1}^{p} w_{TA_l} = 1, w_{TA_l} > 0 \\ \sum_{i'=1}^{2} \sum_{j'=1}^{M_i} \sum_{k'=1}^{C'_{ij}} Q_{ijk-i'j'k'} \varepsilon_{i'j'k'} = \begin{cases} 0 & \varepsilon_{ijk} = 0,\ Q_{ijk-i'j'k'} = 1 \\ 0 & \varepsilon_{ijk} = 1,\ Q_{ijk-i'j'k'} = -1 \end{cases} \end{cases}$$

(5.19)

### 5.2.2 Problem-Solving Process Based on NSGA-II

Multi-objective GA appears to be suitable for PSS configuration considering its nature of multi-objectives and combination. NSGA-II is the underlying algorithm for PSS configuration, and it is derived from NSGA (non-dominated sorting genetic algorithm) that was developed by Deb et al. (2002). An overview of NSGA-II is described as follows.

NSGA can handle more complex and higher dimensional multi-objective problems. Srinivas and Deb (1994) considered that it could find more Pareto frontiers and kept diversity of the population in subsequent generations. However, NSGA has been criticized due to the requirement of assigning sharing parameter, complicacy of non-dominated sorting, and a lack of elitism (Deb et al. 2002). NSGA-II is expected to overcome the above problems. To simplify the process of computation, NSGA-II adopts fast non-dominated sorting method. Furthermore, the selection operator of NSGA is improved to build the mating pool through merging the populations of parent and offspring and choosing the best solutions of population size.

In this chapter, NSGA-II is used to solve multi-objective optimization of PSS configuration. For many problems of multi-objective optimization in the real world, there may be conflicts among optimization objectives. What we can obtain is a set of relative optimal solutions for different objectives, e.g. Pareto-optimal set. This is because no single optimal solution exists to satisfy all objectives. Figure 5.4 shows the algorithm process of NSGA-II.

Step 1: Firstly, a random parent population ($P_t$) with size of $N$ is created.
Step 2: Determine the non-dominant individuals, calculate crowding distance for each individual and perform non-dominated sorting of parent population and classify them into several fronts.
Step 3: Select individuals with binary tournament, and use operators of crossover and mutation to produce offspring population $O_t$;

## 5.2 Methodology for PSS Configuration Optimization

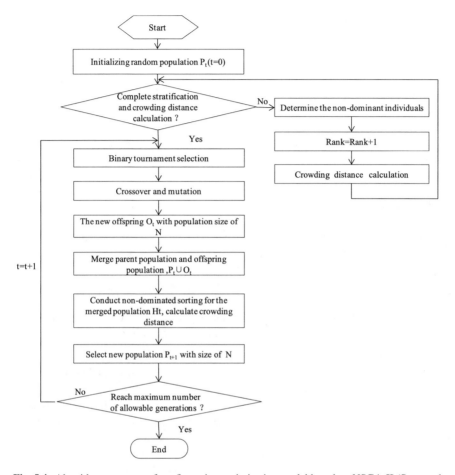

**Fig. 5.4** Algorithm processes of configuration optimization model based on NSGA-II (Song and Chan 2015)

Step 4: Combine the parent population $P_t$ and offspring population $O_t$ to generate population $H_t$ with size of $2N$;

Step 5: Perform fast non-dominated sorting for the population $H_t$, and calculate stratified crowding distance. Select $N$ individuals to form a new parent population $P_{t+1}$;

Step 6: Determine whether to reach the maximum allowable number of generation;

Step 7: If it doesn't reach the maximum allowable number of generation, make $t = t + 1$, and repeat steps (3)–(6) until the maximum allowable number of generations is reached.

Step 8: The algorithm ends if maximum allowable number of iterations is reached.

## 5.2.3 Case Study: Configuration Optimization for Elevator PSS

Elevator Company M is a well known manufacturer who offers different types of elevators such as passenger/freight elevator, hospital elevator, escalator, and elevator monitoring system. The growth rate of profit and revenue of new elevators in Company M gradually decreased because of intense competition in the industry. Company M decided to transform from a manufacturer to a service provider to find a sustainable business model. In order to ensure efficiency and effectiveness of elevator operation, it decided to provide customized elevator services. In this way, Company M wants to enhance its competitiveness in the elevator service market. The company offers elevator service including installation, maintenance, repair, remote monitoring, elevator upgrading and spare parts supply, etc. The elevator service modules and module instances are illustrated in Table 5.1. The designers and managers in Company M provide the data of cost and response time of each service module instance in Table 5.1.

The goal of elevator service configuration optimization is to find a suitable module instance combination to achieve relative optimum of overall service performance, service cost and response time. Considering requirements of company M and customer, the service configuration will also satisfy the following constraints:

- Company M's expected profit margin is 25%;
- The highest elevator service price that customer can afford is ¥300,000;
- The tolerable total response time of customer is 50 h;
- Mutually inclusive and exclusive constraints are as follows: If the first instance of repair service module ($M_{151}$) is chosen, the second instance of spare parts supply module ($M_{172}$) should not be chosen. If the fifth instance of refurbishment service module ($M_{225}$) is chosen, the first instance of energy saving module ($M_{211}$) should not be chosen. If the first instance of emergency repair module ($M_{161}$) is selected, the first instance of service planning module ($M_{1101}$) must be also selected. If the second instance of emergency repair module ($M_{162}$) is selected, the first instance of remote monitoring module ($M_{191}$) must be also selected.

Elevator service attributes are as follows: reasonable recommendations of elevator selection ($TA_1$), fast and professional installation ($TA_2$), broad coverage of condition monitoring ($TA_3$), convenient and accurate failure diagnosis ($TA_4$), professional and timely maintenance ($TA_5$), elevator operation training ($TA_6$), repair service of high standard ($TA_7$), low cost of spare parts ($TA_8$), wide coverage of service network ($TA_9$), quick dispatching for maintenance and repair ($TA_{10}$), 7d × 24 h emergency repair ($TA_{11}$), and elevator upgrading ($TA_{12}$). Matrix of relationships between service attributes and service module instances is shown in Table 5.3. The relationships are represented with scores of 0, 1, 3, and 9. Score of 0 represents no relationship, while score of 9 shows the strongest relationship between service attribute and service module instance. Weights of each service attribute are

## 5.2 Methodology for PSS Configuration Optimization

**Table 5.1** Service modules and module instances of passenger elevator (Song and Chan 2015)

| Service module name | Service module instance | Instance code | Cost | Response time | Module property |
|---|---|---|---|---|---|
| Knowledge support module of elevator service | Online knowledge support | $M_{111}$ | 1.25 | 0.3 | ▲ |
| | Remote knowledge support | $M_{112}$ | 1.54 | 0.3 | ▲ |
| | On-site knowledge training | $M_{113}$ | 2.55 | 1.5 | ▲ |
| Consulting module for elevator purchase | Expert advisory | $M_{121}$ | 0.50 | 3.5 | ▲ |
| | Self advisory with computer | $M_{122}$ | 0.30 | 0.2 | ▲ |
| Module of installation and commissioning | Remote installation guidance | $M_{131}$ | 1.25 | 8 | ▲ |
| | On-site installation guidance | $M_{132}$ | 0.62 | 16 | ▲ |
| | Installation and commissioning | $M_{133}$ | 2.50 | 8 | ▲ |
| Module of customer care | Regular telephone visit | $M_{141}$ | 1.55 | 0.5 | ▲ |
| | Random visit | $M_{142}$ | 0.96 | 6.2 | ▲ |
| | Visits based on complaints | $M_{143}$ | 1.24 | 5.5 | ▲ |
| Repair service module | Maintenance with original spare parts | $M_{151}$ | 1.53 | 3.5 | ▲ |
| | Maintenance with non-original spare parts | $M_{152}$ | 0.86 | 2.5 | ▲ |
| Emergency repair module | Collaborative emergency repair | $M_{161}$ | 0.66 | 0.2 | ▲ |
| | Independent emergency repair | $M_{162}$ | 1.50 | 0.3 | ▲ |
| Module of spare parts supply | One-stop spare parts supply | $M_{171}$ | 2.43 | 2.2 | ▲ |
| | Traditional spare parts supply | $M_{172}$ | 1.54 | 1.8 | ▲ |
| Maintenance module | Maintenance/semimonthly | $M_{181}$ | 2.56 | 3 | ▲ |
| | Maintenance/trimonthly | $M_{182}$ | 1.88 | 3 | ▲ |
| | Maintenance/biannual | $M_{183}$ | 0.86 | 3 | ▲ |
| Remote monitoring module | Basic condition monitoring | $M_{191}$ | 0.78 | 0.2 | ▲ |
| | Operation monitoring | $M_{192}$ | 1.25 | 0.3 | ▲ |

(continued)

**Table 5.1** (continued)

| Service module name | Service module instance | Instance code | Cost | Response time | Module property |
|---|---|---|---|---|---|
| Service planning module | Outsourced dispatching | $M_{1101}$ | 1.68 | 2.5 | ▲ |
|  | Dispatching of company M | $M_{1102}$ | 1.33 | 3.6 | ▲ |
| Energy saving module (optional) | Energy-saving benefit sharing | $M_{211}$ | 3.58 | 8 | △ |
|  | Energy management contract | $M_{212}$ | 5.16 | 8 | △ |
| Rehabilitation module (optional) | Decoration refurbishment | $M_{221}$ | 1.22 | 4 | △ |
|  | … | … | … | … | … |
|  | Elevator shaft upgrading | $M_{224}$ | 2.15 | 8 | △ |
|  | Intellectualized upgrading | $M_{225}$ | 3.35 | 6 | △ |
| Module of life cycle data analysis(optional) | Life cycle alert of component | $M_{231}$ | 0.64 | 0.5 | △ |
|  | Maintenance information inquiry and reporting | $M_{232}$ | 0.88 | 0.5 | △ |

*Note* Measuring unit of cost is ten thousand yuan, measuring unit of response time is hour; ▲ indicates mandatory service module, and △ indicate optional service module. Only part of data is listed here due to privacy restrictions and space limitation

calculated using the method proposed in Song et al. (2014). The weights of service attribute are also shown in Table 5.2.

Parameters for the NSGA-II algorithm are set as follows: population size for elevator service configuration optimization is 300, crossover probability is 0.9, mutation probability is 0.1, and evolution generation is 300. The optimization results are demonstrated in Figs. 5.5 and 5.6. As can be seen from Fig. 5.5, with the generations of algorithm iteration increases, the solution of elevator service configuration optimization mode gradually approaches the optimal solution. However, because objectives of service performance, service costs and response time are not consistent with each other, the final solution for elevator service configuration is not a single point but a solution set. Thus, a Pareto optimal solution set of the elevator service configuration can be obtained. Because the NSGA-II algorithm uses binary tournament selection strategy to keep diversity of the population, the Pareto solution set in Fig. 5.5 has a rational distribution.

Each point in Fig. 5.5 represents an optimized elevator service configuration scheme. The average curves of service performance, service cost and response time in the evolution process of 300 generations are respectively shown in Fig. 5.6. Obviously, after 30 generations' evolution, the averages of service performance, service

## 5.2 Methodology for PSS Configuration Optimization

**Table 5.2** Matrix of correlations between elevator service attributes and service module instances (Song and Chan 2015)

| Service attribute ($TA_i$) | $TA_1$ | $TA_2$ | $TA_3$ | $TA_4$ | $TA_5$ | $TA_6$ | $TA_7$ | $TA_8$ | $TA_9$ | $TA_{10}$ | $TA_{11}$ | $TA_{12}$ | $\sum y_{ijkl} w_{TAl}$ |
|---|---|---|---|---|---|---|---|---|---|---|---|---|---|
| Weight of $TA_i$ ($w_{TAi}$) | 0.0815 | 0.0834 | 0.0852 | 0.0826 | 0.0867 | 0.0827 | 0.0823 | 0.0829 | 0.0826 | 0.0829 | 0.0834 | 0.0839 | |
| $M_{111}$ | 3 | 3 | 3 | 9 | 1 | 3 | 3 | 3 | 3 | 3 | 9 | 3 | 3.8229 |
| $M_{112}$ | 3 | 3 | 1 | 3 | 1 | 1 | 3 | 3 | 3 | 3 | 3 | 1 | 2.3233 |
| $M_{113}$ | 9 | 9 | 1 | 9 | 3 | 3 | 9 | 1 | 1 | 1 | 1 | 3 | 4.1451 |
| $M_{121}$ | 9 | 3 | 0 | 3 | 0 | 3 | 3 | 0 | 0 | 3 | 3 | 3 | 2.4771 |
| $M_{122}$ | 3 | 1 | 0 | 1 | 0 | 3 | 1 | 0 | 0 | 1 | 3 | 1 | 1.1579 |
| $M_{131}$ | 0 | 9 | 3 | 0 | 0 | 0 | 1 | 0 | 3 | 9 | 0 | 1 | 2.1663 |
| $M_{132}$ | 0 | 3 | 1 | 0 | 0 | 0 | 1 | 0 | 1 | 1 | 0 | 3 | 0.8349 |
| $M_{133}$ | 0 | 9 | 1 | 0 | 0 | 0 | 3 | 0 | 1 | 1 | 0 | 3 | 1.4999 |
| $M_{141}$ | 3 | 0 | 0 | 3 | 3 | 0 | 3 | 0 | 3 | 3 | 1 | 0 | 1.5792 |
| $M_{142}$ | 1 | 0 | 0 | 1 | 1 | 0 | 1 | 0 | 1 | 1 | 1 | 0 | 0.582 |
| $M_{143}$ | 1 | 0 | 0 | 3 | 1 | 0 | 1 | 0 | 1 | 1 | 1 | 0 | 0.7472 |
| $M_{151}$ | 0 | 0 | 3 | 1 | 3 | 0 | 9 | 3 | 1 | 1 | 9 | 3 | 2.7555 |
| $M_{152}$ | 0 | 0 | 9 | 3 | 1 | 0 | 3 | 9 | 9 | 9 | 3 | 1 | 3.9179 |
| $M_{161}$ | 0 | 0 | 9 | 9 | 0 | 0 | 1 | 1 | 9 | 3 | 9 | 0 | 3.4181 |
| ⋮ | ⋮ | ⋮ | ⋮ | ⋮ | ⋮ | ⋮ | ⋮ | ⋮ | ⋮ | ⋮ | ⋮ | ⋮ | ⋮ |
| $M_{221}$ | 0 | 1 | 0 | 0 | 1 | 0 | 0 | 3 | 1 | 3 | 0 | 1 | 0.834 |
| $M_{222}$ | 1 | 1 | 0 | 0 | 3 | 0 | 0 | 1 | 0 | 0 | 0 | 9 | 1.263 |
| $M_{223}$ | 3 | 1 | 0 | 0 | 3 | 0 | 0 | 3 | 0 | 0 | 0 | 3 | 1.0884 |
| $M_{224}$ | 3 | 1 | 0 | 0 | 3 | 0 | 0 | 3 | 0 | 0 | 0 | 3 | 1.0884 |
| $M_{225}$ | 3 | 1 | 0 | 0 | 3 | 0 | 0 | 1 | 0 | 0 | 0 | 9 | 1.426 |
| $M_{231}$ | 0 | 1 | 9 | 3 | 3 | 0 | 1 | 9 | 0 | 3 | 1 | 9 | 3.2737 |
| $M_{232}$ | 0 | 1 | 3 | 1 | 9 | 0 | 1 | 3 | 0 | 0 | 3 | 3 | 2.0348 |

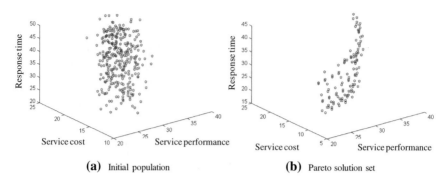

**Fig. 5.5** Initial population and Pareto solution set of elevator service concepts (Song and Chan 2015)

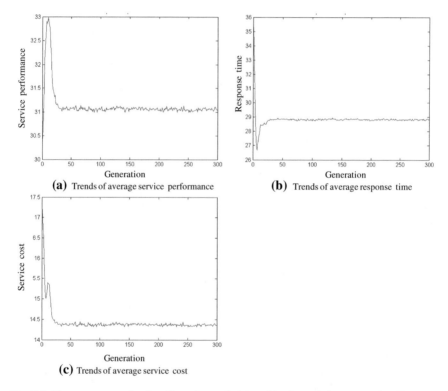

**Fig. 5.6** The average trends of configuration optimizing objectives of elevator service (Song and Chan 2015)

cost and response time in each generation become stable, which indicates that the algorithm of optimization function has better convergence.

Then, the service designers can select an optimized configured service scheme from the Pareto solution set for customers. The service configuration optimization

## 5.2 Methodology for PSS Configuration Optimization

**Table 5.3** The five recommended elevator service schemes (Song and Chan 2015)

| No. | Service module instance | Service performance | Service cost | Response time | Number of modules |
|---|---|---|---|---|---|
| A1 | $M_{113},M_{121},M_{131},M_{141},M_{152},$ $M_{161},M_{171},M_{181},M_{192},M_{1101},$ $M_{211},M_{224},M_{231}$ | 38.80 | 21.66 | 40.7 | 13 |
| A2 | $M_{111},M_{121},M_{131},M_{143},M_{152},$ $M_{161},M_{171},M_{181},M_{192},M_{1101},$ $M_{211},M_{221},M_{231}$ | 37.39 | 19.12 | 40.5 | 13 |
| A3 | $M_{111},M_{121},M_{131},M_{141},M_{152},$ $M_{161},M_{172},M_{181},M_{192},M_{1101},$ $M_{211},M_{231}$ | 35.39 | 17.32 | 31.1 | 12 |
| A4 | $M_{113},M_{121},M_{131},M_{141},M_{152},$ $M_{161},M_{171},M_{181},M_{192},M_{1101},$ $M_{211},M_{222},M_{231}$ | 38.97 | 21.94 | 38.7 | 13 |
| A5 | $M_{111},M_{122},M_{131},M_{141},M_{152},$ $M_{161},M_{171},M_{181},M_{192},M_{1101},$ $M_{212},M_{231}$ | 36.56 | 19.59 | 28.2 | 12 |

model can help to make more informed choices for designers by offering customized PSS for different customers, and it improves the efficiency of PSS design due to its quickly finding the optimized configured service from many feasible solutions.

In this case study, five service schemes are chosen based on customer preference for service performance, service cost and response time (see Table 5.3).

It can be seen from Table 5.3 that the five recommended elevator service schemes have their own advantages and disadvantages. For example, service scheme A1 has higher service performance (38.80) than that of service scheme A3 (35.39). However, A1 (40.7 h) responds relatively slower to customer requirements than A3 (31.1 h). Besides, the service scheme A1 also has higher service cost (21.66) than that of service scheme A3 (17.32). Similar situations also exist in other configured service schemes. This is because the proposed PSS configuration model considers three objectives at the same time (e.g. service performance, service cost and response time), which are in conflict with each other. There is no single best PSS solution but a set of valid optimal solutions exists. In other words, the solution set of elevator service configuration is Pareto-optimal.

In order to analyze the influence of service attribute's weights on the final optimal values (optimal performance, optimal cost, and optimal response time), a sensitivity analysis is conducted. The results of the sensitivity analysis are shown in Fig. 5.7. The results show that the optimal service performance is generally more sensitive to most of technical attributes' weights than optimal service cost and optimal response time. Specifically, "7d × 24 h emergency repair" ($TA_{11}$), "low cost of spare parts" ($TA_8$), and "convenient and accurate failure diagnosis" ($TA_4$) are the top three important factors affecting the optimal service performance (see Fig. 5.7a). The optimal service performance increases obviously as the three technical attributes' weights become larger, while it is generally independent of the weights of $TA_1$ ("reasonable recommendations of elevator selection") and $TA_{12}$ ("elevator upgrading"). The

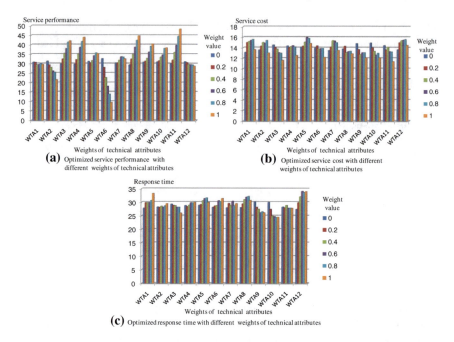

**Fig. 5.7** Sensitivity analysis (Song and Chan 2015)

optimal service cost decreases with the increase of the $TA_3$'s weight ("broad coverage of condition monitoring") (see Fig. 5.7b). It can be seen from the Fig. 5.7c that $TA_{10}$ ("quick dispatching for maintenance and repair") is an important factor for the optimal response time, because the optimal response time will gradually decline when $TA_{10}$ is given higher weights. The optimal response time is also generally independent of the weights of $TA_2$ ("fast and professional installation").

### 5.2.4 Comparisons and Discussion

To reveal the characteristics of the proposed method for PSS configuration optimization, comparisons are made between the proposed model and the method in Gonzalez-Zugasti and Otto (2000). Gonzalez-Zugasti and Otto (2000) combined different objectives into a single objective function and used GA to solve the optimization model. Different characteristics of the two methods are summarized as follows:

Firstly, the method used in Gonzalez-Zugasti and Otto (2000) only produce one optimal solution each time, while the proposed optimization method can provides a set of optimal solutions for customer selection. For example, in the case study of elevator service, only one solution is produced if use the method of Gonzalez-

## 5.2 Methodology for PSS Configuration Optimization

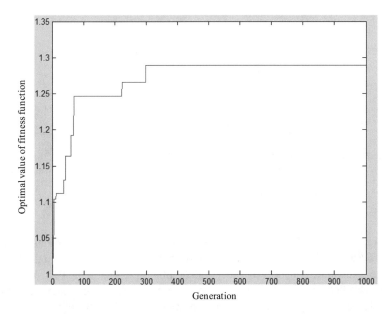

**Fig. 5.8** The optimal value of fitness function with the method in Gonzalez-Zugasti and Otto (2000) (Song and Chan 2015)

Zugasti and Otto (2000), then, the service module instance $M_{111}$, $M_{122}$, $M_{131}$, $M_{141}$, $M_{152}$, $M_{162}$, $M_{171}$, $M_{183}$, $M_{191}$, $M_{1101}$, $M_{211}$, $M_{222}$, and $M_{231}$ are selected to configure into a elevator service scheme. The optimal service performance, the optimal service cost and the optimal response time of the configured service scheme are 33.20, 19.11 and 34.20, respectively. However, the proposed configuration optimization method provides customers with different choices (a Pareto solution set), moreover, some optimal values are completely superior to that of the method in Gonzalez-Zugasti and Otto (2000). For example, the optimal service performance, the optimal service cost and the optimal response time of the elevator service scheme $A_3$ in Table 5.3 ($M_{111}$, $M_{121}$, $M_{131}$, $M_{141}$, $M_{152}$, $M_{161}$, $M_{172}$, $M_{181}$, $M_{192}$, $M_{1101}$, $M_{211}$, $M_{231}$) is 35.39, 17.32 and 31.10. The three optimal values are all superior to that of the method in Gonzalez-Zugasti and Otto (2000). This is because the method used in Gonzalez-Zugasti and Otto (2000) converts the three objectives (service performance, service cost, and response time) into a single objective by giving weights (0.33, 0.33, and 0.33) to them. The average trends of optimal value of fitness function by using the method in Gonzalez-Zugasti and Otto (2000) is shown in Fig. 5.8. On the contrary, the proposed configuration optimization method can simultaneously optimize different objective functions with the NSGA-II-based approach.

Secondly, there are different ways of solution searching between the method in Gonzalez-Zugasti and Otto (2000) and the proposed configuration optimization method for PSS. The entire population in the former method only evolves to a peak of non-inferior solution set, but the population in latter method evolves to the non-

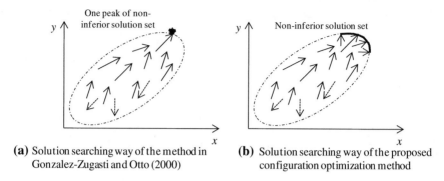

**Fig. 5.9** Different ways of solution searching (Song and Chan 2015)

inferior solution set (Pareto set). Therefore, the method used in Gonzalez-Zugasti and Otto (2000) can only get one solution for the muti-objective optimizing model. Figure 5.9 illustrates the different ways of solution searching in the two methods. In fact, the conflicting objective functions cannot always achieve optimal values simultaneously. In this respect, the final solution of the muti-objective optimizing model is a Pareto set, but not a single solution. To obtain other possible optimal values, the method in Gonzalez-Zugasti and Otto (2000) has to re-set the weights for the objective functions. For instance, when weights of objectives (service performance, service cost and response time) are given 0.3, 0.1 and 0.6, respectively, the corresponding optimal values then transform into 30.19, 13.48, and 24.10. So the module instance $M_{111}$, $M_{122}$, $M_{131}$, $M_{141}$, $M_{152}$, $M_{161}$, $M_{171}$, $M_{183}$, $M_{191}$, $M_{1101}$, $M_{221}$, and $M_{231}$ are selected to configure into an elevator service scheme.

Thirdly, the method used in Gonzalez-Zugasti and Otto (2000) belongs to the category of "decision before solving", while the configuration optimization method in this chapter is in the category of "decision after solving". The former firstly uses some approaches (e.g. weighted sum method) to convert the problem of multi-objective optimization into a single objective optimization problem, and then, it uses the genetic algorithm to solve the model to get one optimal solution. The method has lower computation load, but it is difficult for decision makers to make tradeoff between conflicting objective functions, because much information is required. However, the method in this chapter firstly searches for the possible solution set that meet requirements of different objective functions. Then, decision makers can select the solutions in the light of their actual situation.

In fact, the proposed multi-objective optimization model provides a tool to satisfy the customer's requirements under certain constraints (service cost, service response time, etc.). This model considers both the manufacturing service provider's capability and customer's 'pain points' (e.g. response time and service price). The Pareto solution sets provide a wider choice for customer. Each Pareto solution represents a satisfying service scheme. Different with the traditional product, the product-related service (e.g. repair and maintenance) is consumed frequently. Moreover, the customer has different requirements at different times due to the change of actual product using

## 5.2 Methodology for PSS Configuration Optimization

conditions. Thus, a wider choice of service solutions would be helpful for different customers, because customers can select the service solution from the Pareto solution sets according to their actual preferences.

To sum up, the proposed method reveals the following features:

The optimization model of service configuration can help designers to effectively and quickly find the optimized service solutions satisfying certain constraints from a large number of feasible solutions. In this respect, it enhances the efficiency of PSS design.

Compared with the conventional configuration model with a single optimization objective, the proposed model comprehensively considers service performance, service cost and response time as optimization objectives, and it can provide a set of optimized service solutions that well balance the multiple objectives of stakeholders.

NSGA-II algorithm based solution avoids unnecessary subjectivity in the process of converting the multi-objective optimization model into a single objective optimization model.

The optimization model of PSS configuration helps service providers to improve their capability to quickly deliver customized service at lower cost, which enhances customer satisfaction and customer value.

## 5.3 Design Concept Selection Under Subjective Environments

For the success of product/service development, one of the most key strageties is identified as concept evaluation. This is because that it has a significant influence on the downstream development activities. But, assessing design concept involves subjective and vague information. To deal with this problem, a new decision tool to select design concepts is developed by Song et al. (2013b). It includes two phases: the calculation of evaluation criteria weights and the selection of the most appropriate concept. These stages are composed of a hybrid approach based on a rough group analytic hierarchy process (AHP) method and a rough group technique for order performance by similarity to ideal solution (TOPSIS) method. The novel approach integrates the strength of rough number in handling vagueness, the advantage of AHP in hierarchy evaluation and the merit of TOPSIS in modeling multi-criteria decision making.

### 5.3.1 Preliminaries

A new concept of rough number is proposed by Zhai et al. (2008), which can quantify experts' vagueness based on the basic principles of rough sets. The lower limit and the upper limit of a rough number indicate its boundary, which is determined by the original data without the requirement for extra information (Khoo et al. 1999; Zhai et al. 2008). Experts' true perceptions can be better captured by rough numbers. According to Zhai et al. (2009c), the definition of rough number is presented as follows.

Assume that $U$ is the universe containing all the objects, and there is a set of $n$ classes of human ideas, $R = \{C_1, C_2, \ldots, C_n\}$, ordered in the manner of $C_1 < C_2 < \ldots < C_n$. $Y$ is an arbitrary objects of $U$, then the lower approximation of $C_i$, upper approximation of $C_i$, and boundary region are defined as:

$$\text{Lower approximation}: \underline{Apr}(C_i) = \cup\{Y \in U/R(Y) \leq C_i\} \quad (5.20)$$

$$\text{Upper approximation}: \overline{Apr}(C_i) = \cup\{Y \in U/R(Y) \geq C_i\} \quad (5.21)$$

$$\text{Boundary region}: Bnd(C_i) = \cup\{Y \in U/R(Y) \neq C_i\}$$
$$= \{Y \in U/R(Y) > C_i\} \cup \{Y \in U/R(Y) < C_i\} \quad (5.22)$$

Thus the class, $C_i$, can be represented by a rough number which is defined by its lower limit $\underline{\lim}(C_i)$ and upper limit $\overline{\lim}(C_i)$, where

$$\underline{\lim}(C_i) = \frac{1}{M_L} \sum R(Y) | Y \in \underline{Apr}(C_i) \quad (5.23)$$

$$\overline{\lim}(C_i) = \frac{1}{M_U} \sum R(Y) | Y \in \overline{Apr}(C_i) \quad (5.24)$$

$M_L$ and $M_U$ are the number of objects included in the lower approximation and upper approximation of $C_i$, respectively.

The human ideas can be represented by rough numbers on the basis of lower limit $\left(\underline{\lim}(C_i)\right)$ and upper limit $\left(\overline{\lim}(C_i)\right)$ that are referred to as the mean of elements in the lower approximation and upper approximation respectively. In this regard, the interval of boundary region denotes the degree of preciseness. A rough number with a larger interval of boundary region is interpreted as vaguer or less precise one. The human idea and interval of boundary region are expressed by following equations:

$$\text{Rough number}: RN(C_i) = [\overline{\lim}(C_i), \underline{\lim}(C_i)] \quad (5.25)$$

$$\text{Interval of boundary region}: IBR(C_i) = \overline{\lim}(C_i) - \underline{\lim}(C_i) \quad (5.26)$$

The arithmetic operations of interval analysis can be applied to rough numbers (Zhai et al. 2010). If $RN_1 = (L_1, U_1)$ and $RN_2 = (L_2, U_2)$ are two rough numbers and $k$ is a nonzero constant, then the arithmetic operations are given by:

$$RN_1 + RN_2 = (L_1, U_1) + (L_2, U_2) = (L_1 + L_2, U_1 + U_2) \quad (5.27)$$

$$RN_1 \times k = (L_1, U_1) \times k = (kL_1, kU_1) \quad (5.28)$$

$$RN_1 \times RN_2 = (L_1, U_1) \times (L_2, U_2) = (L_1 \times L_2, U_1 \times U_2) \quad (5.29)$$

## 5.3 Design Concept Selection Under Subjective Environments

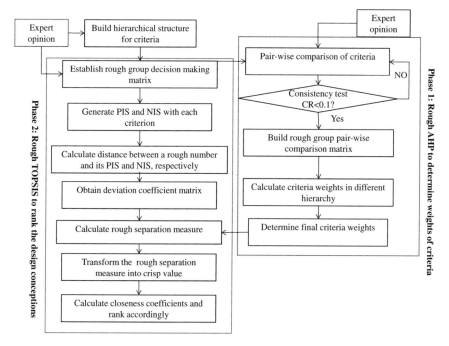

**Fig. 5.10** The proposed concept evaluation framework using Rough AHP-Rough TOPSIS (Song et al. 2013b)

### 5.3.2 The Method for Design Concept Selection

The AHP method is an effective approach to evaluate multiple-criteria alternatives with subjective and vague information, the TOPSIS method is one of the well-known outranking approaches for decision-making and can be easily adopted by practitioners to rank alternatives, and rough number concept is an efficient mechanism for subjectivity manipulation. In this section, the rough number is integrated into the AHP and TOPSIS methods to assess concepts in uncertain environment. The developed approach includes two consequent phases as shown in Fig. 5.10. Firstly, evaluation criteria's weights are determined by constructing a rough AHP model. Secondly, the design concepts are evaluated by proposing an extended TOPSIS model based on rough number.

**Phase I: Evaluation criteria weights determination using Rough AHP approach**

(1) Construct a hierarchical structure for evaluation criteria. The criteria are decomposed from the first level to the second level and from second level to third level, etc. Thus, we can obtain a hierarchical structure for evaluation criteria.

(2) Conduct AHP survey to obtain group decision matrix. Invite expert team to make pair-wise comparisons of criteria importance to obtain weights evaluation

**Table 5.4** Random index $RI(n)$ (Saaty 1977)

| Dimension | 1 | 2 | 3 | 4 | 5 | 6 | 7 | 8 | 9 |
|---|---|---|---|---|---|---|---|---|---|
| RI | 0 | 0 | 0.58 | 0.9 | 1.12 | 1.24 | 1.32 | 1.41 | 1.45 |

data matrix. The pair-wise comparison matrix $D_k$ provided by the $k$th expert can be described as follows:

$$D_k = \begin{bmatrix} 1 & r_{12}^k & \cdots & r_{1m}^k \\ r_{21}^k & 1 & \cdots & r_{2m}^k \\ \vdots & \vdots & \ddots & \vdots \\ r_{m1}^k & r_{m2}^k & \cdots & 1 \end{bmatrix} \quad (5.30)$$

where $r_{ij}^k$ is the $k$th expert's judgment value for the $i$th criterion importance compared with the $j$th criterion.

It is necessary for testing pair-wise comparison matrix consistency. Consistency test can be conducted as follows.

$$CI = \frac{\lambda_{\max} - n}{n - 1} \quad (5.31)$$

$$CR^* = \left(\frac{CI}{RI(n)}\right), \quad (5.32)$$

$CI$ is consistency index, and $\lambda_{\max}$ is the largest eigenvalue of matrix $D_k$, $n$ is the dimension of the matrix $D_k$. $CR^*$ is consistency ratio, and $RI(n)$ is random index depending on the dimension of the matrix (see Table 5.4).

When $CR^* < 0.1$, pair-wise comparison matrix pass the consistency test, experts judgments are in consistency and acceptable. While $CR^* > 0.1$, experts need to adjust their judgments until they pass the consistency test.

After the consistency test, expert team then builds group decision matrix $\tilde{D}$ as follows:

$$\tilde{D} = \begin{bmatrix} 1 & \tilde{r}_{12} & \cdots & \tilde{r}_{1m} \\ \tilde{r}_{21} & 1 & \cdots & \tilde{r}_{2m} \\ \vdots & \vdots & \ddots & \vdots \\ \tilde{r}_{m1} & \tilde{r}_{m2} & \cdots & 1 \end{bmatrix} \quad (5.33)$$

where $\tilde{r}_{ij} = \{r_{ij}^1, r_{ij}^2, \cdots, r_{ij}^m\}$

## 5.3 Design Concept Selection Under Subjective Environments

(3) Transform the element $\tilde{r}_{ij}$ in group decision matrix $\tilde{D}$ into rough number form to obtain rough group decision-making matrix R. We can get rough number form $RN(r_{ij}^k)$ of $\tilde{r}_{ij}$ using Eq. (5.20)–(5.25).

$$RN(r_{ij}^k) = [r_{ij}^{kL}, r_{ij}^{kU}] \tag{5.34}$$

$r_{ij}^{kL}$ and $r_{ij}^{kU}$ are the lower limit and upper limit of rough number $RN(r_{ij}^k)$ in the $k$th pair-wise comparison matrix.

Thus, we can get rough sequence $RN(\tilde{r}_{ij})$,

$$RN(\tilde{r}_{ij}) = \{[r_{ij}^{1L}, r_{ij}^{1U}], [r_{ij}^{2L}, r_{ij}^{2U}], \ldots, [r_{ij}^{mL}, r_{ij}^{mU}]\} \tag{5.35}$$

The average rough interval $\overline{RN(\tilde{r}_{ij})}$ can be obtained by using rough computation principles (5.27)–(5.29):

$$\overline{RN(\tilde{r}_{ij})} = [r_{ij}^L, r_{ij}^U] \tag{5.36}$$

$$r_{ij}^L = (r_{ij}^{1L} + r_{ij}^{2L} + \cdots + r_{ij}^{mL})/m \tag{5.37}$$

$$r_{ij}^U = (r_{ij}^{1U} + r_{ij}^{2U} + \cdots + r_{ij}^{mU})/m \tag{5.38}$$

$r_{ij}^L$ and $r_{ij}^U$ are lower limit and upper limit of rough number $[r_{ij}^L, r_{ij}^U]$ respectively. Then we can get rough group decision matrix R as follows:

$$R = \begin{bmatrix} [1,1] & [r_{12}^L, r_{12}^U] & \cdots & [r_{1n}^L, r_{1m}^U] \\ [r_{21}^L, r_{21}^U] & [1,1] & \cdots & [r_{2m}^L, r_{2m}^U] \\ \vdots & \vdots & \ddots & \vdots \\ [r_{m1}^L, r_{m1}^U] & [r_{m2}^L, r_{m2}^U] & \cdots & [1,1] \end{bmatrix} \tag{5.39}$$

(4) Calculate the rough weight $W_i$ of each criterion in different hierarchy using the following equation.

$$W_i = [\sqrt[m]{\prod_{i=1}^m r_{ij}^L}, \sqrt[m]{\prod_{i=1}^m r_{ij}^U}] \tag{5.40}$$

$i = 1, 2, \ldots, m$

In the same way, we can get weights for other criteria in any other hierarchies.

Finally, each criterion's overall weight is calculated using multiplication synthesis method from top level to bottom level.

## Phase II: Concept evaluation with Rough TOPSIS

(1) Establish decision-making matrixes by identifying alternatives with respect to each criterion, and transform it into rough number form according to the Formulas (5.20)–(5.25). Assume that there are $m$ data sequences represented in the form of rough numbers (intervals) and each data sequence is evaluated by $n$ criteria. The data sequences would compose the following matrix $M$:

$$M = \begin{bmatrix} [x_{11}^L, x_{11}^U] & [x_{12}^L, x_{12}^U] & \cdots & [x_{1n}^L, x_{1n}^U] \\ [x_{21}^L, x_{21}^U] & [x_{22}^L, x_{22}^U] & \cdots & [x_{2n}^L, x_{2n}^U] \\ \vdots & \vdots & \ddots & \vdots \\ [x_{m1}^L, x_{m1}^U] & [x_{m2}^L, x_{m2}^U] & \cdots & [x_{mn}^L, x_{mn}^U] \end{bmatrix} \quad (5.41)$$

$[x_{ij}^L, x_{ij}^U]$ represents a rough number, and $x_{ij}^L, x_{ij}^U$ are the lower and upper limits respectively, $i = 1, 2, \ldots, m, j = 0.1, 2, \ldots, m$.

(2) Obtain the Positive Ideal Solution (PIS) and Negative Ideal Solution (NIS) based on the characteristic of each criterion. Apparently, for benefit criterion, its PIS and the NIS are the largest and the lowest value, respectively. Thus, the largest upper limit of all the rough numbers that this criterion takes is selected as its PIS value, and the lowest lower limit of all the rough numbers that the criterion takes is selected as its NIS value. For cost criterion, on the contrary, the largest upper limit of all the rough numbers that this criterion takes is selected as its NIS value, and the lowest lower limit of all the rough numbers that the criterion takes is selected as its PIS value.

$$x^+(j) = \{\max_{i=1}^m (x_{ij}^U), \text{ if } j \in B; \min_{i=1}^m (x_{ij}^L), \text{ if } j \in C\},$$

$$x^-(j) = \{\min_{i=1}^m (x_{ij}^L), \text{ if } j \in B; \max_{i=1}^m (x_{ij}^U), \text{ if } j \in C\}. \quad (5.42)$$

where $x^+(j)$ and $x^-(j)$ are PIS and NIS value with respect to criterion $j$. $B$ and $C$ represent benefit criterion and cost criterion respectively.

(3) Compute the deviation coefficient based on the characteristic of each criterion: benefit criterion, cost criterion. The deviation coefficient is essentially a measure to depict the distance from a rough number to its PIS and NIS values. It is still a rough number in the form of an interval bound by its lower and upper limits.

The deviation coefficient (in the form of rough number) is calculated using the distance between the rough number and its PIS and NIS value as follows.

$$\begin{aligned} d_{ij}^{+L} &= x^+(j) - x_{ij}^U = \max_{i=1}^m (x_{ij}^U) - x_{ij}^U, \quad \text{if } j \in B, \\ d_{ij}^{+U} &= x^+(j) - x_{ij}^L = \max_{i=1}^m (x_{ij}^U) - x_{ij}^L, \quad \text{if } j \in B. \end{aligned} \quad (5.43)$$

## 5.3 Design Concept Selection Under Subjective Environments

$$d_{ij}^{+L} = x_{ij}^{L} - x^{+}(j) = x_{ij}^{L} - \min_{i=1}^{m}(x_{ij}^{L}), \quad \text{if } j \in C,$$
$$d_{ij}^{+U} = x_{ij}^{U} - x^{+}(j) = x_{ij}^{U} - \min_{i=1}^{m}(x_{ij}^{L}), \quad \text{if } j \in C. \quad (5.44)$$

$[d_{ij}^{+L}, d_{ij}^{+U}]$ represents the distance between a rough number and its PIS (also is a rough number). $d_{ij}^{+L}$ and $d_{ij}^{+U}$ represent the lower and upper limits respectively.

$$d_{ij}^{-L} = x_{ij}^{L} - x^{-}(j) = x_{ij}^{L} - \min_{i=1}^{m}(x_{ij}^{L}), \quad \text{if } j \in B,$$
$$d_{ij}^{-U} = x_{ij}^{U} - x^{-}(j) = x_{ij}^{U} - \min_{i=1}^{m}(x_{ij}^{L}), \quad \text{if } j \in B. \quad (5.45)$$
$$d_{ij}^{-L} = x^{-}(j) - x_{ij}^{U} = \max_{i=1}^{m}(x_{ij}^{U}) - x_{ij}^{U}, \quad \text{if } j \in C,$$
$$d_{ij}^{-U} = x^{-}(j) - x_{ij}^{L} = \max_{i=1}^{m}(x_{ij}^{U}) - x_{ij}^{L}, \quad \text{if } j \in C. \quad (5.46)$$

$[d_{ij}^{-L}, d_{ij}^{-U}]$ represents the distance between a rough number and its NIS (also is a rough number). $d_{ij}^{-L}$ and $d_{ij}^{-U}$ represent the lower and upper limits respectively.

Next, we can establish the deviation coefficient matrix $d^{+}$ and $d^{-}$ as follows:

$$d^{+} = \begin{bmatrix} [d_{11}^{+L}, d_{11}^{+U}] & [d_{12}^{+L}, d_{12}^{+U}] & \cdots & [d_{1n}^{+L}, d_{1n}^{+U}] \\ [d_{21}^{+L}, d_{21}^{+U}] & [d_{22}^{+L}, d_{22}^{+U}] & \cdots & [d_{2n}^{+L}, d_{2n}^{+U}] \\ \vdots & \vdots & \ddots & \vdots \\ [d_{m1}^{+L}, d_{m1}^{+U}] & [d_{m2}^{+L}, d_{m2}^{+U}] & \cdots & [d_{mn}^{+L}, d_{mn}^{+U}] \end{bmatrix} \quad (5.47)$$

$$d^{-} = \begin{bmatrix} [d_{11}^{-L}, d_{11}^{-U}] & [d_{12}^{-L}, d_{12}^{-U}] & \cdots & [d_{1n}^{-L}, d_{1n}^{-U}] \\ [d_{21}^{-L}, d_{21}^{-U}] & [d_{22}^{-L}, d_{22}^{-U}] & \cdots & [d_{2n}^{-L}, d_{2n}^{-U}] \\ \vdots & \vdots & \ddots & \vdots \\ [d_{m1}^{-L}, d_{m1}^{-U}] & [d_{m2}^{-L}, d_{m2}^{-U}] & \cdots & [d_{mn}^{-L}, d_{mn}^{-U}] \end{bmatrix} \quad (5.48)$$

Normalize the deviation coefficients of alternatives with respect to each criterion as follows:

$$d_{ij}^{+'L} = \frac{d_{ij}^{+L}}{\max_{i=1}^{m}\{\max[d_{ij}^{+L}, d_{ij}^{+U}]\}}, \quad d_{ij}^{+'U} = \frac{d_{ij}^{+U}}{\max_{i=1}^{m}\{\max[d_{ij}^{+L}, d_{ij}^{+U}]\}} \quad (5.49)$$

$$d_{ij}^{-'L} = \frac{d_{ij}^{-L}}{\max_{i=1}^{m}\{\max[d_{ij}^{-L}, d_{ij}^{-U}]\}}, \quad d_{ij}^{-'U} = \frac{d_{ij}^{-U}}{\max_{i=1}^{m}\{\max[d_{ij}^{-L}, d_{ij}^{-U}]\}} \quad (5.50)$$

$d_{ij}^{+'L}$ and $d_{ij}^{+'U}$ represent the lower and upper limits of normalized deviation coefficients between a rough number and PIS. $d_{ij}^{-'L}$ and $d_{ij}^{-'U}$ represent the lower and upper limits of normalized deviation coefficients between a rough number and NIS. Then we can obtain the normalized deviation coefficient matrix $d^{+'}$ and $d^{-'}$ as follows:

$$d^{+'} = \begin{bmatrix} [d_{11}^{+'L}, d_{11}^{+'U}] & [d_{12}^{+'L}, d_{12}^{+'U}] & \cdots & [d_{1n}^{+'L}, d_{1n}^{+'U}] \\ [d_{21}^{+'L}, d_{21}^{+'U}] & [d_{22}^{+'L}, d_{22}^{+'U}] & \cdots & [d_{2n}^{+'L}, d_{2n}^{+'U}] \\ \vdots & \vdots & \ddots & \vdots \\ [d_{m1}^{+'L}, d_{m1}^{+'U}] & [d_{m2}^{+'L}, d_{m2}^{+'U}] & \cdots & [d_{mn}^{+'L}, d_{mn}^{+'U}] \end{bmatrix} \quad (5.51)$$

$$d^{-'} = \begin{bmatrix} [d_{11}^{-'L}, d_{11}^{-'U}] & [d_{12}^{-'L}, d_{12}^{-'U}] & \cdots & [d_{1n}^{-'L}, d_{1n}^{-'U}] \\ [d_{21}^{-'L}, d_{21}^{-'U}] & [d_{22}^{-'L}, d_{22}^{-'U}] & \cdots & [d_{2n}^{-'L}, d_{2n}^{-'U}] \\ \vdots & \vdots & \ddots & \vdots \\ [d_{m1}^{-'L}, d_{m1}^{-'U}] & [d_{m2}^{-'L}, d_{m2}^{-'U}] & \cdots & [d_{mn}^{-'L}, d_{mn}^{-'U}] \end{bmatrix} \quad (5.52)$$

(4) Calculate the separation measure $S_i^+$ and $S_i^-$ (weighted normalized deviation) of each alternative. Basically, the separation measure $S_i^+$ and $S_i^-$ are defined to indicate the dissimilarity of a data sequence from its PIS and NIS value, which is represented in the form of rough numbers. The separation measure is calculated as follows.

$$S_i^+ = [S_i^{+L}, S_i^{+U}] = \sum_{j=1}^{n} [w_j \times d_{ij}^{+'}] \quad (5.53)$$

$$S_i^- = [S_i^{-L}, S_i^{-U}] = \sum_{j=1}^{n} [w_j \times d_{ij}^{-'}] \quad (5.54)$$

$S_i^+$ and $S_i^-$ represent weighted normalized deviation of alternative $i$ from its PIS and NIS value respectively. $w_j$ is weight of the *j*th evaluation criterion obtained from Rough AHP method in 3.1.

(5) In this step, optimistic indicator $\alpha$ ($0 \leq \alpha \leq 1$) is introduced to transform the separation measure $S_i^+$ and $S_i^-$ into crisp value. If decision makers are more optimistic, they can select $\alpha$ with a bigger value ($\alpha > 0.5$). If decision makers are more pessimistic, they select a smaller value for $\alpha$ ($\alpha < 0.5$). If decision makers keep a realistic and moderate attitude, in other words, neither more optimistic nor more pessimistic, they give $\alpha$ a certain value of 0.5. The transformation calculation is as follows.

$$S_i^{+*} = (1 - \alpha) S_i^{+L} + \alpha S_i^{+U} \quad (5.55)$$
$$S_i^{-*} = \alpha S_i^{-L} + (1 - \alpha) S_i^{-U} \quad (5.56)$$

where $S_i^{+*}$ and $S_i^{-*}$ represent the crisp value of rough number $S_i^+$ and $S_i^-$ respectively.

(6) Calculate the distance closeness coefficients ($CC_i$) of all alternatives.

## 5.3 Design Concept Selection Under Subjective Environments

$$CC_i = \frac{S_i^{-*}}{S_i^{-*} + S_i^{+*}} \tag{5.57}$$

Prioritize the data sequences based on the $CC_i$. An alternative with a larger $CC_i$ is a better choice because it is probably closer to the positive ideal solution and farther from the negative ideal solution.

### 5.3.3 Case Study: Design Concept Selection of Mini Fridge

To verify the effectiveness of the proposed method, it is applied into design concept evaluation of a mini-fridge. Further, several comparisons are conducted among the proposed rough approach, the traditional fuzzy method (fuzzy AHP-fuzzy TOPSIS), and the crisp method (AHP-TOPSIS). H Company is a manufacturer in eastern China that designs mini refrigerator for the small family and people with increasing mobility. During the conceptual design stage, eight mini refrigerator concepts (i.e. $A_1, A_2, A_3, A_4, A_5, A_6, A_7$ and $A_8$) have been designed by designers. The aim of the evaluation is to select the best design concept from the eight design alternatives.

To assess the eight concepts, experts commission selects three types of criteria, namely, Function ($C_1$), Environmental impact ($C_2$), and External feature ($C_3$). Each criterion includes several sub-criteria which are described in detail as follows.

(1) Function criterion ($C_1$) includes three sub-criteria, i.e. Effective volume ($C_{11}$), Preservation capabilities ($C_{12}$) and Service life ($C_{13}$). Effective volume ($C_{11}$) and Preservation capability ($C_{12}$) are critical. This is because that market investigation indicates that customers in single people and small family often store much food for several days or even a week. To keep enough effective volume and high preservation capability of the mini-fridge, designers should modify internal structure and choose the refrigeration compressor with better performance. Besides, long Service life ($C_{13}$) is expected by both designer and customer. But, if long Service life ($C_{13}$) exceeds the designed life, it may lead to poor preservation capability, high power consumption and noise, etc.

(2) Environmental impact ($C_2$) is a more complex criterion which includes various elements, for example pollution of air, soil and water, etc. According to the standard of "Eco-design of household and similar electrical appliances: Particular requirements for refrigerator" (GB/T 23109-2008) implemented in China from 2009, analysis should be carried on the trade-offs among energy efficiency, noise, and recovery in the stage of concept design. In the following system design stage, other detailed environmental factors would be taken into account. Thus, the unreasonable Refrigerant ($C_{21}$) selection, Noise ($C_{22}$) caused by unreasonable structure, and little Recovery consideration ($C_{23}$), and much Power consumption ($C_{24}$) can be identified as the causes for the latent environ-

mental problems of the mini-fridge in concept design phase. CFC-free refrigerants (e.g. R600a and R134a) are frequently used refrigerants in the production of the mini-fridge. Although these materials have no destructive influence on ozone layer, they are inflammable and explosive. In addition, the amount of refrigerant influences the refrigeration effect of the mini-fridge, and the power consumption amount. Noise ($C_{22}$) is always a big problem plaguing many mini-refrigerator users. It comes mainly from the compressor, scuffing or resonance between the pipes, thermal expansion and contraction of evaporator. This would affect the daily living environment of users, and eventually undermine customer satisfaction and loyalty. Recovery consideration ($C_{23}$) can reduce environmental pollution pressure from scrapped fridge. Designers should select suitable material, and modify the mini-fridge structure (e.g. modular design of some parts) to facilitate the demolition and reuse. Power consumption ($C_{24}$) of the mini-fridge in smaller family accounts for a larger proportion of total energy consumption. This will increase $CO_2$ and other greenhouse gas emissions since thermal power is still the main power generation method in China.

(3) External feature ($C_3$) should also be considered by designers to meet the aesthetic requirements of users. It consists of three sub-criteria ($C_{31}$: Weight; $C_{32}$: External dimensions; $C_{33}$: Styling). Weight ($C_{31}$) is one of selling points of the mini-fridge according to the market research. Designers should select proper material to reduce the mini-fridge weight to satisfy customers. Meanwhile, External dimension ($C_{32}$) is also an important element. Most users in the selected markets tend to choose mini-fridges with "compact size" because they believe smaller fridge is "easy to move" and "occupy limited space". Styling ($C_{33}$) of mini-refrigerator should be designed to meet the ergonomic requirements. Customers would be impressed by a mini-fridge with good design style (e.g., bright color, fashion), and tend to make purchase decisions.

The criteria $C_{11}$, $C_{12}$, $C_{13}$, $C_{23}$, and $C_{33}$ are the types of benefit criterion with the characteristic of "larger-the-better", while the rest of sub-criteria are the types of cost criterion with the characteristic of "smaller-the-better". The hierarchical structure of evaluation criteria can be seen in Fig. 5.11.

The whole assessment framework can be divided into two parts, i.e. the determination of criteria weights using Rough AHP approach, and design concept evaluation under the criteria with Rough TOPSIS. In order to demonstrate the advantages of the proposed evaluation approach, comparison and analysis are then carried out among the rough method (rough AHP-rough TOPSIS), fuzzy approach (fuzzy AHP-fuzzy TOPSIS) and crisp method (AHP-TOPSIS) in the mini-fridge case.

**Phase I: Evaluation criteria weights computation with Rough AHP method**

Step 1: Build a hierarchical structure of evaluation criteria for mini fridge concept, see Fig. 5.11. Design managers can easily understand and apply the hierarchical structure. Meanwhile, the expert team has a deeper insight into the problem systematically in terms of relevant criteria and sub-criteria. In

## 5.3 Design Concept Selection Under Subjective Environments

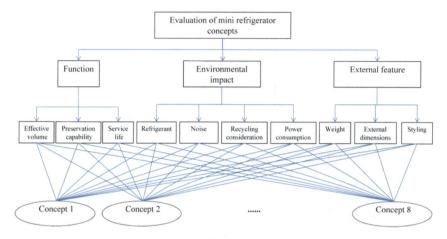

**Fig. 5.11** The hierarchical structure of evaluation criteria (Song et al. 2013b)

addition, the weights of the criteria and sub-criteria can be compared and determined systemically by the expert team.

Step 2: Conduct AHP survey until each AHP comparison matrix can get through the consistency test and obtain group decision matrix.

Take the environmental sub-criteria for example ($C_{21}$: Refrigerant; $C_{22}$: Noise; $C_{23}$: Recovery consideration and $C_{24}$: Power consumption) to illustrate computation process. The four experts' AHP comparison matrixes of environmental sub-criteria are as follows.

$$D_1 = \begin{array}{c} C_{21} \\ C_{22} \\ C_{23} \\ C_{24} \end{array} \begin{bmatrix} 1 & 5 & 3 & 4 \\ 1/5 & 1 & 1/3 & 1/2 \\ 1/3 & 3 & 1 & 3 \\ 1/4 & 2 & 1/3 & 1 \end{bmatrix} \quad D_2 = \begin{array}{c} C_{21} \\ C_{22} \\ C_{23} \\ C_{24} \end{array} \begin{bmatrix} 1 & 3 & 6 & 5 \\ 1/3 & 1 & 2 & 4 \\ 1/6 & 1/2 & 1 & 3 \\ 1/5 & 1/4 & 1/3 & 1 \end{bmatrix}$$

$$D_3 = \begin{array}{c} C_{21} \\ C_{22} \\ C_{23} \\ C_{24} \end{array} \begin{bmatrix} 1 & 4 & 3 & 3 \\ 1/4 & 1 & 1/2 & 1/3 \\ 1/3 & 2 & 1 & 1/2 \\ 1/3 & 3 & 2 & 1 \end{bmatrix} \quad D_4 = \begin{array}{c} C_{21} \\ C_{22} \\ C_{23} \\ C_{24} \end{array} \begin{bmatrix} 1 & 5 & 3 & 2 \\ 1/5 & 1 & 1/3 & 1/2 \\ 1/3 & 3 & 1 & 1/2 \\ 1/2 & 2 & 2 & 1 \end{bmatrix}$$

According to the Formulas (5.31) and (5.32), consistency ratio $CR_1 = 0.04 < 0.1$, $CR_2 = 0.06 < 0.1$, $CR_3 = 0.03 < 0.1$, and $CR_4 = 0.04 < 0.1$, so the consistency of each pair-wise comparison matrix of environmental sub-criteria is acceptable.

Then, we can get group decision matrix of function evaluation criteria $\tilde{D}_{Enviromental}$ by combining the above four pair-wise matrixes together.

$$\tilde{D}_{Enviromental} = \begin{bmatrix} 1,1,1,1 & 5,3,4,5 & 3,6,3,3 & 4,5,3,2 \\ 1/5,1/3,1/4,1/5 & 1,1,1,1 & 1/3,2,1/2,1/3 & 1/2,4,1/3,1/2 \\ 1/3,1/6,1/3,1/3 & 3,1/2,2,3 & 1,1,1,1 & 3,3,1/2,1/2 \\ 1/4,1/5,1/3,1/2 & 2,1/4,3,2 & 1/3,1/3,2,2 & 1,1,1,1 \end{bmatrix}$$

The same procedure can be conducted to other creteria and sub-creteria to get their group decision matrixes. Other group decision matrixes are not listed here due to space limitations.

Step 3: Get the group rough comparison matrix R with the original group comparison matrix from Step 2. To get the rough form of group comparison matrix, we must transform the elements $\tilde{r}_{ij}$ in group decision matrix $\tilde{D}$ into the rough number form according to the Formulas (5.20), (5.21), (5.23), (5.24), and (5.25).

Take the element in $\tilde{r}_{12} = \{5, 3, 4, 5\}$ in $\tilde{D}_{Enviromental}$ to illustrate the rough number transformation process,

$$\underline{\lim}(3) = 3 \quad \overline{\lim}(3) = \tfrac{1}{4}(3+4+5+5) = 4.25$$
$$\underline{\lim}(4) = \tfrac{1}{2}(4+3) = 3.5 \quad \overline{\lim}(4) = \tfrac{1}{3}(4+5+5) = 4.67$$
$$\underline{\lim}(5) = \tfrac{1}{4}(3+4+5+5) = 4.25 \quad \overline{\lim}(5) = \tfrac{1}{2}(5+5) = 5$$

Thus, $r_{12}^k$ can be expressed in the rough number form of $RN(r_{13}^k)$.

$$RN(r_{13}^1) = RN(r_{13}^4) = RN(5) = [4.25, 5],$$
$$RN(r_{13}^2) = RN(3) = [3, 4.25],$$
$$RN(r_{13}^3) = RN(4) = [3.5, 4.67].$$

According to the Eqs. (5.36)–(5.38), the average rough interval of $\overline{RN(\tilde{r}_{12})} = [3.75, 4.73]$. Similarly, we can get rough number forms and average rough intervals for other elements in the group decision matrix $\tilde{D}_{Environmental}$.

Therefore, we get the rough group comparison matrix $\tilde{D}_{Environmental}$,

$$\tilde{R}_{Enviromental} = \begin{bmatrix} [1,1] & [3.75, 4.73] & [3.19, 4.31] & [2.75, 4.25] \\ [0.22, 0.28] & [1,1] & [0.46, 1.21] & [0.64, 2.17] \\ [0.26, 0.32] & [1.50, 2.70] & [1,1] & [1.13, 2.38] \\ [0.25, 0.40] & [1.22, 2.37] & [0.75, 1.58] & [1,1] \end{bmatrix}$$

## 5.3 Design Concept Selection Under Subjective Environments

**Table 5.5** Rough weights of evaluation criteria (Song et al. 2013b)

| Criteria | Sub-criteria | Rough weight |
|---|---|---|
| $C_1$ (Function) [0.814, 1] | $C_{11}$ (Effective volume), [0.366, 0.717] | [0.298, 0.717] |
| | $C_{12}$ (Preservation capabilities), [0.586, 1] | [0.477, 1.000] |
| | $C_{13}$ (Service life), [0.156, 0.287] | [0.127, 0.287] |
| $C_2$ (Environment) [0.318, 0.495] | $C_{21}$ (Refrigerant), [0.785, 1] | [0.249, 0.495] |
| | $C_{22}$ (Noise), [0.165, 0.303] | [0.052, 0.150] |
| | $C_{23}$ (Recycling consideration), [0.267, 0.393] | [0.085, 0.195] |
| | $C_{24}$ (Power consumption), [0.227, 0.363] | [0.072, 0.179] |
| $C_3$ (Product image) [0.206, 0.339] | $C_{31}$ (Weight), [0.262, 0.657] | [0.054, 0.223] |
| | $C_{32}$ (Dimensions), [0.235, 0.567] | [0.048, 0.192] |
| | $C_{33}$ (Styling), [0.585, 1] | [0.121, 0.339] |

In the same way, the other criteria's group comparison matrix in rough number form can be obtained. Other group comparison matrixes in rough number form are not listed here due to space limitations.

Step 4: Calculate rough weights of criteria and sub-criteria (see Table 5.5) in the light of the Formula (5.40).

For the sub-criteria of function, we can get the second hierarchy criteria weight $w_{C_2} = \{w_{C_{21}}, w_{C_{22}}, w_{C_{23}}, w_{C_{24}}\} = \{[2.394, 3.051], [0.502, 0.925], [0.814, 1.199], [0.693, 1.107]\}$.

Then normalize $w_{C_2}$ to obtain its normalization form $w'_{C_2}$, $w'_{C_2} = \{[0.785, 1.000], [0.165, 0.303], [0.267, 0.393], [0.227, 0.363]\}$.

Normalized weights for other criteria are also calculated similarly in Table 5.5. The final overall weight is calculated using multiplication synthesis method from top level to bottom level. The results are also listed in Table 5.5.

### Phase II: Design concepts evaluation using Rough TOPSIS approach

Eight mini fridge design concepts are generated in the conceptual design phase. These eight design concepts with respect to the ten criteria are evaluated by the four selected experts. For quantitative criteria, an appropriate value is suggested by each expert according to his own experience and knowledge, for instance, the values of '9 years', '10 years', '12 years', and '13 years' are chosen by the four experts respectively for the service life of concept 1 ($A_1$). For qualitative criteria ($C_{23}$ and $C_{33}$), experts use the scale of 1, 3, 5, 7, and 9 to assess the design concepts in relation to the criterion. They represent 'very low', 'low', 'medium', 'high', and 'very high', respectively. Thus, the performance of a design concept with respect to each evaluation criterion can be expressed by a set of such values from expert's estimation. Table 5.6 presents the four domain experts' evaluation values for concept 1 ($A_1$) in relation to the ten criteria. Other concepts estimation values are not listed here due to space limitation.

Step 1: Convert the original evaluation matrix into a rough decision matrix M according to the Formulas (5.20)–(5.25). (Table 5.7)

Step 2: Obtain the Positive Ideal Solution (PIS) and Negative Ideal Solution (NIS) for each criterion in Table 5.8 with the Formula (5.42).

Step 3: Compute the distance from each concept evaluation data to PIS and NIS in relation to each criterion according to the Eqs. (5.43)–(5.48). Then, establish the distance matrix $d^+$ and $d^-$, and normalize $d^+$ and $d^-$ according to the Formulas (5.49)–(5.52) to obtain the normalized distance matrix $d^{+'}$ and $d^{-'}$ in Tables 5.9 and 5.10 respectively.

Step 4: Calculate the separation measure $S^+$ and $S^-$ (weighted normalized deviation) for each mini fridge design concept in Table 5.11 using the Formulas (5.53)–(5.54).

Step 5: In this step, expert team introduces the optimistic indicator $\alpha = 0.5$, and transforms the separation measure $S^+$ and $S^-$ into crisp value with the Formulas (5.55)–(5.56) in Table 5.11.

Step 6: Also shown in Table 5.11, closeness coefficient $CC_i$ for each mini fridge design concept can be obtained according to the Formula (5.57). The ranking order of design concepts is: $A_8 > A_3 > A_1 > A_6 > A_4 > A_7 > A_2 > A_5$. We can clearly see that the concept 8 ($A_8$) is the best one among the eight design alternatives when decision makers have a moderate risk propensity ($\alpha = 0.5$).

In order to analyze the effect of decision makers' risk propensity on the final rank of product concepts, a sensitivity analysis is conducted. Table 5.12 shows the results of the sensitivity analysis and Fig. 5.12 illustrates the graphical representation of these results. The results reveal that concept 3 ($A_3$) has a maximum priority when decision makers have pessimistic propensity ($\alpha < 0.5$). While decision makers have optimistic risk propensity ($\alpha > 0.5$), concept 8 ($A_8$) has higher priority than concept 3 ($A_3$). Ranks of some concepts [e.g. concept 2 ($A_2$) and concept 5 ($A_5$)] are independent on the risk propensity of decision makers.

### 5.3.4 Comparisons and Discussion

In order to demonstrate the strength of the proposed concept evaluation approach, it is compared with AHP-TOPSIS method based on fuzzy number (symmetrical triangular fuzzy number) and traditional AHP-TOPSIS approach.

5.3 Design Concept Selection Under Subjective Environments

**Table 5.6** Evaluation data of concept 1 ($A_1$) in relation to each criteria (Song et al. 2013b)

| Expert | $C_{11}$ (L) | $C_{12}$ (kg/24 h) | $C_{13}$ (year) | $C_{21}$ (g) | $C_{22}$ (db) | $C_{23}$ | $C_{24}$ (KWH/24H) | $C_{31}$ (kg) | $C_{32}$ (m$^2$) | $C_{33}$ |
|---|---|---|---|---|---|---|---|---|---|---|
| 1 | 70 | 0.83 | 9  | 52 | 32 | 7 | 0.52 | 26 | 0.164 | 3 |
| 2 | 72 | 0.93 | 10 | 55 | 31 | 3 | 0.52 | 27 | 0.165 | 3 |
| 3 | 76 | 1.00 | 12 | 52 | 34 | 5 | 0.55 | 30 | 0.165 | 5 |
| 4 | 70 | 0.95 | 13 | 54 | 35 | 5 | 0.54 | 31 | 0.168 | 7 |

**Table 5.7** Rough decision matrix M of all the mini-fridge concepts in relation to each criterion (Song et al. 2013b)

| No. | $C_{11}$ | ... | $C_{21}$ | $C_{22}$ | $C_{23}$ | $C_{24}$ | ... | $C_{33}$ |
|---|---|---|---|---|---|---|---|---|
| A1 | [70.667, 73.500] | ... | [52.479, 54.000] | [31.958, 34.042] | [4.167, 5.833] | [0.525, 0.540] | ... | [3.542, 5.500] |
| A2 | [71.500, 74.500] | ... | [54.833, 57.333] | [33.250, 34.667] | [2.167, 3.833] | [0.528, 0.548] | ... | [4.292, 6.792] |
| A3 | [72.500, 73.500] | ... | [53.417, 56.750] | [32.250, 33.667] | [6.167, 7.833] | [0.517, 0.538] | ... | [2.917, 7.083] |
| A4 | [71.500, 74.500] | ... | [54.063, 54.438] | [33.271, 34.250] | [6.167, 7.833] | [0.516, 0.548] | ... | [4.500, 5.917] |
| A5 | [71.167, 72.833] | ... | [53.479, 57.271] | [33.104, 34.354] | [1.500, 2.500] | [0.521, 0.542] | ... | [2.167, 3.833] |
| A6 | [71.292, 73.792] | ... | [55.375, 58.625] | [32.229, 34.188] | [3.125, 3.875] | [0.538, 0.553] | ... | [4.292, 6.792] |
| A7 | [72.500, 73.500] | ... | [52.729, 56.000] | [33.750, 34.729] | [3.542, 5.500] | [0.533, 0.548] | ... | [5.500, 6.500] |
| A8 | [72.500, 75.333] | ... | [55.500, 58.104] | [32.750, 33.729] | [4.167, 5.833] | [0.523, 0.552] | ... | [4.167, 5.833] |

*Note:* Part of the evaluation results are listed due to space limitations

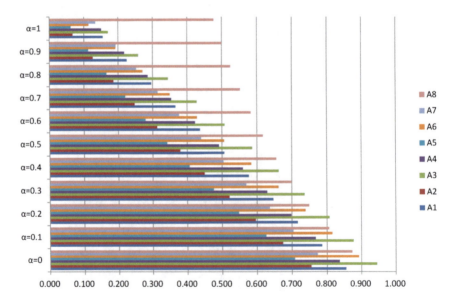

**Fig. 5.12** Sensitivity analysis (Song et al. 2013b)

The evaluation criteria weight is an important input of concept evaluation which influences the final reliability of concept ranks. Thus, we firstly compare the subjectivity manipulating mechanisms of criteria weights in fuzzy AHP (using symmetrical

### 5.3 Design Concept Selection Under Subjective Environments

**Table 5.8** Positive Ideal Solution (PIS) and Negative Ideal Solution (NIS) of each criteria (Song et al. 2013b)

|  | $C_{11}$ | $C_{12}$ | $C_{13}$ | $C_{21}$ | $C_{22}$ | $C_{23}$ | $C_{24}$ | $C_{31}$ | $C_{32}$ | $C_{33}$ |
|---|---|---|---|---|---|---|---|---|---|---|
| PIS | 75.333 | 1.095 | 12.042 | 52.479 | 31.958 | 7.833 | 0.516 | 25.750 | 0.164 | 7.083 |
| NIS | 70.667 | 0.836 | 8.271 | 58.625 | 34.729 | 1.500 | 0.553 | 30.833 | 0.172 | 2.167 |

**Table 5.9** The normalized difference coefficient matrix $d^{+\prime}$ (Song et al. 2013b)

| No. | $C_{11}$ | ... | $C_{21}$ | $C_{22}$ | $C_{23}$ | $C_{24}$ | ... | $C_{33}$ |
|---|---|---|---|---|---|---|---|---|
| A1 | [0.393, 1.000] | ... | [0.000, 0.247] | [0.000, 0.870] | [0.316, 0.579] | [0.235, 0.665] | ... | [0.322, 0.720] |
| A2 | [0.179, 0.821] | ... | [0.383, 0.790] | [0.539, 1.130] | [0.632, 0.895] | [0.329, 0.882] | ... | [0.059, 0.568] |
| A3 | [0.393, 0.607] | ... | [0.153, 0.695] | [0.122, 0.713] | [0.000, 0.263] | [0.012, 0.600] | ... | [0.000, 0.847] |
| A4 | [0.179, 0.821] | ... | [0.258, 0.319] | [0.548, 0.957] | [0.000, 0.263] | [0.000, 0.882] | ... | [0.237, 0.525] |
| A5 | [0.536, 0.893] | ... | [0.163, 0.780] | [0.478, 1.000] | [0.842, 1.000] | [0.141, 0.729] | ... | [0.661, 1.000] |
| A6 | [0.330, 0.866] | ... | [0.471, 1.000] | [0.113, 0.930] | [0.625, 0.743] | [0.594, 1.000] | ... | [0.059, 0.568] |
| A7 | [0.393, 0.607] | ... | [0.041, 0.573] | [0.748, 1.157] | [0.368, 0.678] | [0.476, 0.876] | ... | [0.119, 0.322] |
| A8 | [0.000, 0.607] | ... | [0.492, 0.915] | [0.330, 0.739] | [0.316, 0.579] | [0.171, 1.000] | ... | [0.254, 0.593] |

**Table 5.10** The normalized difference coefficient matrix $d^{-\prime}$ (Song et al. 2013b)

| No. | $C_{11}$ | ... | $C_{21}$ | $C_{22}$ | $C_{23}$ | $C_{24}$ | ... | $C_{33}$ |
|---|---|---|---|---|---|---|---|---|
| A1 | [0.000, 0.607] | ... | [0.753, 1.000] | [0.248, 1.000] | [0.421, 0.684] | [0.351, 0.778] | ... | [0.280, 0.678] |
| A2 | [0.179, 0.821] | ... | [0.210, 0.617] | [0.023, 0.534] | [0.105, 0.368] | [0.135, 0.684] | ... | [0.432, 0.941] |
| A3 | [0.393, 0.607] | ... | [0.305, 0.847] | [0.383, 0.895] | [0.737, 1.000] | [0.415, 1.000] | ... | [0.153, 1.000] |
| A4 | [0.179, 0.821] | ... | [0.681, 0.742] | [0.173, 0.526] | [0.737, 1.000] | [0.135, 1.000] | ... | [0.475, 0.763] |
| A5 | [0.107, 0.464] | ... | [0.220, 0.837] | [0.135, 0.586] | [0.000, 0.158] | [0.287, 0.871] | ... | [0.000, 0.339] |
| A6 | [0.134, 0.670] | ... | [0.000, 0.529] | [0.195, 0.902] | [0.257, 0.375] | [0.000, 0.421] | ... | [0.432, 0.941] |
| A7 | [0.393, 0.607] | ... | [0.427, 0.959] | [0.000, 0.353] | [0.322, 0.632] | [0.140, 0.538] | ... | [0.678, 0.881] |
| A8 | [0.000, 0.607] | ... | [0.085, 0.508] | [0.361, 0.714] | [0.421, 0.684] | [0.018, 0.842] | ... | [0.407, 0.746] |

## 5.3 Design Concept Selection Under Subjective Environments

**Table 5.11** The value of separation measure, closeness coefficient and ranking results (Song et al. 2013b)

| No. | Rough number form S⁺ | Rough number form S⁻ | Crisp value (α = 0.5) S⁺ | Crisp value (α = 0.5) S⁻ | $CC_i$ (α = 0.5) | Rank |
|---|---|---|---|---|---|---|
| $A_1$ | [0.458, 2.651] | [0.487, 2.706] | 1.554 | 1.596 | 0.507 | 3 |
| $A_2$ | [0.708, 3.223] | [0.234, 2.171] | 1.965 | 1.202 | 0.380 | 7 |
| $A_3$ | [0.193, 2.516] | [0.517, 3.319] | 1.355 | 1.918 | 0.586 | 2 |
| $A_4$ | [0.507, 2.676] | [0.475, 2.597] | 1.591 | 1.536 | 0.491 | 5 |
| $A_5$ | [0.785, 3.307] | [0.218, 1.900] | 2.046 | 1.059 | 0.341 | 8 |
| $A_6$ | [0.356, 2.888] | [0.370, 2.950] | 1.622 | 1.660 | 0.506 | 4 |
| $A_7$ | [0.662, 2.748] | [0.424, 2.252] | 1.705 | 1.338 | 0.440 | 6 |
| $A_8$ | [0.406, 3.065] | [0.302, 2.796] | 1.736 | 2.796 | 0.617 | 1 |

triangular fuzzy number), rough AHP and crisp AHP (see Fig. 5.13). It can be seen clearly from Fig. 5.13 that the three methods produce almost the same rank of criteria weights ($C_{12} > C_{11} > C_{21} > C_{33} > C_{13} > C_{23} > C_{31} > C_{32} > C_{24} > C_{22}$), but most of the criteria weights are different in size. The conventional AHP evaluation approach only presents crisp weights for criteria without considering the subjectivity and vagueness. On the contrary, both the fuzzy AHP and the rough AHP provide interval boundary indicating the confidence level for the weights evaluation. For example, the rough weights and fuzzy weights of criterion of $C_{31}$ ("Weight") in Fig. 5.13 are respectively [0.054, 0.223] and [0.124, 0.306] denoting both importance of criteria and evaluation confidence level. The rough confidence level for criterion of $C_{31}$ is 0.169, and the fuzzy confidence level is 0.182. The rough weights and fuzzy weights have different interval boundaries denoting different level of subjectivity and vagueness because of different subjectivity manipulating mechanisms. In fact, the weights from the fuzzy AHP lose some subjective information in the evaluation process. For instance, both fuzzy and rough criterion weights of $C_{21}$ ("Refrigerant") are [0.137, 0.322] and [0.249, 0.495] respectively, and the fuzzy interval (0.185) is less than that of rough interval (0.245). The four experts judgments on the importance of $C_{21}$ relative to other criteria are (1,1,1,1), (5,3,4,5), (3,6,3,3) and (4,5,3,2) respectively. Those ratings can be converted into rough number forms holistically. The rough numbers are [1, 1], [3.75, 4.729], [3.188, 4.312], and [2.75, 4.25]. They can be also transformed into fuzzy numbers [1, 1], [3.25, 5.25], [2.75, 4.75] and [2.5, 4.5]. Apparently, the rough number forms of experts' judgments present flexible intervals according to

Table 5.12 Sensitivity analysis (Song et al. 2013b)

| | $\alpha = 0$ | $\alpha = 0.1$ | $\alpha = 0.2$ | $\alpha = 0.3$ | $\alpha = 0.4$ | $\alpha = 0.5$ | $\alpha = 0.6$ | $\alpha = 0.7$ | $\alpha = 0.8$ | $\alpha = 0.9$ | $\alpha = 1$ |
|---|---|---|---|---|---|---|---|---|---|---|---|
| $A_1$ | 0.855 | 0.786 | 0.716 | 0.646 | 0.577 | 0.507 | 0.437 | 0.366 | 0.296 | 0.226 | 0.155 |
| $A_2$ | 0.754 | 0.673 | 0.596 | 0.521 | 0.449 | 0.380 | 0.313 | 0.248 | 0.186 | 0.126 | 0.068 |
| $A_3$ | 0.945 | 0.877 | 0.807 | 0.736 | 0.662 | 0.586 | 0.508 | 0.427 | 0.344 | 0.259 | 0.170 |
| $A_4$ | 0.837 | 0.767 | 0.698 | 0.629 | 0.560 | 0.491 | 0.423 | 0.354 | 0.286 | 0.218 | 0.151 |
| $A_5$ | 0.708 | 0.625 | 0.548 | 0.475 | 0.406 | 0.341 | 0.279 | 0.221 | 0.165 | 0.112 | 0.062 |
| $A_6$ | 0.892 | 0.816 | 0.738 | 0.661 | 0.584 | 0.506 | 0.428 | 0.350 | 0.271 | 0.192 | 0.114 |
| $A_7$ | 0.773 | 0.704 | 0.636 | 0.569 | 0.504 | 0.440 | 0.376 | 0.314 | 0.253 | 0.193 | 0.134 |
| $A_8$ | 0.873 | 0.806 | 0.749 | 0.699 | 0.655 | 0.617 | 0.583 | 0.552 | 0.525 | 0.500 | 0.477 |

## 5.3 Design Concept Selection Under Subjective Environments

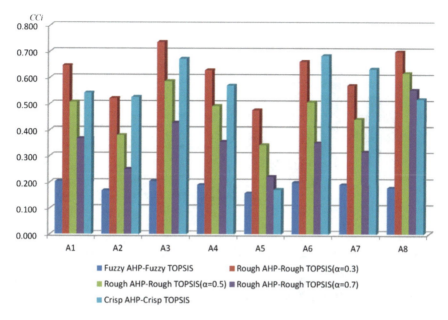

**Fig. 5.13** Criteria weights from fuzzy AHP, rough AHP, and conventional AHP (Song et al. 2013b)

the general distribution of judgments. However, the fuzzy number forms of experts' judgments provide fixed and static interval (2) because of the preset membership function. The fixed interval in the fuzzy AHP may finally lead to deviations of the criteria weights which cannot well flexibly reflect the realistic importance of criteria (e.g. the final fuzzy weight of $C_{21}$ [0.137, 0.322] is generally lower than that of rough weight [0.249, 0.495]). In sum, rough AHP can provide more flexible and realistic weights incorporating subjectivity than fuzzy AHP and crisp AHP.

To reveal the features of the novel concept evaluation method based on rough number, comparisons also made between fuzzy AHP-fuzzy TOPSIS, rough AHP-rough TOPSIS and crisp AHP-crisp TOPSIS (see Fig. 5.14). The ranks are different in the three evaluation approaches. According to Fig. 5.14, the proposed rough AHP-rough TOPSIS has clearer and more flexible closeness coefficients than that of fuzzy integrated approach and crisp integrated method. The best alternative is the concept $A_8$ when optimistic indicator $\alpha = 0.5$ and 0.7 in the proposed approach. Concept $A_3$ ranks the first among the eight alternatives when the decision makers have pessimistic attitude ($\alpha = 0.3$). However, the fuzzy AHP-fuzzy TOPSIS only provides one rank result, because it calculates crisp separation measure without incorporating subjectivity. In addition, the ranking results of most concepts obtained from the fuzzy method almost have the same level. For example, concept $A_1$ and concept $A_3$ both rank the first; concept $A_4$ and concept $A_7$ also have the same rank, etc. Similarly, in crisp integrated evaluation approach, the concept $A_2$ and concept $A_8$ nearly have the same rank of closeness coefficient. These almost equal closeness coefficients would

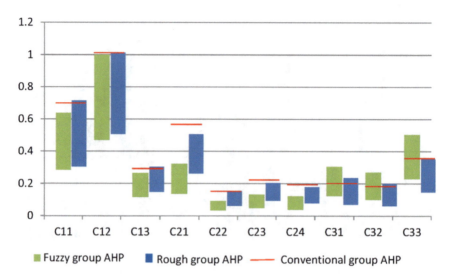

**Fig. 5.14** The closeness coefficients from fuzzy AHP-fuzzy TOPSIS, rough AHP-rough TOPSIS and crisp AHP- crisp TOPSIS (Song et al. 2013b)

lead to illusion in the final concept selection. Thus, the rough integrated approach has a clearer differentiation and can obtain realistic ranks in the light of decision maker's risk propensity.

In sum, the proposed approach has the features as follows: The AHP-TOPSIS evaluation structure based on the rough number can generally describe experts' opinions, provide a more holistic judgment, and deal with the inconsistency of decision makers' judgments in criteria weights determination and concept evaluation. Concept evaluation using AHP-TOPSIS structure integrates rough number with flexible boundary, which can well reflect decision maker's subjective and vague judgment. The rough number enabled AHP-TOPSIS concept evaluation method can avoid using much priori information and assumptions (e.g. pre-set membership functions). The rough integrated group method can discern the change of decision makers' preferences. The introduction of the optimistic indicator α can help decision makers obtain flexible and realistic concept ranks in line with their risk propensities.

# References

Deb, K., Pratap, A., Agarwal, S., & Meyarivan, T. A. M. T. (2002). A fast and elitist multiobjective genetic algorithm: NSGA-II. *IEEE Transactions on Evolutionary Computation, 6*(2), 182–197.

Gonzalez-Zugasti, J. P., & Otto, K. N. (2000). Modular platform-based product family design. In ASME Advances in Design Automation Conference. Baltimore, MD.

Khoo, L. P., Tor, S. B., & Zhai, L. Y. (1999). A rough-set-based approach for classification and rule induction. *The International Journal of Advanced Manufacturing Technology, 15*(6), 438–444.

# References

Moon, S. K., Shu, J., Simpson, T. W., & Kumara, S. R. (2010). A module-based service model for mass customization: Service family design. *IIE Transactions, 43*(3), 153–163.

Nilsson, C. (1990). *Handbok i QFD*. Sverige, Stockholm: Mekanförbundets förlag.

Saaty, T. L. (1977). A scaling method for priorities in hierarchical structures. *Journal of Mathematical Psychology, 15*(3), 234–281.

Shen, J., Wang, L., & Sun, Y. (2012). Configuration of product extension services in servitisation using an ontology-based approach. *International Journal of Production Research, 50*(22), 6469–6488.

Song, W., Ming, X., Han, Y., & Wu, Z. (2013a). A rough set approach for evaluating vague customer requirement of industrial product-service system. *International Journal of Production Research, 51*(22), 6681–6701.

Song, W., Ming, X., & Han, Y. (2014). Prioritising technical attributes in QFD under vague environment: A rough-grey relational analysis approach. *International Journal of Production Research, 52*(18), 5528–5545.

Song, W., & Chan, F. T. (2015). Multi-objective configuration optimization for product-extension service. *Journal of Manufacturing Systems, 37,* 113–125.

Song, W., Ming, X., & Wu, Z. (2013b). An integrated rough number-based approach to design concept evaluation under subjective environments. *Journal of Engineering Design, 24*(5), 320–341.

Srinivas, N., & Deb, K. (1994). Muiltiobjective optimization using nondominated sorting in genetic algorithms. *Evolutionary Computation, 2*(3), 221–248.

Zhai, L. Y., Khoo, L. P., & Zhong, Z. W. (2008). A rough set enhanced fuzzy approach to quality function deployment. *The International Journal of Advanced Manufacturing Technology, 37*(5–6), 613–624.

Zhai, L. Y., Khoo, L. P., & Zhong, Z. W. (2009). A rough set based QFD approach to the management of imprecise design information in product development. *Advanced Engineering Informatics, 23*(2), 222–228.

Zhai, L. Y., Khoo, L. P., & Zhong, Z. W. (2010). Towards a QFD-based expert system: A novel extension to fuzzy QFD methodology using rough set theory. *Expert Systems with Applications, 37*(12), 8888–8896.

# Chapter 6
# Personalized Recommendation of Customizable PSS to Customers

Many manufacturers today are trying hard to provide a large number of value-added PSSs. Potential buyers are impeded by the increased number of PSS to effectively find the most suitable PSS to meet their personalized needs. In order to accurately discover the needed or wanted PSS with lower search costs, it is effective to recommend suitable PSS solutions to the appropriate buyers. To help potential buyers effectively find the most suitable PSS with lower search costs, Song and Sakao (2018) develop a multi-criteria recommendation method based on rough collaborative filtering (CF) method to proactively provide customers with customizable suggesting proposals of PSS. Specifically, rough DEMATEL (Decision-Making and Trial Evaluation Laboratory) (Song and Cao 2017) is used to manipulate the interactions of vague user preferences. Furthermore, a rough collaborative filtering method is developed to make PSS recommendation in a vague environment.

## 6.1 The Proposed Method for Personalized PSS Recommendation

The method can be applied to both industrial and consumer services. Its overall process consists of two phases as shown in Fig. 6.1: Phase I is weight determination for recommendation criteria, and Phase II is PSS multi-criteria recommendation. In Phase I, a rough DEMATEL is used to manipulate the vague ratings and the interactions of criteria. Then, Phase II makes the personalized PSS recommendation based on a rough collaborative filtering method.

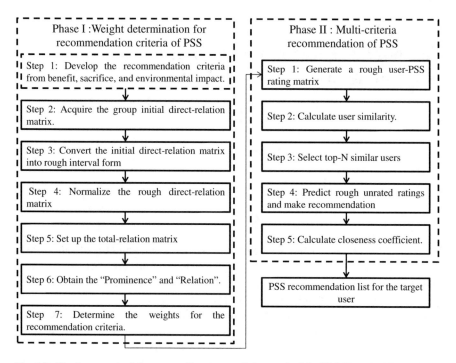

**Fig. 6.1** The framework of the proposed recommendation method for PSS (Song and Sakao 2018)

## 6.1.1 Phase I: Weight Determination for PSS Recommendation Criteria

The following steps shows the determination of rough weight of PSS recommendation criteria based on the rough DEMATEL method.

***Step 1: Develop the evaluation criteria for the PSS.***

The evaluation criteria are developed according to characteristics of the PSS in question and originate of all three categories: (1) users' benefit, (2) users' sacrifice, and (3) environmental impact. This classification is a result of the deployment of a widely recognized value definition in the industrial marketing field by Ulaga and Chacour (2001), which is the trade-off between perceived benefits and sacrifices. All the criteria from the three categories are denoted as $C_1, C_2,...,C_n$. Note that the category of a criterion is not mathematically important, so the category is not visible in the following mathematical formulation.

Some criteria are more important to the user than the others, such as the *service response time* may be more important than the *service cost* for him, and thus, the two criteria shouldn't be treated equally on the same rating scale. In addition, some criteria may influence each other, such as reducing *service response time* may lead to an increase in the *service cost*. Therefore, to achieve accurate PSS recommendation,

## 6.1 The Proposed Method for Personalized PSS Recommendation

it is necessary to learn about the highest predominant criteria among the others and the interactions between the evaluation criteria.

***Step 2: Acquire the group initial direct-relation matrix.***

To measure the correlations between criteria $C = \{C_i | i = 1, 2, \ldots, n\}$, a decision group of $p$ customers is invited to make sets of pair-wise comparisons in terms of crisp scores (Very high influence = 4, High influence = 3, Low influence = 2, Very low influence = 1, No influence = 0). Thus, $p$ crisp matrices $Z^{(1)}, Z^{(2)}, \ldots, Z^{(p)}$, each corresponding to an expert and with crisp scores as its elements, are obtained. The initial direct-relation matrix $Z^{(k)}$ of customer $k$ is represented as:

$$Z^{(k)} = \begin{bmatrix} 0 & z_{12}^{(k)} & \cdots & z_{1n}^{(k)} \\ z_{21}^{(k)} & 0 & \cdots & z_{2n}^{(k)} \\ \vdots & \vdots & \ddots & \vdots \\ z_{n1}^{(k)} & z_{n2}^{(k)} & \cdots & 0 \end{bmatrix} \quad (6.1)$$

where $z_{ij}^{(k)}$ is the crisp score of the $k$th customer.

Hence, the group initial direct-relation matrix $Z$ can be obtained as follows:

$$Z = \begin{bmatrix} \{0,0,\ldots,0\} & \{z_{12}^{(1)}, z_{12}^{(2)}, \ldots, z_{12}^{(p)}\} & \cdots & \{z_{1n}^{(1)}, z_{1n}^{(2)}, \ldots, z_{1n}^{(p)}\} \\ \{z_{21}^{(1)}, z_{21}^{(2)}, \ldots, z_{21}^{(p)}\} & \{0,0,\ldots,0\} & \cdots & \{z_{2n}^{(1)}, z_{2n}^{(2)}, \ldots, z_{2n}^{(p)}\} \\ \vdots & \vdots & \ddots & \vdots \\ \{z_{n1}^{(1)}, z_{n1}^{(2)}, \ldots, z_{n1}^{(p)}\} & \{z_{n2}^{(1)}, z_{n2}^{(2)}, \ldots, z_{n2}^{(p)}\} & \cdots & \{0,0,\ldots,0\} \end{bmatrix} \quad (6.2)$$

***Step 3: Convert the judgments $z_{ij}^{(k)}$ in group initial direct-relation matrix $Z$ into rough form.***

Assume that there is a set of $m$ classes of human judgments, $J = \{r_{ij}^1, r_{ij}^2, \ldots, r_{ij}^k, \ldots, r_{ij}^m\}$ ordered in the manner of $r_{ij}^1 < r_{ij}^2 < \cdots < r_{ij}^k < \cdots < r_{ij}^m$. $U$ is the universe including all the objects and $Y$ is an arbitrary object of $U$, and then the lower approximation of $r_{ij}^k$ and the upper approximation of $r_{ij}^k$ can be defined as:

$$\text{Lower approximation: } \underline{Apr}(r_{ij}^k) = \cup\{Y \in U / J(Y) \leq r_{ij}^k\} \quad (6.3)$$

$$\text{Upper approximation: } \overline{Apr}(r_{ij}^k) = \cup\{Y \in U / J(Y) \geq r_{ij}^k\} \quad (6.4)$$

Then, the judgment, $r_{ij}^k$, can be represented with a rough number defined by its lower limit $\underline{Lim}(r_{ij}^k)$ and upper limit $\overline{Lim}(r_{ij}^k)$ as follows:

$$\underline{Lim}(r_{ij}^k) = \frac{\sum_{m=1}^{N_{ijL}} x_{ij}}{N_{ijL}} \quad (6.5)$$

$$\overline{Lim}(r_{ij}^k) = \frac{\sum_{m=1}^{N_{ijU}} y_{ij}}{N_{ijU}} \qquad (6.6)$$

$x_{ij}$ and $y_{ij}$ are the elements of lower and upper approximation for $r_{ij}^k$. $N_{ijL}$ and $N_{ijU}$ are the number of objects contained in the lower approximation and upper approximation of $r_{ij}^k$, respectively.

Then, all the crisp judgments $z_{ij}^{(k)}$ in initial direct-relation matrix $Z^{(k)}$ can be transformed into rough number form $RN(z_{ij}^{(k)})$ can be obtained using Eqs. (6.3)–(6.6),

$$RN(z_{ij}^{(k)}) = \left[\underline{Lim}(z_{ij}^{(k)}), \overline{Lim}(z_{ij}^{(k)})\right] = \left[z_{ij}^{(k)L}, z_{ij}^{(k)U}\right], \qquad (6.7)$$

where $z_{ij}^{(k)L}$ and $z_{ij}^{(k)U}$ are the lower limit and upper limit of rough number $RN(z_{ij}^{(k)})$ in the $k$th pair-wise comparison matrix. The interval of boundary region (i.e. $z_{ij}^{(k)U} - z_{ij}^{(k)L}$) represents the degree of vagueness. A rough number with a smaller interval of boundary region is interpreted as more precise one.

Thus, the rough initial direct-relation matrix $R(Z^{(k)})$ for each customer can be obtained as follows:

$$R(Z^{(k)}) = \begin{bmatrix} RN(z_{11}^{(k)}) & RN(z_{12}^{(k)}) & \cdots & RN(z_{1n}^{(k)}) \\ RN(z_{21}^{(k)}) & RN(z_{22}^{(k)}) & \cdots & RN(z_{2n}^{(k)}) \\ \vdots & \vdots & \ddots & \vdots \\ RN(z_{n1}^{(k)}) & RN(z_{n2}^{(k)}) & \cdots & RN(z_{nn}^{(k)}) \end{bmatrix} \qquad (6.8)$$

**Step 4: Acquire the normalized direct-relation rough matrix.**

Then, the linear scale transformation is used as a normalization formula to convert the criteria scales into comparable scales. The normalized direct-relation rough matrix of the $k$th customer, indicated as $\overline{R(Z^{(k)})}$, is given by

$$\overline{R(Z^{(k)})} = \begin{bmatrix} \overline{RN(z_{11}^{(k)})} & \overline{RN(z_{12}^{(k)})} & \cdots & \overline{RN(z_{1n}^{(k)})} \\ \overline{RN(z_{21}^{(k)})} & \overline{RN(z_{22}^{(k)})} & \cdots & \overline{RN(z_{2n}^{(k)})} \\ \vdots & \vdots & \ddots & \vdots \\ \overline{RN(z_{n1}^{(k)})} & \overline{RN(z_{n2}^{(k)})} & \cdots & \overline{RN(z_{nn}^{(k)})} \end{bmatrix}; \ k = 1, 2, \ldots, p \qquad (6.9)$$

where

$$\overline{RN(z_{ij}^{(k)})} = \frac{RN(z_{ij}^{(k)})}{\gamma^{(k)}} = \left[\frac{z_{ij}^{(k)L}}{\gamma^{(k)}}, \frac{z_{ij}^{(k)U}}{\gamma^{(k)}}\right], \qquad (6.10)$$

## 6.1 The Proposed Method for Personalized PSS Recommendation

$$r^{(k)} = \max_{1 \le i \le n} \left( \sum_{j=1}^{n} z_{ij}^{(k)U} \right). \tag{6.11}$$

**Step 5: Set up the total-relation matrix $T^{(k)}$.**

The total-relation matrix $T^{(k)}$ of the $k$th customer can be obtained as follows:

$$T^{(k)} = [t_{ij}^{(k)L}, t_{ij}^{(k)U}], \tag{6.12}$$

$$T^{(k)s} = [t_{ij}^{(k)s}]_{n \times n} = \overline{R(Z^{(k)})}^s (I - \overline{R(Z^{(k)})}^s)^{-1}, s = L, U \tag{6.13}$$

where $t_{ij}^{(k)L}$ and $t_{ij}^{(k)U}$ are the lower limit and upper limit of rough interval in the total-relation matrix $T^{(k)}$, and I is the unit matrix.

**Step 6: Obtain the "Prominence" and "Relation".**

After acquiring the total-relation matrix $T^{(k)}$, the sum of rows and the sum of columns are separately represented as $D^{(k)}$ and $R^{(k)}$ within the total-relation matrix $T^{(k)}$ through the following formula:

$$D^{(k)} = \left( [d_{ij}^{(k)L}, d_{ij}^{(k)U}] \right)_{n \times 1} = \left( \left[ \sum_{j=1}^{n} t_{ij}^{(k)L}, \sum_{j=1}^{n} t_{ij}^{(k)U} \right] \right)_{n \times 1} \tag{6.14}$$

$$R^{(k)} = \left( [r_{ij}^{(k)L}, r_{ij}^{(k)U}] \right)_{1 \times n} = \left( \left[ \sum_{i=1}^{n} t_{ij}^{(k)L}, \sum_{i=1}^{n} t_{ij}^{(k)U} \right] \right)_{1 \times n} \tag{6.15}$$

To effectively determine the "Prominence" and "Relation", it is necessary to transform the $D^{(k)}$ and $R^{(k)}$ into crisp values. The de-"roughness" of any rough number $X_i = [x_i^L, x_i^U]$ can be conducted as follows:

(1) Normalization

$$\tilde{x}_i^L = (x_i^L - \min_i x_i^L) \Big/ \Delta_{\min}^{\max}, \tilde{x}_i^U = (x_i^U - \min_i x_i^L) \Big/ \Delta_{\min}^{\max}$$

$$\Delta_{\min}^{\max} = \max_i x_i^U - \min_i x_i^L \tag{6.16}$$

where $\tilde{x}_i^L$ and $\tilde{x}_i^U$ are the normalized form of the $x_i^L$ and $x_i^U$, respectively.

(2) Determination of a total normalized crisp value

$$\alpha_i = \frac{\tilde{x}_i^L \times (1 - \tilde{x}_i^L) + \tilde{x}_i^U \times \tilde{x}_i^U}{1 - \tilde{x}_i^L + \tilde{x}_i^U} \tag{6.17}$$

(3) Computation of final crisp values $x_i$ for $X_i$

$$x_i = \min_i x_i^L + \alpha_i \Delta_{\min}^{\max} \qquad (6.18)$$

We can obtain the final crisp values $d_i$ for $D^{(k)}$, and crisp values $r_i$ for $R^{(k)}$.

The vector $m_i$ called "Prominence" is made by adding $d_i$ to $r_j$. Similarly, the vector $n_i$ called "Relation" is made by subtracting $d_i$ to $r_j$.

$$m_i = d_i + r_j, \quad n_i = d_i - r_j, \quad i = j \qquad (6.19)$$

The vector $m_i$ reveals how much importance the criteria have. The larger the value of $m_i$ the greater the overall prominence of the criterion $i$ in terms of overall relationships with other criteria. The vector $n_i$ divide the criteria into the cause and effect groups. When the value $n_i$ is positive, the criterion belongs to the cause group. Then the criterion $i$ is a cause for other criteria. If the value $n_i$ is negative, the criterion belongs to the effect group. Then the criterion is reliant on fulfillment of other criteria. Therefore, the causal diagram can be acquired by mapping the dataset of the $(m_i, n_i)$, providing valuable insight for making decisions.

### Step 7: Determine the weights for the recommendation criteria.

The importance of the criteria $\omega_i^k$ is calculated with the following equation:

$$\omega_i^k = \sqrt{m_i^2 + n_i^2} \qquad (6.20)$$

The importance of any criterion can be normalized as follows:

$$W_i^k = \frac{\omega_i^k}{\sum_{1 \le i \le n} \omega_i^k} \qquad (6.21)$$

$W_i^k$ is the rough weight of the $i$th criterion.

## 6.1.2 Phase II: Multi-criteria PSS Recommendation

The analysis process of the proposed rough CF (Collaborative Filtering)-based recommendation method is concisely described as follows.

### Step 1: Generate a rough user-PSS rating matrix.

Each user is represented by a set of PSS-rating pairs and the summary of all those pairs can be collected into a user-PSS rating matrix in which for the $i$th user on the $j$th item under the $k$th criterion, a rating, $s_{ijk}$, is given. These ratings are described in the crisp scores (Strongly Interested=5, More Interested=4, Interested=3, Less

## 6.1 The Proposed Method for Personalized PSS Recommendation

Interested $=2$, Not Interested $=1$) according to Lu et al. (2010). There are $m$ customers in total and $n$ PSSs are provided. If user $i$ has not rated item $j$, then $r_{ijk} =$ Null. Note that more than one of the PSSs can be provided at the same time to an identical customer.

To convert the user-item rating matrix into rough user-item rating matrix (see Table 6.1), all the crisp scores $s_{ijk}$ in user-item rating matrix are transformed into rough number form $RN(s_{ijk})$ using Eqs. (6.3)–(6.6), $RN(s_{ijk}) = [s_{ijk}^L, s_{ijk}^U]$, where $s_{ijk}^L$ and $s_{ijk}^U$ are the lower limit and upper limit of the $RN(s_{ijk})$, respectively (Table 6.2).

Normalize the rough user-item rating matrix by using the follow equations: 6.22

$$s_{ijk}^{'L} = \frac{s_{ijk}^L}{\max_{i=1}^{P}\left\{\max\left[s_{ijk}^L, s_{ijk}^U\right]\right\}}, s_{ijk}^{'U} = \frac{s_{ijk}^U}{\max_{i=1}^{P}\left\{\max\left[s_{ijk}^L, s_{ijk}^U\right]\right\}} \quad (6.22)$$

$[s_{ijk}^{'L}, s_{ijk}^{'U}]$ indicates the lower and upper limits of normalized from of interval $[s_{ijk}^L, s_{ijk}^U]$. The normalization method mentioned above is to preserve the property that the ranges of normalized interval numbers belong to [0, 1]. Then calculate the comprehensive rough user-item rating matrix

$$S_{ij} = \sum_{k=1}^{n} W_i^k \times RN(S_{ijk}) = [S_{ij}^L, S_{ij}^U], \quad (6.23)$$

where $s_{ij}^L$ and $s_{ij}^U$ are the lower limit and upper limit of the $RN(s_{ijk})$, respectively (Table 6.3).

***Step 2: Calculate user similarity.***

The similarity of users can be measured by the distance between their ratings on the same PSS.

$$d_{rating}\left(R(U, j), R(U', j)\right) = \sqrt{\frac{(S_{ij}^L - S_{ij}^{L'})^2 + (S_{ij}^U - S_{ij}^{U'})^2}{2}} \quad (6.24)$$

where $R(U, j)$ is the user $U$'s rating on the $j$th PSS, and $R(U', j)$ is the rating of user $U$ on the $j$th PSS; $d_{rating}(R(U, j), R(U', j))$ denotes the distance between the rating $R(U, j)$ and $R(U', j)$.

Then, the distance $d_{user}(U, U')$ between the user $U$ and $U'$ can be acquired as follows:

$$d_{user}(U, U') = \frac{\sum_{j \in N(U,U')} d_{rating}(R(U, j), R(U', j))}{N(U, U')} \quad (6.25)$$

where $N(U, U')$ is the number of PSS which the user $U$ and $U'$ simultaneously rate. The smaller the $d_{user}(U, U')$ is, the larger of the similarity between the user $U$ and $U'$.

**Table 6.1** User-PSS rating matrix (Song and Sakao 2018)

|    | PSS1 |   |   |   | PSS2 |   |   |   | ... | PSSq |   |   |   |
|----|------|------|-----|--------|------|------|-----|--------|-----|------|------|-----|--------|
|    | $C_1$ | $C_2$ | ... | $C_n$ | $C_1$ | $C_2$ | ... | $C_n$ | ... | $C_1$ | $C_2$ | ... | $C_n$ |
| U1 | $S_{111}$ | $S_{112}$ | ... | $S_{11n}$ | $S_{121}$ | $S_{122}$ | ... | $S_{12n}$ | ... | $S_{1q1}$ | $S_{1q2}$ | ... | $S_{1qn}$ |
| U2 | $S_{211}$ | $S_{212}$ | ... | $S_{21n}$ | $S_{221}$ | $S_{222}$ | ... | $S_{22n}$ | ... | $S_{2q1}$ | $S_{2q2}$ | ... | $S_{2qn}$ |
| ... | ... | ... | ... | ... | ... | ... | ... | ... | ... | ... | ... | ... | ... |
| Up | $S_{p11}$ | $S_{p12}$ | ... | $S_{p1n}$ | $S_{p21}$ | $S_{p22}$ | ... | $S_{p2n}$ | ... | $S_{pq1}$ | $S_{pq2}$ | ... | $S_{pqn}$ |

## 6.1 The Proposed Method for Personalized PSS Recommendation

**Table 6.2** Rough user-item rating matrix (Song and Sakao 2018)

|    | PSS1 | | | | ... | PSSq | | | |
|----|------|------|------|------|-----|------|------|------|------|
|    | $C_1$ | $C_2$ | ... | $C_n$ | ... | $C_1$ | $C_2$ | ... | $C_n$ |
| U1 | $RN(S_{111})$ | $RN(S_{112})$ | ... | $RN(S_{11n})$ | ... | $RN(S_{1q1})$ | $RN(S_{1q2})$ | ... | $RN(S_{1qn})$ |
| U2 | $RN(S_{211})$ | $RN(S_{212})$ | ... | $RN(S_{21n})$ | ... | $RN(S_{2q1})$ | $RN(S_{2q2})$ | ... | $RN(S_{2qn})$ |
| ... | ... | ... | ... | ... | ... | ... | ... | ... | ... |
| Up | $RN(S_{p11})$ | $RN(S_{p12})$ | ... | $RN(S_{p1n})$ | ... | $RN(S_{pq1})$ | $RN(S_{pq2})$ | ... | $RN(S_{pqn})$ |

**Table 6.3** The comprehensive rough user-item rating matrix (Song and Sakao 2018)

|     | PSS1     | PSS2     | ... | PSSk     | ... | PSSq     |
|-----|----------|----------|-----|----------|-----|----------|
| U1  | $S_{11}$ | $S_{12}$ | ... | $S_{1k}$ | ... | $S_{1q}$ |
| U2  | $S_{21}$ | $S_{22}$ | ... | $S_{2k}$ | ... | $S_{2q}$ |
| ... | ...      | ...      | ... | ...      | ... | ...      |
| Up  | $S_{p1}$ | $S_{p2}$ | ... | $S_{pk}$ | ... | $S_{pq}$ |

The similarity $sim(U, U')$ between the user $U$ and $U'$ is calculated as follows:

$$sim(U, U') = \frac{1}{1 + d_{user}(U, U')} \quad (6.26)$$

### Step 3: Select top-N similar users.

We need to choose a number of neighbor users to predict ratings. In our method, we use the top-N technique for neighbor selection (Herlocker et al. 2002). A certain number of most similar users will be selected as neighbors by using this method. Before the user neighbor selection, the number of neighbors is predetermined.

### Step 4: Predict rough unrated ratings and make recommendation.

This step is to predict the ratings of every unrated PSS for target users. In this step, all the unrated ratings can be calculated and all the empty cells in the user-item rating table will be filled except the ratings to the new items which have been rated less than twice. The algorithm for prediction is as follows:

$$P_{U,j} = \bar{R}_U + \frac{\sum_{V \in N} sim(U, V) \times (R_{V,j} - \bar{R}_V)}{\sum_{V \in N} sim(U, V)} = [P^l_{U,j}, P^u_{U,j}] \quad (6.27)$$

where $P_{U,j}$ indicates the final predicted ratings of user U on the jth PSS. $R_{V,j}$ indicates the ratings of user V on the jth PSS. N is the number of selected neighbors. $sim(U, V)$ is the similarity between the user $U$ and user $V$. $\bar{R}_U$ is the average of all ratings from user U, and $\bar{R}_V$ is the average of all ratings from user V. $P^l_{U,j}$ and $P^u_{U,j}$ are the lower limit and upper limit of the $P_{U,j}$.

### Step 5: Calculate Closeness Coefficient.

In this final step, the ranking order of all PSSs' prediction values is determined by computing a closeness coefficient. First, the distance between each $P_{U,j}$ and value of "strongly interested (SI = 5)" ($d^+_{U,j}$), and the distance between each $P_{U,j}$ and value of "not interested (NI = 1)" ($d^-_{U,j}$) can be calculated as follows:

$$d^+_{U,j} = \sqrt{\frac{(P^l_{U,j} - SI)^2 + (P^u_{U,j} - SI)^2}{2}} \quad (6.28)$$

## 6.1 The Proposed Method for Personalized PSS Recommendation

$$d_{U,j}^- = \sqrt{\frac{(P_{U,j}^l - NI)^2 + (P_{U,j}^u - NI)^2}{2}} \quad (6.29)$$

When the $d_{U,j}^+$ and $d_{U,j}^-$ has been calculated, a closeness coefficient is defined to determine the ranking order of all PSSs' prediction values. The closeness coefficient $CC_{U,j}$ is defined as:

$$CC_{U,j} = \frac{d_{U,j}^-}{d_{U,j}^- + d_{U,j}^+}, \quad j = 1, 2, \ldots, m. \quad (6.30)$$

There are various ways to present recommendations to the user: either by offering the best PSS, or by presenting the top-K PSSs as a recommendation list. Because we target the certainty of PSS recommendations for increasing the trust and confidence of the user towards the recommendation, it's more advisable to recommend the highly certain among the top-K most interesting PSSs. The rough predicted value $P_{U,j}$ that corresponds to Min $(CC_{U,j}, j = 1, 2, \ldots, m)$ is the top predicted value and the top-$N$ PSSs that correspond to the top-$N$ higher raking $CC_{U,j}$ are selected as the final recommendation list for the target user.

## 6.2 Case Study: Personalized Recommendation of Elevator PSS

### 6.2.1 Case Background

To verify the effectiveness of the proposed the PSS recommendation method, it was applied to an elevator manufacturing Company M. The proposed approach is implemented step by step. Elevator Company M is a leading manufacturer who provides various types of elevators (e.g., passenger/freight elevator, hospital elevator, and escalator). Besides, it also provides service offerings including "Installation & commissioning" (PSS1), "Expert advisory" (PSS2), "Life cycle data analysis" (PSS3), "Customer care" (PSS4), "Maintenance/semimonthly" (PSS5), "Emergency repair" (PSS6), "One-stop spare parts supply" (PSS7), "Operation monitoring" (PSS8), "Energy management contract" (PSS9), and "Online knowledge support" (PSS10). Considering the dynamic change of requirements over time, Company M decided to conduct PSS personalized recommendation. In this way, Company M can actively provide differentiated PSS and improve their response ability to increase customer value and satisfaction.

## 6.2.2 Implementation of the PSS Recommendation Approach

**Phase I: Weight determination for elevator PSS criteria**

***Step 1: Develop the evaluation criteria for the PSS.***

All the three categories (benefit, sacrifice, and environmental impact) are taken into account, as a result, this step selects six evaluation criteria according to the characteristics of PSS, namely, $C_1$: Service Infrastructure (Benefit criterion), $C_2$: Service Reliability (Benefit criterion), $C_3$: Service Cost (Sacrifice criterion), $C_4$: Service Response (Benefit criterion), $C_5$: Service Competence (Benefit criterion), $C_6$: Environmental Concern (Criterion of environmental impact).

***Step 2: Acquire the group initial direct-relation matrix.***

To measure the correlations between different criteria, eight users are invited to make sets of pair-wise comparisons according to crisp scores of 4, 3, 2, 1, 0. The group initial direct-relation matrix Z can be acquired as follows:

$$Z = \begin{bmatrix} \{0,0,0,0,0,0,0,0\} & \{0,1,1,0,2,2,0,2\} & \cdots & \{2,0,1,2,1,0,1,0\} \\ \{4,2,2,4,3,1,1,4\} & \{0,0,0,0,0,0,0,0\} & & \{1,2,3,4,3,1,4,2\} \\ \{2,0,0,0,4,3,4,3\} & \{0,1,0,0,3,1,0,0\} & \cdots & \{1,2,1,2,3,2,3,3\} \\ \vdots & \vdots & \ddots & \vdots \\ \{3,2,3,1,4,2,3,2\} & \{1,2,3,1,0,2,1,0\} & \cdots & \{0,0,0,0,0,0,0,0\} \end{bmatrix}$$

***Step 3: All the crisp judgments in initial direct-relation matrix Z are converted into rough number form.***

According to the Formulas (6.3)–(6.8), the rough initial direct-relation matrix $R(Z^{(k)})$ (k = 1, 2, ..., 8) for each customer can be obtained. For example, when k = 1, the first user's rough initial direct-relation matrix $R(Z^{(1)})$ is as follows:

$$R(Z^{(1)}) = \begin{bmatrix} [0.000, 0.000] & [0.000, 1.000] & [2.167, 3.500] \\ [2.625, 4.000] & [0.000, 0.000] & [1.500, 3.000] \\ [0.500, 3.200] & [0.000, 0.625] & [0.000, 0.000] \\ [3.375, 4.000] & [1.286, 3.500] & [2.000, 3.400] \\ [2.500, 3.333] & [1.571, 3.333] & [1.600, 2.667] \\ [2.286, 3.250] & [0.600, 1.667] & [2.500, 3.333] \end{bmatrix}$$

## 6.2 Case Study: Personalized Recommendation of Elevator PSS

$$\begin{bmatrix} [0.000, 0.500] & [0.000, 1.875] & [0.875, 2.000] \\ [0.714, 1.167] & [2.875, 4.000] & [1.000, 2.500] \\ [0.000, 1.125] & [0.000, 1.375] & [1.000, 2.125] \\ [0.000, 0.000] & [1.500, 3.000] & [2.333, 3.333] \\ [0.500, 1.600] & [0.000, 0.000] & [2.000, 2.750] \\ [0.429, 1.250] & [2.000, 2.625] & [0.000, 0.000] \end{bmatrix}$$

### Step 4: Acquire the normalized rough direct-relation matrix.

To convert the criteria scales into comparable scales, the normalized direct-relation rough matrix of the $k$th user $\overline{R(Z^{(k)})}$ is obtained in accordance with the Formulas (6.9)–(6.11). For example, the first user's normalized direct-relation rough matrix $R(Z^{(1)})$ is acquired as follows:

$$\overline{R(Z^{(1)})} = \begin{bmatrix} [0.000, 0.000] & [0.000, 0.058] & [0.126, 0.203] \\ [0.152, 0.232] & [0.000, 0.000] & [0.087, 0.174] \\ [0.029, 0.186] & [0.000, 0.036] & [0.000, 0.000] \\ [0.196, 0.232] & [0.075, 0.203] & [0.116, 0.197] \\ [0.145, 0.193] & [0.091, 0.193] & [0.093, 0.155] \\ [0.133, 0.189] & [0.035, 0.097] & [0.145, 0.193] \end{bmatrix}$$

$$\begin{bmatrix} [0.000, 0.029] & [0.000, 0.109] & [0.051, 0.116] \\ [0.041, 0.068] & [0.167, 0.232] & [0.058, 0.145] \\ [0.000, 0.065] & [0.000, 0.080] & [0.058, 0.123] \\ [0.000, 0.000] & [0.087, 0.174] & [0.135, 0.193] \\ [0.029, 0.093] & [0.000, 0.000] & [0.116, 0.160] \\ [0.025, 0.073] & [0.116, 0.152] & [0.000, 0.000] \end{bmatrix}$$

### Step 5: Set up the total-relation matrix $T^{(k)}$.

The total-relation matrix $T^{(1)}$ of the first user can be acquired in the light of the Formulas (6.12)–(6.13).

$$T^{(1)} = \begin{bmatrix} [0.014, 0.263] & [0.003, 0.197] & [0.137, 0.416] \\ [0.212, 0.621] & [0.025, 0.240] & [0.155, 0.548] \\ [0.040, 0.412] & [0.003, 0.178] & [0.015, 0.241] \\ [0.260, 0.701] & [0.093, 0.456] & [0.196, 0.639] \\ [0.198, 0.576] & [0.103, 0.393] & [0.157, 0.517] \\ [0.177, 0.516] & [0.051, 0.284] & [0.194, 0.497] \end{bmatrix}$$

**Table 6.4** The $D^{(1)}, R^{(1)}$, $m_i$ and $n_i$ of the total-relation matrix $T^{(1)}$ (Song and Sakao 2018)

|  | C1 | C2 | C3 | C4 | C5 | C6 |
|---|---|---|---|---|---|---|
| $D^{(1)}$ | [0.225,1.580] | [0.738,2.572] | [0.130,1.535] | [0.868,3.034] | [0.684,2.458] | [0.629,2.142] |
| $R^{(1)}$ | [0.901,1.489] | [0.277,1.489] | [0.854,1.489] | [0.136,1.489] | [0.498,1.489] | [0.606,1.489] |
| $m_i$ | 2.811 | 2.486 | 2.514 | 2.477 | 2.837 | 2.676 |
| $n_i$ | −1.439 | 0.88 | −1.338 | 1.74 | 0.297 | −0.04 |

**Table 6.5** The weighs for the criteria of different users (Song and Sakao 2018)

|  | $\omega_1^k$ | $\omega_2^k$ | $\omega_3^k$ | $\omega_4^k$ | $\omega_5^k$ | $\omega_6^k$ |
|---|---|---|---|---|---|---|
| User 1 | 0.184 | 0.153 | 0.166 | 0.176 | 0.166 | 0.156 |
| User 2 | 0.147 | 0.169 | 0.179 | 0.145 | 0.193 | 0.167 |
| User 3 | 0.175 | 0.171 | 0.159 | 0.152 | 0.163 | 0.18 |
| User 4 | 0.166 | 0.168 | 0.171 | 0.147 | 0.168 | 0.18 |
| User 5 | 0.164 | 0.156 | 0.19 | 0.148 | 0.186 | 0.156 |
| User 6 | 0.168 | 0.149 | 0.182 | 0.168 | 0.189 | 0.144 |
| User 7 | 0.169 | 0.152 | 0.182 | 0.161 | 0.17 | 0.166 |
| User 8 | 0.182 | 0.159 | 0.173 | 0.123 | 0.192 | 0.171 |

$$\begin{bmatrix} [0.002, 0.125] & [0.008, 0.283] & [0.061, 0.296] \\ [0.051, 0.217] & [0.188, 0.504] & [0.108, 0.442] \\ [0.002, 0.150] & [0.008, 0.257] & [0.062, 0.297] \\ [0.012, 0.180] & [0.125, 0.520] & [0.181, 0.538] \\ [0.038, 0.230] & [0.038, 0.302] & [0.151, 0.440] \\ [0.032, 0.194] & [0.132, 0.388] & [0.043, 0.262] \end{bmatrix}$$

Similarly, the total-relation matrix $T^{(k)}$ of the other users can also be acquired.

***Step 6: Obtain the "Prominence" and "Relation".***

The sum of rows and the sum of columns are respectively expressed as $D^{(k)}$ and $R^{(k)}$ within the total-relation matrix $T^{(k)}$ according to the Formulas (6.14)–(6.15). $M_i$ and $N_i$ are computed with the Formulas (6.16)–(6.19). Table 6.4 provides the $D^{(1)}$, $R^{(1)}$, $m_i$ and $n_i$ of the user 1 (U1). Other $D^{(k)}$, $R^{(k)}$, $m_k$ and $n_k$ can be calculated in the same way.

***Step 7: Determine the weighs for the recommendation criteria.***

The importance of the criteria $\omega_i^k$ is calculated by using the Eqs. (6.20)–(6.21). All the weighs for the criteria of different users are offered in Table 6.5.

## Phase II: Multi-criteria recommendation of elevator PSS

### Step 1: Generate a rough user-PSS rating matrix.

Eight users' ratings under different criteria are collected to construct the initial user-elevator PSS rating matrix (see Table 6.6). User 1's ratings on "Life cycle data analysis" (PSS3), "Emergency repair" (PSS6), "Energy management contract" (PSS9), and "Online knowledge support" (PSS10) are not available. Hence, they are represented with "Null".

Then, all the crisp ratings in the initial user-elevator PSS rating matrix are converted into rough intervals using Eqs. (6.3)–(6.6) to acquire the rough user- elevator PSS rating matrix (see Table 6.7).

Through the normalization of the rough user-elevator PSS rating matrix (see Table 6.8), the comprehensive rough user-PSS rating matrix was computed (see Table 6.9) according to the Eqs. (6.22)–(6.23).

### Step 2: Calculate user similarity.

The user 1 doesn't provide ratings on several of the PSSs (e.g., PSS3, PSS6, PSS9 and PSS10), because the user 1 has not previously purchased those PSSs. Therefore, the company decided to recommend PSSs to user 1 in this case. The similarities between user 1 and the other users (see Table 6.10) can be calculated according to the Formulas (6.24)–(6.26).

### Step 3: Select top-N similar users.

With this method of top-N technique, 3 of most similar users are selected as neighbors to predict ratings. They are U5 $(sim(U_1, U_5) = 0.963)$, U8 $(sim(U_1, U_8) = 0.958)$ and U2 $(sim(U_1, U_2) = 0.943)$.

### Step 4: Predict unrated rough ratings and make recommendation.

All the unrated ratings $P_{U,j}$ ($j = 3, 6, 9, 10$) are computed with the Formula (6.27). The ratings of PSS3, PSS6, PSS9, and PSS10 are provided in the Table 6.11.

### Step 5: Calculating Closeness Coefficient.

The closeness coefficients of PSS3, PSS6, PSS9, and PSS10 are calculated to determine the ranking order of their prediction values by using the Formulas (6.28)–(6.30). Table 6.12 presents the distance between each $P_{U,j}$ and value of "strongly interested (SI=5)" $\left(d^+_{U,j}\right)$, the distance between each $P_{U,j}$ and value of "not interested (NI=1)" $\left(d^-_{U,j}\right)$, and the closeness coefficients.

According to the Table 6.12, because the rough predicted value of "Life cycle data analysis" (PSS3) has the smallest closeness coefficients (0.052), PSS3 is selected as the highly recommended item. In this case study, PSSs corresponding to the smaller $CC_{U,j}$ serve as the final recommendation list for the target user 1 (U1), i.e., the final recommendation list is {PSS3 "Life cycle data analysis" (highly recommended), PSS6 "Emergency repair" and PSS10 "Online knowledge support" (fairly recommended)}.

**Table 6.6** User-elevator PSS rating matrix (Song and Sakao 2018)

| | PSS1 | | | | | | PSS2 | | | | | | ... | PSS9 | | | | | | PSS10 | | | | | |
|---|---|---|---|---|---|---|---|---|---|---|---|---|---|---|---|---|---|---|---|---|---|---|---|---|---|
| | C1 | C2 | C3 | C4 | C5 | C6 | C1 | C2 | C3 | C4 | C5 | C6 | ... | C1 | C2 | C3 | C4 | C5 | C6 | C1 | C2 | C3 | C4 | C5 | C6 |
| U1 | 4 | 3 | 1 | 3 | 2 | 1 | 3 | 4 | 4 | 2 | 3 | 2 | ... | Null | Null | Null | Null | Null | Null | Null | Null | Null | Null | Null | Null |
| U2 | 4 | 3 | 2 | 3 | 3 | 3 | 2 | 4 | 4 | 2 | 4 | 3 | ... | 2 | 3 | 4 | 3 | 3 | 4 | 3 | 4 | 3 | 3 | 3 | 4 |
| U3 | 4 | 4 | 2 | 4 | 3 | 2 | 2 | 3 | 3 | 2 | 4 | 3 | ... | 3 | 3 | 3 | 2 | 2 | 3 | 3 | 3 | 3 | 3 | 3 | 3 |
| U4 | 3 | 2 | 1 | 2 | 2 | 1 | 3 | 2 | 3 | 1 | 4 | 4 | ... | 2 | 3 | 2 | 4 | 4 | 3 | 2 | 3 | 1 | 2 | 4 | 2 |
| U5 | 3 | 4 | 1 | 2 | 4 | 2 | 3 | 3 | 4 | 2 | 3 | 3 | ... | 2 | 2 | 3 | 2 | 2 | 4 | 2 | 4 | 2 | 2 | 3 | 2 |
| U6 | 4 | 3 | 2 | 2 | 3 | 1 | 2 | 4 | 4 | 2 | 3 | 2 | ... | 1 | 4 | 2 | 2 | 2 | 3 | 2 | 2 | 2 | 3 | 2 | 3 |
| U7 | 3 | 3 | 1 | 3 | 3 | 1 | 2 | 4 | 3 | 1 | 4 | 2 | ... | 1 | 3 | 3 | 2 | 4 | 4 | 3 | 2 | 3 | 4 | 3 | 3 |
| U8 | 3 | 3 | 1 | 2 | 3 | 3 | 2 | 3 | 4 | 1 | 3 | 3 | ... | 3 | 2 | 3 | 3 | 3 | 4 | 2 | 4 | 2 | 4 | 3 | 4 |

*Note* Strongly Interested = 5, More Interested = 4, Interested = 3, Less Interested = 2, Not Interested = 1. Null denote that no rating is available. Some ratings in the table are omitted due to the space limitations

## 6.2 Case Study: Personalized Recommendation of Elevator PSS

**Table 6.7** The rough user-elevator PSS rating matrix (Song and Sakao 2018)

| | PSS1 | | | | | ... | PSS10 | | | | |
|---|---|---|---|---|---|---|---|---|---|---|---|
| | C1 | C2 | ... | C5 | C6 | ... | C1 | C2 | ... | C5 | C6 |
| U1 | [3.500,4.000] | [2.833,3.286] | ... | [2.000,2.875] | [1.000,1.750] | ... | Null | Null | ... | Null | Null |
| U2 | [3.500,4.000] | [2.833,3.286] | ... | [2.714,3.167] | [1.750,3.000] | ... | [2.429,3.000] | [3.143,4.000] | ... | [2.833,3.167] | [3.000,4.000] |
| U3 | [3.500,4.000] | [3.125,4.000] | ... | [2.714,3.167] | [1.333,2.500] | ... | [2.429,3.000] | [2.500,3.600] | ... | [2.833,3.167] | [2.600,3.400] |
| U4 | [3.000,3.500] | [2.000,3.125] | ... | [2.000,2.875] | [1.000,1.750] | ... | [2.000,2.429] | [2.500,3.600] | ... | [3.000,4.000] | [2.000,3.000] |
| U5 | [3.000,3.500] | [3.125,4.000] | ... | [2.875,4.000] | [1.333,2.500] | ... | [2.000,2.429] | [3.143,4.000] | ... | [2.833,3.167] | [2.000,3.000] |
| U6 | [3.500,4.000] | [2.833,3.286] | ... | [2.714,3.167] | [1.000,1.750] | ... | [2.000,2.429] | [2.000,3.143] | ... | [2.000,3.000] | [2.600,3.400] |
| U7 | [3.000,3.500] | [2.833,3.286] | ... | [2.714,3.167] | [1.000,1.750] | ... | [2.429,3.000] | [2.000,3.143] | ... | [2.833,3.167] | [2.600,3.400] |
| U8 | [3.000,3.500] | [2.833,3.286] | ... | [2.714,3.167] | [1.750,3.000] | ... | [2.000,2.429] | [3.143,4.000] | ... | [2.833,3.167] | [3.000,4.000] |

*Note* Some rough intervals are omitted in the table due to the space limitations

**Table 6.8** The normalized rough user-elevator PSS rating matrix (Song and Sakao 2018)

|  | PSS1 | | | | | | PSS10 | | | | |
|---|---|---|---|---|---|---|---|---|---|---|---|
|  | C1 | C2 | ... | C5 | C6 | ... | C1 | C2 | ... | C5 | C6 |
| U1 | [0.875,1.000] | [0.708,0.821] | ... | [0.500,0.719] | [0.333,0.583] | ... | Null | Null | ... | Null | Null |
| U2 | [0.875,1.000] | [0.708,0.821] | ... | [0.679,0.792] | [0.583,1.000] | ... | [0.810,1.000] | [0.786,1.000] | ... | [0.708,0.792] | [0.750,1.000] |
| U3 | [0.875,1.000] | [0.781,1.000] | ... | [0.679,0.792] | [0.444,0.833] | ... | [0.810,1.000] | [0.625,0.900] | ... | [0.708,0.792] | [0.650,0.850] |
| U4 | [0.750,0.875] | [0.500,0.781] | ... | [0.500,0.719] | [0.333,0.583] | ... | [0.667,0.810] | [0.625,0.900] | ... | [0.750,1.000] | [0.500,0.750] |
| U5 | [0.750,0.875] | [0.781,1.000] | ... | [0.719,1.000] | [0.444,0.833] | ... | [0.667,0.810] | [0.786,1.000] | ... | [0.708,0.792] | [0.500,0.750] |
| U6 | [0.875,1.000] | [0.708,0.821] | ... | [0.679,0.792] | [0.333,0.583] | ... | [0.667,0.810] | [0.500,0.786] | ... | [0.500,0.750] | [0.650,0.850] |
| U7 | [0.750,0.875] | [0.708,0.821] | ... | [0.679,0.792] | [0.333,0.583] | ... | [0.810,1.000] | [0.500,0.786] | ... | [0.708,0.792] | [0.650,0.850] |
| U8 | [0.750,0.875] | [0.708,0.821] | ... | [0.679,0.792] | [0.583,1.000] | ... | [0.667,0.810] | [0.786,1.000] | ... | [0.708,0.792] | [0.750,1.000] |

*Note* Some rough intervals are omitted in the table due to the space limitations

## 6.2 Case Study: Personalized Recommendation of Elevator PSS

**Table 6.9** The comprehensive rough user-PSS rating matrix (Song and Sakao 2018)

| | PSS1 | PSS2 | PSS3 | PSS4 | PSS5 | PSS6 | ... | PSS9 | PSS10 |
|---|---|---|---|---|---|---|---|---|---|
| U1 | [0.594,0.776] | [0.770,0.931] | Null | [0.727,0.949] | [0.626,0.877] | Null | ... | Null | Null |
| U2 | [0.688,0.902] | [0.797,0.936] | [0.690,0.862] | [0.683,0.869] | [0.581,0.823] | [0.611,0.821] | ... | [0.668,0.889] | [0.744,0.938] |
| U3 | [0.686,0.936] | [0.735,0.894] | [0.670,0.856] | [0.588,0.871] | [0.471,0.700] | [0.669,0.862] | ... | [0.629,0.814] | [0.701,0.899] |
| U4 | [0.512,0.716] | [0.688,0.930] | [0.638,0.823] | [0.654,0.858] | [0.564,0.785] | [0.562,0.782] | ... | [0.636,0.865] | [0.562,0.829] |
| U5 | [0.617,0.843] | [0.769,0.929] | [0.713,0.930] | [0.699,0.913] | [0.577,0.818] | [0.586,0.805] | ... | [0.598,0.779] | [0.627,0.822] |
| U6 | [0.638,0.816] | [0.753,0.896] | [0.694,0.852] | [0.660,0.882] | [0.529,0.766] | [0.615,0.823] | ... | [0.540,0.763] | [0.590,0.812] |
| U7 | [0.594,0.760] | [0.690,0.866] | [0.691,0.881] | [0.620,0.881] | [0.581,0.852] | [0.688,0.903] | ... | [0.629,0.820] | [0.700,0.907] |
| U8 | [0.627,0.812] | [0.703,0.864] | [0.645,0.822] | [0.669,0.882] | [0.579,0.869] | [0.727,0.977] | ... | [0.656,0.875] | [0.704,0.897] |

*Note* Some rough intervals are omitted in the table due to the space limitations

Table 6.10 The similarities between user 1 and other users (Song and Sakao 2018)

| $d_{rating}(R(U_1,j), R(U_k,j))$ | PSS1 | PSS2 | PSS4 | PSS5 | PSS7 | PSS8 | $d_{user}(U_1, U_k)$ | $sim(U_1, U_k)$ |
|---|---|---|---|---|---|---|---|---|
| U1–U2 | 0.111 | 0.019 | 0.065 | 0.049 | 0.094 | 0.025 | 0.061 | 0.943 |
| U1–U3 | 0.131 | 0.036 | 0.113 | 0.166 | 0.060 | 0.013 | 0.086 | 0.920 |
| U1–U4 | 0.072 | 0.058 | 0.082 | 0.078 | 0.108 | 0.033 | 0.072 | 0.933 |
| U1–U5 | 0.05 | 0.001 | 0.032 | 0.054 | 0.055 | 0.039 | 0.039 | 0.963 |
| U1–U6 | 0.042 | 0.027 | 0.067 | 0.104 | 0.091 | 0.046 | 0.063 | 0.941 |
| U1–U7 | 0.012 | 0.073 | 0.113 | 0.036 | 0.046 | 0.082 | 0.060 | 0.942 |
| U1–U8 | 0.035 | 0.067 | 0.063 | 0.034 | 0.036 | 0.029 | 0.044 | 0.958 |

**Table 6.11** The average of all ratings and the predicted ratings of user $U_1$ (Song and Sakao 2018)

| The average of all ratings from user 1 and its similar users | $\bar{R}_{U_1}$ | [0.662,0.870] |
|---|---|---|
| | $\bar{R}_{U_5}$ | [0.643,0.850] |
| | $\bar{R}_{U_8}$ | [0.660,0.875] |
| | $\bar{R}_{U_2}$ | [0.648,0.854] |
| The predicted ratings of user $U_1$ | $P_{U,3}$ | [0.694,0.888] |
| | $P_{U,6}$ | [0.678,0.905] |
| | $P_{U,9}$ | [0.639,0.834] |
| | $P_{U,10}$ | [0.688,0.885] |

**Table 6.12** $d^+_{U,j}, d^-_{U,j}$ and the closeness coefficients (Song and Sakao 2018)

| | $d^+_{U,j}$ | $d^-_{U,j}$ | $CC_{U,j}$ |
|---|---|---|---|
| PSS3 | 4.210 | 0.230 | 0.052 |
| PSS6 | 4.210 | 0.237 | 0.053 |
| PSS9 | 4.264 | 0.281 | 0.062 |
| PSS10 | 4.215 | 0.235 | 0.053 |

## 6.3 Comparisons and Discussion

To verify the effectiveness and advantages of the proposed approach, the fuzzy recommendation approach based on symmetrical triangular fuzzy number has also been applied to solve the same problem. Figure 6.2 illustrates the comparative results of the proposed and fuzzy recommendation approach.

Criteria weights for user 1 are different in the two approaches (see Fig. 6.2). As can be seen in Fig. 6.2, the most important criterion for user 1 is Service Infrastructure ($C_1$) by the proposed method. However, it is Service Response ($C_4$) in the fuzzy method. The reason for this difference is that calculation by the proposed method is more accurate.

In addition to recommendation, the designers can also know which aspect of PSS should be improved based on the different criteria weights. For example, it is better for designers to increase tangibility of the PSS9 with appropriate service infrastructure and improve the response speed when recommending it to user 1, because user 1 pays more attention to the criterion of Service Infrastructure ($C_1$) and Service Response ($C_4$).

Moreover, the causal diagram by the proposed method is different from that by the fuzzy method. For instance, from the perspective of user 7, the recommendation criteria Service Infrastructure ($C_1$), Service Cost ($C_3$), and Service Competence ($C_5$), Environmental Concern ($C_6$) are all considered as the effect criteria which receive influences from other criteria by the proposed method, because the "Relation" $n_1$,

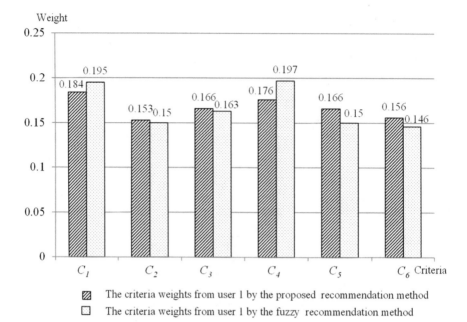

**Fig. 6.2** Comparisons between the proposed rough approach and the fuzzy approach (Song and Sakao 2018)

$n_3$, $n_5$ and $n_6$ are all negative (see Fig. 6.3a). However, both Service Cost ($C_3$) and Environmental Concern ($C_6$) are regarded as the cause criteria which may dispatch influence on other criteria in the fuzzy recommendation method, because both the "Relation" $n_3$ and $n_6$ are all positive (see Fig. 6.3b). This information can provide valuable suggestions for the future improvement of PSS.

Figure 6.4 illustrates the different closeness coefficients to U1 by the proposed method and those by the fuzzy recommendation method. PSS3 "Life cycle data analysis" is selected as the highly recommended solution for U1 in the proposed method and the fuzzy recommendation method, because the $CC_3$ is the smallest in both methods. Both PSS6 "Emergency repair" and PSS10 "Online knowledge support" are considered as fairly recommended in the proposed method, because $CC_6$ and $CC_{10}$ are the second smallest among different closeness coefficients ($CC_6 = CC_{10} = 0.053$). However, only PSS6 "Emergency repair" is considered as fairly recommended in the fuzzy recommendation method, because $CC_6$ is the second smallest closeness coefficient ($CC_6 = 0.053$). This is because the proposed rough recommending method flexibly considers the vagueness and rating distribution throughout the recommending process.

The differences between the proposed method and the fuzzy recommendation approach are mainly caused by their different rating manipulating mechanism. The proposed method considers not only the individual user ratings but also the rating distribution among all the users' ratings under the same criteria. For exam-

## 6.3 Comparisons and Discussion

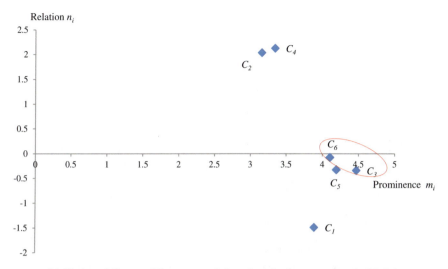

(a). The casual diagram of the recommendation criteria by the proposed method Relation $n_i$

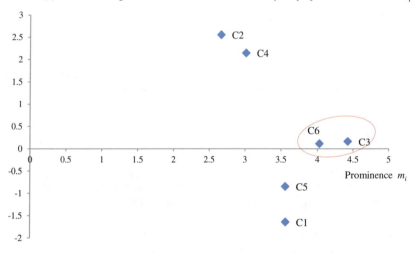

(b). The casual diagram of the recommendation criteria by fuzzy method

**Fig. 6.3** The causal diagrams of user 7 by the two different methods (Song and Sakao 2018)

ple, when rating *PSS1* (Installation & commissioning) under the criterion $C_4$ (Service Response), eight users give their scores as {3,3,4,2,2,2,3,2}. The rough approach transforms their scores into {[2.429,3.250], [2.429,3.250], [2.625,4.000], [2.000,2.625], [2.000,2.625], [2.000,2.625], [2.429,3.250], [2.000,2.625]}, which considers the vagueness in group decision making process with flexible intervals. In contrast, the fuzzy recommendation method transforms their scores into {[2,4], [2,4], [3,5], [1,3], [1,3], [1,3], [2,4], [1,3]}, and these interval numbers

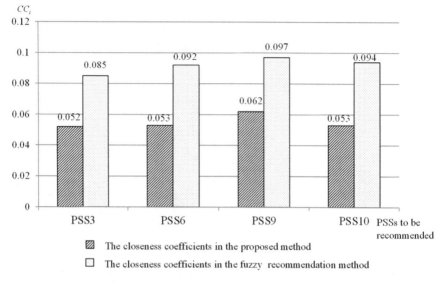

**Fig. 6.4** The closeness coefficients by the proposed method and the fuzzy recommendation method (Song and Sakao 2018)

all have fixed interval of 2. The fixed interval of 2 is used by the fuzzy method to indicate vagueness in different user rating. This is not consistent with the practice, because different users have different experience and knowledge which leads to different vagueness and subjectivity in their ratings. When the original scores {3,3,4,2,2,2,3,2} change into {2,2,4,3,3,3,4,3}, the rough method converts this judgment set into {[2.000,3.000], [2.000,3.000], [3.000,4.000], [2.667,3.333], [2.667,3.333], [2.667,3.333], [3.000,4.000], [2.667,3.333]}, which reflects the variation of vagueness in ratings with the flexible intervals. However, in the fuzzy recommendation method, the new judgment set is transformed into {[1,3], [1,3], [3,5], [2,4], [2,4], [2,4], [3,5], [2,4]}, which are still with fixed interval of 2. Therefore, the fuzzy conversion does not reflect rating changes in vagueness. This is mainly caused by the pre-set fuzzy membership function in the fuzzy recommendation approach. Thus, the proposed method is more flexible and close to the reality than the fuzzy recommendation approach.

Although the well-known AHP/ANP (Saaty 1988, 1996)-based approaches are good MCDM (multi-criteria decision-making) approaches, they cannot be directly applied into the personalized recommendation of PSS. This is because the AHP/ANP approaches lack appropriate mechanism for addressing similarity calculation (e.g. user similarity) which is critical to the success of personalized recommendation. On the contrary, the proposed method not only has the mechanism of criterion weight determination, but also has the mechanism of user similarity calculation for PSS recommendation. Thus, the proposed method can be used to achieve personalized recommendation of PSS.

## 6.4 Theoretical and Practical Implications

This chapter introduces a multi-criteria recommendation method for PSSs from the theoretical perspective. This research fills the gap of PSS recommendation identified by a comprehensive evaluation (Song 2017). In this way, manufactures can actively provide differentiated PSSs (Song and Sakao 2017) to achieve proactive response to dynamic change of requirements. This helps to distinguish the company's offerings from those by competitors. In addition, the proposed recommendation method can also identify the interdependencies between different PSS recommendation criteria, which has not been noticed in the literature on PSS. With the help of the proposed method, managers can understand the interdependencies mechanism between recommendation criteria. With such a decision-making tool, PSS design and marketing can achieve positive strategy (Frambach et al. 1997), because it can support improving the PSS features in advance by discovering how recommendation criteria interact with each other. Finally, the proposed method can effectively and flexibly deal with fuzzy and inaccurate information with less priori information in decision making of PSS recommendation.

In summary, the proposed method reveals the following features: first, unlike the single rating-based recommendation approach, this research proposes a rough multi-criteria method of personalized PSS recommendation, which reduces the users' burden on time-consuming and error-prone manual PSS selection, and helps PSS providers proactively to respond to user's personal preferences. Second, by using rough aggregation approach, the proposed method successfully extends the DEMATEL method, and can well deal with the problem of recommendation criteria evaluation in vague environment. Therefore, it can effectively handle vague and imprecise information. Third, the rough DEMATEL-based weighting method considers the interactions between different criteria. Hence, the complexity of PSS features is easier to be captured and more information can be obtained for the PSS recommendation. Fourth, in the proposed recommendation method, not only the user's subjective rating on PSS is dealt with, but also the objective distribution of the rating is considered with the rough number concept. And the proposed approach handles ratings in rough scale to precisely capture user preferences and ratings to obtain the reasonable recommendation results.

Beside the theoretical implications, the proposed method provides several practical benefits. First, the time and efforts needed to get data for the method in practice from a provider and a customer can be marginal. This is positive for dissemination of the method into industry. Second, the method can be used as a standardized process at a company to avoid discussion based on subjective or biased opinions of different users of the method. This helps to improve the efficiency of making decision at a company. Furthermore, risk of human errors can be reduced by the method, especially in case the method is implemented as computer software. Third, inexperienced staffs can be guided by the method to make decision, avoiding risk of improper decision making due to lack of knowledge. Fourth, the method can suggest proposals of new offerings that may be not easily found, then, the company can make proposals to customers in a proactive manner. This has potential to increase loyalty of customers to the provider and the sales of the provider. Fifth, the method can be applied to a wide range of areas, from business to business and from business to consumer.

## References

1. Frambach, R. T., Wels-Lips, I., & Gündlach, A. (1997). Proactive product service strategies: an application in the European health market. *Industrial Marketing Management, 26*(4), 341–352.
2. Herlocker, J., Konstan, J. A., & Riedl, J. (2002). An empirical analysis of design choices in neighborhood-based collaborative filtering algorithms. *Information Retrieval, 5*(4), 287–310.
3. Lu, J., Shambour, Q., Xu, Y., Lin, Q., & Zhang, G. (2010). BizSeeker: a hybrid semantic recommendation system for personalized government-to-business e-services. *Internet Research, 20*(3), 342–365.
4. Saaty, T. L. (1988). What is the analytic hierarchy process? In *Mathematical models for decision support* (pp. 109–121). Heidelberg: Springer, Berlin.
5. Saaty, T. L. (1996). *Decision making with dependence and feedback: The analytic network process* (Vol. 4922). Pittsburgh: RWS Publications.
6. Song, W. (2017). Requirement management for product-service systems: Status review and future trends. *Computers in Industry, 85,* 11–22.
7. Song, W., & Cao, J. (2017). A rough DEMATEL-based approach for evaluating interaction between requirements of product-service system. *Computers & Industrial Engineering, 110,* 353–363.
8. Song, W., & Sakao, T. (2017). A customization-oriented framework for design of sustainable product/service system. *Journal of Cleaner Production, 140,* 1672–1685.
9. Song, W., & Sakao, T. (2018). An environmentally conscious PSS recommendation method based on users' vague ratings: A rough multi-criteria approach. *Journal of Cleaner Production, 172,* 1592–1606.
10. Ulaga, W., & Chacour, S. (2001). Measuring Customer Perceived Value in Business Markets. *Industrial Marketing Management, 30,* 525–540.

Printed in the United States
By Bookmasters